LET CHAR SHOW Y... [obscured by barcode sticker: W9-CPY-620]
INTUITION TO...

. . . "home in" on missing or misplaced objects
. . . psychically contact people or "accidentally"
run into them
. . . choose or change a career intuitively
. . . do an intuitive health check, including
discerning specific conditions
. . . ease the pain of grief and losing a loved one
. . . expand your wisdom and happiness
. . . increase your ability to love
. . . prevent problems and attain goals in your life

"Char is an enormously talented psychic medium . . . She
skillfully teaches you how to recognize, trust, and develop
your own intuitive wisdom. In doing this, you find *for
yourself* the inner pathway to love and happiness . . . You
are your own best psychic. Char teaches you how in this
magnificent and practical book."
—Brian L. Weiss, M.D., bestselling author of
*Many Lives, Many Masters*

"Char shared her gift on my TV show for the first time years
ago and she was amazing. Now, years later, she's still doing it,
and I still don't know how she does it. And I'm still amazed."
—Regis Philbin

"Char never ceases to amaze me. Her book QUESTIONS
FROM EARTH, ANSWERS FROM HEAVEN will show
you how to tap into your intuition to achieve peace and
happiness even when life throws you unexpected curves."
—Joan Lunden

"I'm so impressed with her intuition and insight. She has
really touched my life."
—Ricki Lake

# Questions *from* Earth, Answers *from* Heaven

## A Psychic Intuitive's Discussion of Life, Death, and What Awaits Us Beyond

# CHAR MARGOLIS

### with Victoria St. George

St. Martin's Paperbacks

QUESTIONS FROM EARTH, ANSWERS FROM HEAVEN

Library of Congress Catalog Card Number: 99-35896

ISBN: 0-312-97514-7

Printed in the United States of America

St. Martin's Press hardcover edition / September 1999
St. Martin's Paperbacks edition / September 2000

10  9  8  7  6  5  4  3  2  1

With my deepest appreciation and love to my
"ACE HI" family—Herbie, Ida, Alicia
and Elaine—for giving me roots and wings.
With a special thank you to my friend Mark
for helping me mend those wings
when they were broken.

# Contents

SECTION THREE
Intuition in Action    189

# Acknowledgments

Throughout the years, I have received so much support from family, friends, clients, students, viewers and media people. It's impossible to thank them all, but I want to mention a few of the many souls who have helped me in my life and my mission.

Many thanks to my parents, Herbert and Ida Margolis (my angels on earth—and Mom's still going strong, God bless her!), my sisters Alicia and Elaine, and their husbands, Paul Tisdale and David Lippitt. Thanks to my nieces and nephews—Ronna, Linda, Lenny and his wife, Cari, and Larry and his wife, Carolyn—as well as their children—Jason, Jordan, Rachel, Lauren, and Ryan. And a special thank you to Katherine Jeffrey, who helped raise me.

No one's life is complete without friends to support them, and I'm happy that my friendship list is so long. Thank you to Malcolm Mills, Bob Sher, and Mark Hundahl, three gentlemen who offered me support, advice and encouragement every step of the way. Much love to Diana Basehart and her family, who opened their home to me in Los Angeles almost from the moment I arrived, not forgetting Diana's mother, Gwenyth Snyder. Thanks to all my friends from Michigan, especially Mary and Harold Sarko, and the people I grew up with who are still part of my life, including my childhood "best girlfriend," Becky Geyer. I'm privileged to have had many wonderful friends over the years, and special mention must go to Raleigh Robinson, Jonathan Hirsh, Garth Ancier, Alana Emhardt, Gary and Sandy Hughes, Ilene and David Techner, Sidney Altman, Dorothy Lucey, Maryann Mitchell, Martha Gresham, Mary and Gary Lycan, Danny and Jeff Fantich, Julee Roth, my girlfriends Michelle Kluck and Cindy Cowan, the great dancer Ann Miller, Craig Tomashoff, Denise Gordon, Jennifer Bassie, Ricci Martin and his family, Bobbie Fisher, Robert Fleisher, and Edgar Castillo. And to all my other friends, in New York, L.A., Michigan and all parts in between, who share my life in ways big and small—thank you!

When I first began my work on television and radio, I got to know and appreciate many of the amazingly talented people who work both in front of and behind the camera and microphone, starting with Regis Philbin, who gave me my first break in L.A. I am also eternally grateful to all the TV producers and people who put me on the air, kept me "out there" through the years, and became my friends along the way, including my steadfast friends Lora Wiley, Joanne Saltzman, Gail Yancosek, and Tisi Alyward, as well as Randy Barone (one of the first producers to put me on the air), Glen Meehan, Bradly Bessey, Mark Itkin, Janet Stevens (producer for the morning show in Cleveland), José Rios, Pat Piper, David Armour, Mindy Moore, Renata Joy, Leslie Gustat, Ron Ziskin, Gail Steinberg, Steve Antionetti, Mark Lipinsky, Eric Schotz, Isabel Rivera, Laura Wadsworth, Faith Beth Lamont, Valerie Schaer (V.P. of programming at ABC), and Jordan Schwartz, Morley Nirenberg, and all the folks at CTV in Canada. Many thanks to all the on-air people like Suzanne Somers, Cheryl Washington, Steve Edwards on *Good Day Los Angeles,* Vicki Lawrence, Rolanda Watts, Tawny Little, Ann Martin, Paul Moyer, Harold Green, Susan Estrich, Marilyn Kagan, Stephanie Miller, Dini Petti and Camilla Scott and the staffs of their shows, Ru Paul, Larry King, Ricki Lake, Sally Jesse Raphael, Cindy Garvey, Christina Ferarre, Alan Thicke, Garry Shandling (a wonderful talent), Joan Lunden, Debbie Matenopoulos, Donny and Marie Osmond (and Mary Ellen DiPrisco, Melanie Chilek, and Zachary Van Amberg, the executives at Columbia), and special love to Barbara Walters, Meredith Viera and everyone at *The View.* Thanks also to the folks on the print media side, especially Larry Jordan of Midwest Today, and Stephanie Sable (Editor-in-Chief of *Woman's World*), and Allison Nemetz. And much gratitude for the creativity and hard work of my dear friend Stuart Krasnow, as well as Rick Jacobson and all the executives and people who worked with me at 20th Television.

The business side of my life is supported by an exceptional team of people. Tom Estey, my publicist and friend, opens doors for me that no one else could. I appreciate the loyalty of Cathy Klarr, my CPA, who keeps my finances straight, and Janie Hendrick, who keeps everything else straight. Thanks also to Audrey Belpasso and Carol Lawson for being part of the business team, and deep appreciation to my attorneys, David Rudich and Chase Mellen III, and their staff—Keri, Gail, and Kathleen.

This book could not have become a reality without the support and help of people who believed, as I did, that this work is important. To begin with, if it weren't for Mark Hundahl, I would never have started writing this. Brian and Carol Weiss encouraged me through the years to write down what I do. George Evans started the initial groundwork, and Iris Martin connected me to my wonderful literary agent, Wendy Keller. (Wendy, thanks—you "got it" right from the beginning.) I deeply appreciate the work of Victoria St. George of Just Write, the best living ghostwriter a psychic could have! Thanks also to Jennifer Enderlin, my editor (I adore her) as well as all the people at St. Martin's Press, especially Sally Richardson, Jeff Capshew, Steve Cohen, John Murphy, Jenny Dworkin, and Michael Storings, for their amazing teamwork and support. They are creative giants and the best friends an author could have, because they work with you unconditionally. Special "thank yous" to all the clients and students who agreed to be interviewed for and/or quoted in this book—Mike Blackman, Chris Blackman, Chantale Bruno, Patty Cimine, Chief Joel Dobis, Jeffrey Fantich, D.C., Hope Neff Grant, Martha Gresham, Cheryl Herbeck, Jackie, Tami Howard, Gary Hughes, Mark Hundahl, Larry Jordan, Wendy Keller, Stuart Krasnow, Julie Krull, Elaine Lippitt, Bob Lorsch, Malcolm Mills, Ricci Martin, Gordon Meltzer, Sandra Messinger, Robin Nemeth, D.C., Nancy Newton, Dr. Mary Sarko, Nancy Spinelli, Jeannie Starrs–Goldizen, Tarrah Sterling, Lois Steup, Alicia Tisdale, and Debby White. Your stories of intuition in action will help thousands of others become aware of what's possible in their own lives.

Lastly, heartfelt thanks to all my clients and students throughout the years. While I can't mention everyone by name, you were all part of my learning and growing and thus, a vital part of this book. And to anyone I may have forgotten, I apologize—please consider yourself thanked!

# Questions
*from* Earth,
# Answers
*from* Heaven

# Introduction

~

# The Age of Awareness

We all have questions we'd like to ask God. Why is my life so difficult? Why did my loved one have to die? Why can't I be successful? Why do I feel so disconnected? Why did I get sick? Why is there so much injustice? How can I be more connected with myself and my loved ones? What happens when I die? Will I know my loved ones on the other side? *Is* there an "other side" and what is it like? Does heaven exist? What about reincarnation and soul mates? And is there an infinite knowledge in the universe that I can connect with and use to help make my life better here on earth, or am I just a random by-product of the chemical processes we call life?

Human beings have been seeking answers to these questions throughout recorded history. Some of their answers are based on faith; some on scientific data; some on fantasy. But a few answers—very few—are based on the actual experience of tapping in to a realm beyond this physical world, where we can speak directly with energies we call "spirits," and, more important, where we can connect directly with the highest level of universal and infinite love, wisdom, and light that we call God.

We connect with these other realms through our

inborn sixth sense—our intuition. This God-given power is a direct connection between each soul and the universe. I was lucky enough to discover this intuitive power within myself at a very young age. As a child I was able to see spirits, read thoughts, and foresee events. At first my abilities frightened me because I did not understand them, but eventually I came to accept them as a gift from the universe. I learned (and continue to learn) from others, as well as through my own efforts, how to develop my intuition to its fullest extent. And ultimately, I learned how to teach others to develop their own intuition as well.

You see, I know with absolute certainty that, in the same way animals have instinct, *every human being has intuition*. It's inherent in our makeup, in the same way we have sight, hearing, touch, taste, and smell. We use our intuition unconsciously all the time in ways too numerous to mention. But intuition can be so much more than something that just helps you find the jewelry you lost or tells you if your child is in trouble. Our intuitive sense is literally a channel between this world and the next. It's an energy conduit through which we can connect with loved ones who have died, speak to our guardian angels and spirit guides, and even touch the highest level of universal consciousness and love.

My purpose for being on this planet is to help others recognize, develop, and use their God-given intuitive abilities to ease suffering and grow in goodness, love, compassion, and wisdom. My mission is to help take away fear—the fear of death, by proving that we don't die and will see our loved ones again, and the fear of living, by showing how we can tap in to our wisest selves and make our lives much happier and easier. My desire is to help each of us connect to the love that is eternal, that is the reason for our existence.

Awakening to our own intuitive powers is more important than ever, because I believe that humanity is going through a metamorphosis—from a material world to a spiritual one. We're moving into a new age of spiritual awareness, a whole new phase for the human race, a time when we must learn to balance the spiritual *and* material. I call it the Age of Awareness, because I believe it's a time when we all will have to become aware of the enormous power we possess.

In the Age of Awareness, we each must take responsibility for our thoughts and our deeds. Human beings have the power to destroy or heal both themselves and the planet. We must learn that the choices we make will reverberate throughout the universe, affecting not just our own lives but the lives of countless others. We must learn also that our choices, thoughts, and deeds will affect what happens to our spirits when we die. And I believe we must finally awaken to the immense power of our own sixth sense.

As a professional psychic intuitive for the past twenty-five years, I have been associated with many people who were part of what's called the "New Age" movement. Truthfully, however, I believe much of the "New Age" was really "Old Age" in disguise. People sought to return to humanity's deepest roots of culture, religion, nature, trying to connect with the power they sensed in themselves and in the universe. But all too often it seemed that they got caught up in the forms they chose. They failed to recognize that all paths lead to the same place, and the best, most direct path to God does not rely on outer forms, but on a direct connection with the universe from within ourselves—a connection that flows naturally through our own intuitive channels, as long as we don't block them with doubts, fears, and misconceptions.

I have written this book in the hopes people everywhere will read it and awaken to their own instinctive, intuitive abilities. I'm not here to "convince" anybody. I don't have to. There are already thousands of documented cases of people who have had near-death experiences. There are many others who have seen and heard spirits, or been warned about something, or found their soul mates. I don't feel I have to convince the world that intuition is real. But for those people who do have an interest, who have had an inkling of that inexplicable sixth sense, who want to connect with loved ones who have passed away, I hope this book will show them they're not alone or crazy—in fact, they're surprisingly ordinary, because everyone has a psychic/intuitive gift.

Intuition has enormous power for either good or evil. Each of us must choose how we will use this power in our own lives. My wish, my desire for you is that in reading this book you will recognize your intuitive gifts, utilizing them as your best guide to the Age of Awareness and thereby bringing peace, healing, and love to yourself and others. Trust your intuition; it can provide the answers you seek from Heaven.

# 1

## I Talk to Dead People
## for a Living

What do you say when someone asks, "What do you do?" If you're a truck driver or CEO or artist or teacher or manager or ditch-digger, it's easy. But what do you say when you're in a profession like mine?

Occasionally I'll say, "I talk to dead people—and what's more, they talk back to me. Some people just never know *when* to shut up!"

For the past twenty-five years, I've given readings for thousands of people, mostly in private sessions, sometimes on TV and radio in front of millions. The media usually calls me a psychic intuitive, but I like to think of myself as "your most affordable long-distance carrier to the other side," since I connect people with loved ones who just happen to be dead!

I'll never forget the time I went shopping for carpeting, and I was chatting with the salesman. He was a nice man but a character: tall, thin, and with a really obvious toupee. He asked me what I did and I told him. He was a little taken aback, so I said, "Let me give you an example," and I proceeded to spell out his grandfather's name, Chaim (a rather unusual name). The reading convinced the salesman I was genuine—and from then on he wouldn't leave me alone! The whole time I was looking at samples and ordering my carpet, he was asking questions about his family, his health, his business. He even followed me out to the parking lot. He was literally running after my car yelling, "Wait! Wait! Should I sell the diamonds?" Needless to say, I got a great deal on my carpet.

Through the years I've made a name for myself because I pick up specific names, facts, images, and relationships that no one could possibly know other than the person I'm reading for. On live television and radio, I'll tell people about their mother, father, spouse, fiancée, boss. Some of the most touching messages are from departed relatives who want to let the living know that death has not obliterated the love they feel for those who are still here.

I recently shot the pilot for my own television show, where I did readings on camera for people I'd never met before. Let me give you a sample of my session with Lois, which we did in front of a studio audience. As with all of my readings, I asked Lois not to lead me in any way but simply to confirm the information I was giving her.

| | |
|---|---|
| Char | What's your name? |
| Lois | Lois. |
| Char | Is there somebody with a J or G? |
| Lois | J. |
| Char | A J? Deceased? Or living? |
| Lois | Living. |
| Char | Is this J a male? |
| Lois | J male. |
| Char | Is there an N or M in his name? |
| Lois | In his last name. |
| Char | In his first name is there an E? Like Jeff, or J-E, or Joseph? Joseph? |
| Lois | Yes—that's his name. |
| Char | Is this family to you? |

Lois    Ex.

Char    Is this your ex-husband?

Lois    Yes.

Char    Did either of you, did you have a problem with a child? Did you lose a child? Was this his child as well?

Lois    *(Nods throughout.)*

Char    You know what? I have a feeling this child's here, but I just can't hear the name. But this is Joseph's child and your child. Is there an R in the name, it starts with R, or it's in it?

Lois    In it.

Char    Is there an E in it? Start with E? Or is it E-R, or R-E in the name?

Lois    *(Nodding.)*

Char    I can't hear the name. This person isn't used to talking to me and I'm not used to talking to them. Maybe . . . was there somebody else deceased that's a J, like on Joseph's side of the family? Did he have a grandfather or father?

Lois    His father.

Char    Was his father's name Joseph, too?

Lois    Yes!

Char    That's who I think is in here. Was he a strong personality, his dad?

Lois    I didn't know him.

Char    I feel him as a strong personality. He wants you to know . . . I don't know how you got along with this man. Did you like him?

Lois    I didn't know him.

Char    Because he's with your child. But this would be his grandchild. And he wants you to know that your child is okay. For some reason . . . there's not a B or D with this name, is there?

Lois    D.

Char    Starts with D and there's an R in it? Is it D-E-R?

*(Lois shakes head no.)* But D-E and there's an R in it. Is it Deborah? It is Deborah?

Lois     *(Nods yes, crying.)*

Char     It's taking me awhile to hear her. But she wants you to know she's all right. Oh, now I'm seeing the balloons. Did you send balloons up for her? She's saying somebody put balloons on her grave site?

Lois     *(Nods yes.)*

Char     She's showing me the balloons. Did somebody also send a balloon up in the air for her?

Lois     I don't know.

Char     You don't know. But she wants you to think of her as free, that her spirit is free. Are you . . . are you wearing anything that was Deborah's?

Lois     *(Nods yes.)*

Char     She's saying, "Mom, you're wearing my jewelry! Let me see!" *(From underneath her turtleneck shirt, Lois pulls out a ring which is on a chain around her neck.)* Was that her class ring?

Lois     She never got to wear it.

Char     She's a good soul. Sometimes different people come into our lives as teachers, and I have a feeling Deborah was here as a teacher, to teach us about love, and to teach you about the relationship between a parent and a child. And there's nothing that I can say that will ever bring her back or make this better. The only good news is, when you pass over to the other side, she'll be there with you. She'll be waiting for you. She says, "Mom, I came to you in a dream!"

Lois     *(Shakes her head no.)*

Char     Who did she come to in a dream? Someone had a dream about her. Think.

Lois     A cousin.

Char    Your cousin. Okay. Maybe it wasn't your dream, it was your cousin's dream. And the cousin gave you a message from Deborah. What did Deborah say in the dream?

Lois    That she's okay.

Char    She *is* okay! I promise she's okay. Her grandpa is keeping an eye out for her on the other side, which even if you're not with her dad is okay, because I think Grandpa was a good guy. You know, when we don't try so hard is when the spirits can come back to us. And you *will* feel her again, you will dream about her, you'll see her.

After our reading, Lois said, "It was breathtaking—more than I expected. I came here hoping I would hear from Debbie; that's all I wanted. Now I feel like my daughter's in a better place." When asked about the balloons, she revealed that for the three years since her daughter's death, on Debbie's birthday every year she had gone to her grave and put a balloon there. "No one could know that but me," she said.

I do this work because I believe it's important. My clients tell me that the information they learn in our readings helps them make decisions, cope with losses, discover undetected health problems, avoid disastrous accidents, or even just get through the bad times because they know good times are just around the corner. Those are some of the concrete results. But it also means a lot to me when I see a smile on the face of a man whose beloved grandmother speaks to him after years of being separated by death . . . or feel the healing of a mother who is reunited with her child who died of cancer . . . or experience the confidence almost everyone feels when they don't just hope, but *know,* that they are still connected with those they love, even after their physical forms are gone.

I call myself "the most affordable long-distance carrier" in jest, but when I read for people, I actually see and hear their loved ones very close by. The spirits communicate by putting thoughts into my head—thoughts that just plain "feel" different than those produced by my own mind. But the actual process of tuning in psychically is very similar to the way we *all* get impressions that don't come from a logical place. Have you ever thought about someone you haven't heard from for a while, and then they call you a short time later? Or had a bad feeling about a particular trip or route, only to have your car break down or some other obstacle arise? Or felt the presence of someone you loved, either living or dead? We get information all the time which simply can't have come from our logical minds yet which turns out to be true. Because I've been tuning in for most of my life, I've gotten very good at using my intuition—but we all do it. Throughout this book, you're going to hear stories of people just like you who are using their intuition simply and easily, just like tuning in a radio or opening a book. And by the time you finish reading, I hope you will have had similar experiences yourself.

My dear friend and fellow intuitive Mark calls this ability "instinctive intuition." Animals have instincts, right? And those instincts are primarily used to survive. Most animals can somehow sense danger even when the cause is out of sight. Humans have a kind of survival instinct, too, but in our case it can help us with a lot more than simply staying alive. When we use our intuition regularly, when we pay attention to the information that doesn't come from our logical, left-brain side, we can pick up on energies and frequencies that are being broadcast by the universe itself. We can tune into the great "field of possibility" described by physicists, which extends beyond the physical universe into other dimensions, other levels, even other times.

# Out of the Blue . . .

It was one of those phone calls anyone would hate getting. I was staying with my good friend, Diana Basehart (actor Richard Basehart's widow), in Beverly Hills. It was March 1987, and I had been dividing my time between L.A. and my home in Michigan for the last several years. When Diana called me to the phone and I picked up the receiver, the voice on the other end sounded desperate. "Char? This is Scott Sandler. Shirley MacLaine suggested I give you a call. I don't know if you've been reading the papers about Dean Paul Martin. . . ."

Of course I had. Everybody in Los Angeles knew about the disappearance of Dean Martin's son, Dean Paul. Dean Paul had been on a training flight with the Air National Guard and the F4 Phantom jet he had been flying had simply disappeared. The air force had been looking for him for five days but had found nothing.

"Dean Paul is my best friend," Scott said. "His family is going out of their minds not knowing what's happened, so they decided to take matters in their own hands. Dean Paul's mom called Shirley MacLaine and someone recommended you. Would you help us?"

I said yes immediately. I'd been using my psychic gift professionally for about ten years at that point, and had already been called in (quietly) on several missing person cases by police agencies in Michigan and California. That afternoon Scott Sandler and Dean Paul's brother, Ricci, came to Beverly Hills to pick me up, and we drove out to March Air Force Base in Riverside, California, about an hour and a half away. Dean Paul's training flight originated at March AFB, and his last radio transmission was sent from an area about thirty miles into the San Bernardino Mountains.

The three of us walked into a big, open room filled with what looked like dozens of military "brass." There were officers everywhere. One of them came up to us and said quietly that the air force had consulted psychics before, but obviously they didn't like the public to know about it. "We like to think we can find our fliers ourselves," he told us.

At that point, the air force had been combing the area with planes and helicopters for five days. President Ronald Reagan had even authorized a couple of spy planes to fly over the area and take infrared photographs to see if that would help spot the wreckage. However, nothing had turned up. So there I was, a civilian, in jeans, amid this sea of air force officers, being asked to do what the entire U.S. military hadn't managed to accomplish: find Dean Paul Martin.

Quite frankly, I'm not the best at remembering a lot of detail about incidents or readings. I do remember asking one of the officers for a map of the area. Ricci Martin remembers that I asked to interview anyone who might have heard or seen anything having to do with Dean Paul's flight. One little girl had reported hearing a big airplane roar by at about the same time Dean Paul had been heard from last. (That day had been cloudy and stormy, so we couldn't find anyone who had actually seen the plane.) I talked to the little girl on the phone. I talked to some of the officers. Again and again I went back to the map. I remember getting initials, names, words that represented different places near where Dean Paul's last transmission had come from. At one point I saw and felt the spirits of air force officers from World Wars I and II in the room. I knew they all wanted to help me find Dean Paul.

Then it all became clear. "Here," I said, pointing to a specific spot on the map. "If you fly over this area in either a helicopter or an airplane, you'll be able to see where Dean Paul is."

The officers protested, telling me they'd already been over that area several times. "It doesn't matter," I said. "He's on the side of a mountain, but the crash site is camouflaged by a tree. If you look for the tree, you'll see something hanging from it, and that's where he is."

At that point I could tell the level of skepticism in the room had risen considerably. Nevertheless, the order was issued for search parties to fly over the area I had pinpointed.

Scott and Ricci wanted to take a helicopter up themselves to check out that location. One of the officers volunteered to drive us over to Riverside Airport where we could hire a civilian chopper. "And I'd like to come with you, if I could," he said, and we agreed to his request.

Ricci told me later he felt a little foolish as our helicopter roared over the valleys and hills, heading for the mountain where I said Dean Paul would be found. "Here I was, with my brother's best friend and a psychic I had met only that day, searching the countryside for my brother based upon her 'knowing' where he would be found—even though the entire U.S. military hadn't been able to locate him after five days! My brother would have said I was out of my mind."

But as we were flying along I almost felt as if I had been in these valleys and mountains before. I knew exactly where to go. I was telling the pilot, "Go right through this canyon and then left here," and he told me that was exactly how to get to the spot I had pointed to on the map.

Then all of a sudden a call came over the radio. "We have located an unidentified object that appears to be wreckage. This airspace must now be considered restricted. No civilian aircraft are permitted in this area. Repeat, all civilian aircraft are to stay out of this area."

What could we do? We turned back. At least they let us land at March AFB rather than sending us back to Riverside. Scott, Ricci, and I drove back to L.A. with no confirmation that they had found Dean Paul—other than the certainty we felt in our hearts.

A few hours later, Dean Paul's family got the call that confirmed his death in a plane crash. He had been flying in formation with three other jets in very stormy, cloudy weather. His radio and radar were not working very well, and he had not been able to get permission to gain "altitude immediately" from the air control tower at Ontario Airport. Unable to see, unable to fly straight up for fear of crossing the path of commercial aircraft in the area, Dean Paul had turned his plane to the left—and slammed straight into the side of a mountain. The impact was so great that the plane's transponder (which normally broadcasts a signal which allows search crews to locate a downed plane) had been completely obliterated.

That same night, I too got a call, from one of the captains at March AFB. It seemed the wreckage had been found exactly where and how I had seen it. Because of the overhanging tree and the complete destruction of the airplane, it would have been next to impossible for anyone to find the site without clear directions about where to look. "I just want you to know, you made a lot of skeptics into believers today," he said.

I felt sad and happy—happy I was able to help, but sad that this family now had to cope with the loss of a beloved son, brother, husband, and father. Based on my years of communicating with the souls of those who have died, I knew without a doubt that Dean Paul's spirit was still alive even though his body was no longer here; yet I also knew the pain his family would be going through.

To this day, I'm glad to say I consider Ricci Martin a friend. He has told me again and again how much it meant to him that I was able to find Dean Paul and end his family's uncertainty. He's complained that I never got the recognition I deserved for my help. But I don't do this work for recognition. I do it because I believe it's important, because I know we and our loved ones will continue to live on, because I want people to understand that we *all* share this gift of intuition, this sixth sense that puts us in touch with things we would never know otherwise. And by reading this book, I want *you* to learn how to tap in to your God-given instinct to help make your life better, safer, and happier than ever before.

# 2

## What It's Like to Grow Up Psychic

People often ask me if I knew I was psychic when I was a child. Well, I think most kids are a lot more "tuned in" than adults are. Many parents have told me fascinating stories of their children reporting encounters with spirits or angels; sometimes the parents themselves remember seeing unexplainable lights or hearing noises when they were young. But a few things stick out in my own childhood as what some would call "psychic phenomena."

I remember when I was about two or three years old standing in my bed and watching my doll walk over to me. My grandfather had given me the doll, and it was beautiful—it walked when you pushed a button on its back. But there it was, the middle of the night, I was alone in the room with no one anywhere near the doll to push its button—and yet it started walking across the floor toward my crib. All I can think of is that either a spirit moved the doll, or I was using my young mind to will the doll to come to me.

For years my mother has told the story of the time my father and I went to the grocery store. When we got back, as my mother was looking at the receipt I blurted out, "They cheated us, Mommy. Those people cheated us!" I was no older than four and hadn't yet learned to add, so I had no way to know the receipt was wrong. But my mother checked it and, sure enough, we had been over-charged. To me, that demonstrates one of the best attributes of intuition: it can help you with little things as well as big ones. Anyone can use their sixth sense to help find their soul mate—or to keep from being overcharged at the market.

For example, my father would never have called himself "psychic," yet he kept pen and paper by his bed to record numbers that would come to him in dreams. Then he would bet those numbers at the track—and win! (He was a very generous man and usually gave all his winnings away. And he would often bet his dream numbers on behalf of someone who was poor, giving them the winnings when the horse came in.)

Another time when I was about seven or eight I wanted to go play in the park across the street from our house in Oak Park, Michigan. All the other kids from the neighborhood were over there having a great time, but on that particular day my father said no. My father never said no to me, so this was very unusual, especially since I went to that park all the time. I screamed and cried, and finally he went against his better judgment and reluctantly let me go.

Well, I ended up falling down a hill in the park and cutting my leg very badly on a piece of broken glass. I went to the hospital and got twenty-two stitches. On the way to the hospital my father kept saying, "I knew she shouldn't go to the park. I just knew it." To this day looking at the scar on my leg reminds me to trust my hunches.

I was eight years old when I first encountered something truly "paranormal." I was always afraid of the dark as a child and had trouble falling asleep. Also, a few weeks earlier our house had been broken into, so I was more afraid than ever. That night I woke up in what must have been the wee hours of the morning. It was pitch black but I could see one thing clearly: a man standing at the foot of my bed. He had a long beard and was dressed in ragged clothing, with a pouch hanging at his waist. He took the pouch in his hand and opened it, and I stuck my head under the covers because I was so scared. I started pinching my arm to make sure I wasn't dreaming.

A few moments later I stuck my head out again, just in time to see the man grab a handful of something from the pouch and throw it at me. To my amazement I saw a shower of little, glittering, golden lights falling all over my body. As they touched me they evaporated. Well, I stuck my head back under the covers and stayed there. I must have shivered myself back to sleep because the next thing I knew it was morning, and my arm was black and blue from where I had pinched it so hard.

When I told my parents what had happened, they were great—they didn't discourage me or tell me I had been dreaming or, worse, lying. They simply said, "Oh, honey, that was just the Sandman," and did their best to reassure me. But I knew I had seen something more than the Sandman. I knew what I had seen had been real—not a dream or a figment of my imagination. To this day I believe it was one of my earliest experiences of seeing spirits.

(A lot of children are afraid of the dark, or tell their parents they've seen the boogyman or monsters under the bed. While there are a lot of different psychological reasons children may be afraid, it's just possible they are sensing the presence of spirits and don't understand what they're feeling. The best thing parents can do is to be matter-of-fact and reassuring. If children say they see something, don't assume what they're seeing is only their imagination or something they're making up. Treat it like a natural occurrence. For example, a young father I know was bathing his three year old son around the time of the holidays. The child looked into a bottle filled with clear shampoo and said, "There's a man in the bottle and he has presents for me." "That's great, Mikey," the father said, humoring him. "Ask him who he is." "He says his name is Grandpa Jake," Mikey replied. The father nearly fell on the floor: Jake was his stepfather's father, who had passed away long before Mikey was born. The father knew that Jake's name had never been mentioned in front of Mikey. To top it all off, since the next night was the start of Hanukkah, Mikey was indeed going to be getting presents very soon. Recovering his composure, Mikey's dad said, "Well, Grandpa Jake obviously loves you since he's bringing you presents!" and continued with his son's bath.)

Somehow I had always believed there were angels and spirits. At summer camp I went to church services every Sunday, and heard the preacher talk about angels. I also remember hearing about the angel who protected the firstborn sons of the Jews at Passover. Even as a child I realized there was something more than what people were admitting. Deep down inside I always knew it was possible to speak to spirits.

# Being Psychic Has Its Advantages

My psychic abilities never did me any good when it came to school—I could never "pick up" the answers on a test, for instance! But I quickly became the person everyone would come to for advice. One girl, Becky, became my best friend in tenth grade. (She's still one of my closest friends in the world.) We were so connected we would know instinctively when the other one was going to phone. I think that most of us have similar experiences with friends when we're growing up. At least most women I know have had them!

Once Becky and I were riding on the bus to a regional choir contest. She had been sitting next to her boyfriend, John, but then came over to sit with me for a while. For some reason I told her that John was going to write, "I love you," on the bus window. About twenty minutes later Becky went back to John, and she saw that he had just written, "Ich liebe dich," in the fog on the window. "Ich liebe dich" means "I love you" in German.

I wasn't the best student in the world but I was really good at music and theater. When I graduated from high school I went to community college for two years and then to Wayne State University, where I managed to pull my grade point average up to a respectable 3.0. I graduated with a degree in secondary education. While I was in college, I also got married. My husband and I moved to a house with some land, where we could have animals— two horses, five cats, and a dog. I did substitute teaching at the local high school. I liked teaching, but it wasn't my real passion. I kept feeling I had these psychic abilities that I wasn't using to their fullest, simply because I didn't know how.

In the meantime, flashes of intuition kept coming up more and more frequently. There was the day someone stole a pair of shoes from a girl in my class. There were at least forty kids in the room and I didn't have a clue who was responsible. Without thinking, I called one boy's name. He denied it vociferously, but I had this feeling he had taken the shoes. I walked straight up to him, looked him in the eye, and said, "Give her back her shoes." He stood up, reached for the shoes (he had been sitting on them), and handed them to me, saying, "You must have eyes in the back of your head."

Eventually, I was introduced to other people who had developed and channeled their psychic abilities. With practice, I too mastered listening to the inner messages which I could now identify as coming from the spirit world. I learned what I had always known instinctively somehow: that people who had died were still watching over those they loved on earth—and, given the opportunity, these spirits were eager to share their insight and caring.

I remember clearly one particular training session. I was in a room with several others who had been in this work for years. I said, "There's somebody here named (a man's name—I don't remember what). It's your father and he has a message." A gentleman in the group started crying and said, "That's my father! I've been waiting for a message from him for twenty years." I was able to give him a series of details which confirmed that the message could only have come from his father.

During this time I mastered many of the same techniques I now teach to people like you—how to focus the mind, how to open ourselves to impressions and images from the other side, how to protect ourselves from negative energy and surround ourselves with light and love. As I continued to get better and better at receiving and interpreting what the spirits and my direct intuition told me, I developed the confidence that I could use my gift to help others.

## Going "Pro"—and Teaching Others

Everyone has different ways of using their intuition to "tune in." (I'll talk about that quite a lot when I describe my own method for accessing your wisest self in Section Two.) I usually get letters of the alphabet and names of people, both living and deceased. (I think it was Sally Jesse Raphael who called me "the alphabet soup psychic.") Nobody taught me that particular technique; it just came to me. But from the first moment I began developing my abilities, I always knew I wanted to be very, very specific. So many people think psychic readings are phony because the information given is usually generic. And unfortunately, I'm sure there are so-called psychics who give readings based entirely on good guesswork. But I knew in my soul there was something different about the information I was getting. I could give people names, dates, places, relationships, secrets that only they knew about and I had no way of discovering.

I wanted to develop my gift to its greatest possible extent. I became obsessed with learning as much as I could from whomever I could. I went to several different psychics to see how they worked. I was constantly calling other intuitives and asking, "What if this happens? What if that happens?" Watching others work gave me a great deal of confidence, especially since I was often more accurate than they were! And the more I knew I could do it, the stronger the communication from the other side seemed to become.

But I'll tell you, this ability to hear spirits can have some pretty funny aspects. For example, by this point in my life I had gotten divorced. (I was actually warned on my wedding day that my marriage wasn't going to work out, but you'll hear more about that later.) One night I was double-dating with a friend of mine. My friend knew I was psychic and believed in my abilities, but when her date found out what I did, he was really skeptical.

During dinner I whispered to my friend, "Ask your date if he has a dead grandmother named Rose." She did so, and he said, "Yeah," a little surprised. Then I whispered to her, "Tell him his grandma Rose is upset with him because she kept kosher all her life and he's not eating kosher right now!" It scared the living daylights out of the guy because there's no way I could have known that about his grandmother. (My friend and I thought his reaction was hysterical!)

Within a couple of years, I started giving readings professionally. It was a big step for me, and I kept looking for confirmation that I was on the right path. Sometime in the first year I read for an older woman who told me, "I've had many readings from different people. In fact, years ago I was fortunate enough to have a reading by

Edgar Cayce, one of the best-known psychics in America—and your reading was comparable to his. I'm very impressed." It was very exciting for me to have a client of Edgar Cayce's give me such a compliment. It also seemed to be the message I was looking for, confirming that I should continue my career as a psychic intuitive.

Through referrals and good word of mouth, my list of private clients kept expanding. Then I was booked on a local radio station, WWJ, for a call-in show. The man who interviewed me was blown away by how accurate my readings were. Other radio and TV shows in Michigan and the Midwest started to ask me to appear, and my client list grew and grew. But I felt my mission on earth was to reach as many people as possible with the message that we don't die, that our loved ones want to speak to us from the other side, and that we all have an instinctive intuitive ability that will help us tap in to a source of wisdom greater than ourselves. So I asked myself, "Where can I go to reach the most people?" The answer came from nowhere: Los Angeles!

I had already appeared on the morning TV interview show in Detroit a couple of times, so I asked one of the producers, "Is there a morning show in Los Angeles?" "Of course," he said. "It's called *AM Los Angeles,* and it's one of the top-rated local shows in the country."

So I went home and called information in L.A. "Can I get the number for *AM Los Angeles?*" I asked the operator.

"I think you mean KABC, because that's the channel that produces it," the operator replied. That shows you how naive I was—even the telephone operator in L.A. knew more about the show than I did!

I called KABC and asked to speak to the show's executive producer. He told me later that he never takes calls from people he doesn't know, but somehow he felt he had to take my call. I said, "I'll only take two minutes of your time. I'm a psychic and I've been on *Kelly and Company* in Detroit. I'd love to appear on *AM Los Angeles*." He asked me to read for his associate producer, and she was astonished at the details I was able to give her. She said, "When can you fly out to L.A. to do the show?"

A couple of weeks later, there I was, this little girl from the Midwest, in L.A. for the very first time, staying at the Beverly Wilshire Hotel (courtesy of the show), being taken by a limousine to appear on one of the top-rated local talk shows in America! I was very nervous. Someone had told me, "If Regis Philbin (the show's cohost) likes you, you'll be a success. If he doesn't, you won't." I was scared but determined. I always knew that once I got there I'd be able to read, and I did. Regis liked me, and that first appearance led to many others on *AM Los Angeles,* and from there to talk shows all over the country.

It was all because I believed in my gifts and my mission. I knew nothing about the entertainment business—I just knew it was important for me to share what I knew about intuition and our innate psychic abilities. I wanted to be the channel that would help people understand that their departed loved ones were still alive in spirit, looking out for them on the other side.

## "I'm Not a Guru!" Teaching Others to Use Intuition

As I kept giving readings, I noticed some clients wanted to become dependent on me. They would call me for advice every time they needed to make the smallest decision. That was absolutely *not* something I would ever allow. I believe we all create our own destiny, and we have to be responsible for our own choices. I wasn't about to become someone's "guru." To me, "guru" means just what it spells: "Gee, You Are You." *You're* in charge of your life, not some psychic, not some spirit, not your loved ones on the other side. It's up to you to make your life the way you want it.

I had always told people they could call me for readings no more than twice a year. If they wanted guidance at other times, I told them to check inside their own heart or gut or whatever they called the place where their own inner wisdom arose. "Listen to your intuition," I would tell them. "It's far more accurate than even I am. You'll find your own instincts are usually right."

Thank heavens, my clients listened to me and started using their own intuition to help guide their lives. Like my good friend Gary Hughes. When I first met Gary twenty years ago, he was building swimming pools for a living and going through what he describes now as a "combination midlife crisis and self-pity party." I told him he was going to be changing his work, moving to a new location, making more money than he ever imagined, and traveling all over the country. I also sensed that he was quite intuitive and suggested he develop his own gift. Well, over the next few years Gary moved from Los Angeles to Sedona, Arizona. He got out of the swimming pool business and became a partner in a time share/resort operation. After a lot of ups and downs (and traveling pretty constantly) he sold the business to investors in New York and San Francisco for $34 million.

Today whenever Gary makes an important decision he listens to his "gut" as well as his head. "Char taught me that we all have this knowledge, but we've been trained to ignore it," he said recently. "We start using logic alone and end up making simple things complicated. Now when I go to do a deal, I listen to that gut feeling first, and then let the logical side have its input. But if my gut says no, I pay attention. And I've been very successful as a result."

Part of my mission here on earth is to teach others how to develop and use their intuition. *Everyone is psychic; everyone has intuition.* It's our God-given, natural sixth sense, one that can enrich our lives as much or even more than the other five senses combined. Once you learn to use your intuition, life doesn't necessarily become easier—after all, we all have our lessons to learn—but it does become a little smoother, and a lot more fun.

I wrote this book to help you develop your own inherent intuitive gift. I hope you'll read it with openness and curiosity, and try the exercises you'll find in later chapters. You may discover a new way of knowing which way to go when faced with a difficult decision. Perhaps you'll be able to avoid danger by listening to your "gut" rather than your head. Maybe you'll be able to "read" what's going on with your husband or wife or child. Maybe you'll be able to find your keys more easily! And maybe, just maybe, you'll discover a new certainty within your own heart about the love that exists inside you and around you, that is radiating to you from souls and guides you may not be able to see but who care for you very much. I believe that's one of the best and most lasting gifts your intuition has to offer.

# 3

## Psychic 900 Lines, or Why I Turned Down the "Opportunity of a Lifetime"

Around 1988, before any of the psychic 900 lines began to appear—and before Dionne Warwick was thought of as anyone other than a great pop singer—I was contacted by Bob Lorsch, who had seen me on *AM Los Angeles*. Bob was one of the first to figure out how to use the telephone to deliver information and entertainment via caller-paid telephone services. He had already done programs for several consumer products companies as well as TV networks and movie studios.

Bob told me, "Char, I understand you're very gifted and your predictions are astonishingly accurate. What do you think about hosting a 900 line on which people could get psychic readings?"

I was assured that any program his company created would be of high quality. But I told him no, I wasn't interested in putting my name on a network and having people call in to a "stable" of psychics to get readings. It's not that I thought there was anything wrong with telephone readings; I just didn't want to be involved with something where I couldn't personally interact with every caller.

Even though I turned down Bob's offer (as well as many other offers of my own psychic hotline from other people through the years), we kept in touch. A couple of years later, Bob called me again, and said, "Did you know that if you had taken my offer, you could have generated millions of dollars?" I said, "I don't care, Bob. The money isn't that important to me. That's simply not the way I choose to share my gift."

I have very strong views about intuition. I think it's important for everyone to develop their *own* abilities and not rely on anyone else exclusively for advice. And I have several issues with psychic hotlines which illustrate some of the incorrect beliefs about intuition floating through our culture today.

## 1. Psychic hotlines set up a "have" and "have not" mentality: *They* have intuition, you don't.

"Call us when you need answers!" "We have the best psychics around!" "Gosh, she knew this and this and this about me. . . ." I'm sure you've heard the commercials advertising different psychic hotlines. But you and I both know, psychic hotlines are all about making a buck. I don't think it's wrong to charge for a reading—a good reading can give you valuable guidance and direction. But psychic hotlines set people up to believe *these* psychics are the only ones who can give you that guidance. Therefore, you'll call them repeatedly and spend lots of money.

Quite frankly, that approach makes me angry. I believe every single one of us has intuition. We all get messages from the universe. We all have loved ones on the other side who want to speak with us, help us, and offer their advice (which we can take or not—more about that in Chapter 6). Intuition is just like athletic ability. Most of us can walk or run, right? If we don't run regularly, we may find it hard to keep going for very long. However, if we start a regular exercise program and walk or run every day, we get better and better at it. It's the same thing with intuition. The more you use it, the easier it is for you to tune in.

Some people are born with more natural athletic ability—Michael Jordan, for example, or Carl Lewis, or
Mary Lou Retton. When they're given training or develop
their abilities on their own, these athletes can become
superstars in their chosen sport. In the same way, some
people are born with a greater ability to tap into their
intuitive powers. But I believe *everyone has some level of
ability—and with focus and practice, everyone can
become a good psychic "athlete."*

The media, some psychics and the businesses that
profit from 900 lines have made psychic ability into
something far more mysterious than it really is. When I
first learned to use my intuition consciously, I was told,
"You have a gift." Yes, it's a gift—in the same way that
athletic ability, or the ability to sing or dance, is a gift. It's
a talent that I have studied, developed, and worked on. I
don't take it for granted, but I know it's not unique. You
have it; your neighbor has it; even the people who run the
psychic networks have it. And *everyone* can be taught to
develop their intuition.

I have spent a lot of time gathering stories about the
ways my students and clients have used their own psychic
abilities. This book contains several accounts of my own
readings, and I hope they'll open your mind to what's
possible when we speak with the spirits. But you'll also
read many, many stories about people just like you using
their intuition to contact loved ones who have passed,
avoid danger and disaster, tune in at work or in their close
relationships, monitor their health or the health of others,
and much more.

## 2. Psychic hotlines can create a relationship of dependency.

I once had a woman call my office to arrange a reading. When I called her back at the appointed time, the first
words out of her mouth were, "My husband would kill

me if he knew I was talking to you. In the last year I've had a $10,000 phone bill to the 900 psychic lines." I was astounded. I asked, "Then why are you calling me?" She replied, "I saw you on television and thought you could help me."

I told her, "First of all, I don't blame your husband. Second, if you really want my help, I'll go ahead and read for you because I want to make sure you get accurate information." But after the reading I said, "Now, I'm putting a note in my computer that you are not allowed to call me again until you've gone through therapy to learn to make your own decisions. When I know you're not going to be dependent on me or any other psychic to help you make choices in your life, then I will consider reading for you again."

A lot of people don't want to make their own decisions; they want somebody else to do it for them. That's especially true of someone who's in an extremely vulnerable place—they've lost someone close, or they're in a bad relationship, or they've had a really bad time. They are looking for answers and desperately need something to lean on. I call people like this "psychic-aholics"—and for them, the psychic 900 lines are the corner bar.

I'm not about to be the bartender for these poor souls. I believe this work is supposed to help people prevent problems and attain goals. It's about facing the truth, not hiding from it. A psychic reading can be an extremely intimate experience, where our issues are revealed as if in a mirror. Many people are in denial about their problems and don't want to face the truth, and they allow their fears to keep them from getting the help they need. If I think that's the case, I'll tell clients they are not allowed to call me for a reading until they get therapy, or see a doctor, or discuss with me how they're dealing with a particular issue.

I don't want anyone becoming dependent on someone else's advice, including mine. I'm interested in people taking charge of their own lives, using their intuition to direct their own destinies. And unless we've healed ourselves through whatever means necessary—therapy, getting out of a destructive situation, and so on—we run the risk of allowing ourselves to become dependent on others.

I'm not saying, don't get a reading from a psychic. But a session with a really good psychic should be like a visit to the doctor. When do most people go to the doctor? Either when there's a change in their physical health, or for a periodic checkup to make sure everything's okay. In the same way, you should consult a psychic when there's a change in your life—a death in the family, an impending job or relationship choice, and so on—or if you want to make sure things in general are okay. The doctor gives you advice on how to handle your physical health; but if you're smart, you check that advice with your own sense of your body and good old-fashioned common sense, right? In the same way, you should check the advice a psychic gives you, using your own intuition and a little healthy skepticism.

Depending on psychics to run your life is like a hypochondriac calling the doctor every time he or she has a real or imagined symptom. Healthy people don't do that. They take care of themselves with good nutrition, exercise, vitamins. Most of the time they can figure out what's wrong with themselves using common sense and a little intuition. The same thing is true about directing your life. It's your responsibility, not your doctor's, not your therapist's—and certainly not your psychic's.

**3. When you call a psychic hotline, you don't know who's on the other end of the line, how (or if) they were trained, how accurate they are, or if they have a conscience.**

All the psychic hotline ads say, "We have the best psychics!" and of course they show people getting great readings. But *you* don't know who's going to be at the other end of the line when you call. You have no idea who this person is, or how (or whether) they've been trained. You don't know until you've paid $2.95 or $3.95 or $4.95 a minute for someone to make a few educated guesses about you and your life.

When psychic hotlines first showed up, I called and got readings from a number of "operators." The accuracy was somewhat variable, to say the least! One woman told me I should be involved with fashion as a career, or be a clothing consultant. Well, considering I've always had to ask my girlfriends to go shopping with me because I can't pick out clothes to save my life, that prediction was not exactly on the money.

One of my clients and students, Jeannie, is a wonderful free spirit. She took my workshop a few years ago and quickly started developing a reputation with her friends as a very accurate psychic. One night she got a call out of the blue from a woman who said, "Hi, I work for so-and-so. I heard you give psychic readings. Do you want to work for our psychic hotline?" Jeannie decided to try it for a lark.

Jeannie is good, so I know the people who got her when they called were very lucky. However, I was disturbed (but not surprised) by what she told me about the way this psychic hotline was run. She said all the psychics were told to keep people on the phone as long as they could. In fact, she was paid according to the length of each phone call. (Since Jeannie wasn't interested in stringing anyone along, she didn't make much money.) She also learned that none of the so-called psychics were ever tested; there was no quality control at all. Worse yet, the hotline company actually gave Jeannie a script that told her how to answer questions generically, phrase things in such a way that the person on the phone gives you the answer, and lead people on to keep them on the line as long as possible. "Needless to say, I never followed their script," Jeannie told me gleefully.

Saddest of all were Jeannie's stories about the people who called in. One man seemed very agitated, and Jeannie kept hearing "sickness" in her head. Then she got a hit, "This man has AIDS." Another woman called and said, "I got this sweepstakes offer in the mail. How much money am I going to win?" "You ain't winning nothing!" Jeannie told her. Then Jeannie asked if the woman's youngest daughter was handicapped. There was a silence, and the woman replied, "I've called a lot of times before, but you're the only one who ever picked that up."

Jeannie finally quit after she spoke to a man whom she knew had something wrong with him. "All I kept getting was 'mental,' but I couldn't put my finger on it. Finally it clicked—he was a paranoid schizophrenic and he wasn't taking his medication. I said to him, 'Listen to me: you must take your medicine. Go to the doctor right away.' I got off the phone and told my girlfriend, 'I can't be part of this anymore.' What if that guy had gotten someone who just wanted to keep him on the phone? You know the damage they could have done?"

I'm not saying that the people who work the psychic hotlines aren't gifted. Some of them probably are. And I believe there are psychics on the hotlines who have great and pure motives. But you have to wonder how many people get hurt by incorrect advice, and how many poor, confused souls call in even though they don't have the money to pay the bills. I'm sorry—it's just too much of a chance when you call someone on a hotline and expect them to give you accurate advice about your life.

How do most people find a psychic if they want a reading? Often it's through the recommendation of a friend. Most of my clientele come to me because someone they knew had a reading with me. Others have seen me on TV or heard me on radio. Yes, I'm on TV and radio, too—but I don't follow a script or make guesses. Usually I'm on in a live interview format, where I have to be absolutely accurate with person after person. I don't hit things exactly every time; no one does. But I'm very, very accurate most of the time, giving names, relationships, past incidents with a precision that has nothing to do with making educated guesses or following a script.

The old saying goes, "The proof of the pudding is in the eating," and the proof of a psychic is the accuracy of his or her readings. I'll always stand behind my own readings, but I can't vouch for the accuracy of anyone else's. Because I feel that way, I would never set up my own psychic hotline even if I could train and verify every single person who answered the phone.

## 4. Someone on a psychic hotline may be feeding you information that comes from a lower, dangerous level.

Even though someone is psychic, it doesn't mean that information is coming to them from the highest level. I'll talk about this a lot in later chapters, but here's the short version: There is good and evil in the universe, both here and in the spirit world, and not all spirits operate from the same high place. There are energies and spirits out there that do not wish us well and want to trick us, and they can use truth to their own ends. A Ouija board is an example of how this can happen. Kids often use things like Ouija boards to tap in to the "spooky" side of things, but unfortunately they can tap in to some very bad energies. The Ouija board may tell them nine things in a row that are true; the pointer will spell out names and situations, and give answers to questions that are absolutely accurate. Then the tenth time it will say, "Break into the school and vandalize the science lab," or "Kill the neighbor's cat," or

"Slash the tires on your teacher's car." Don't laugh—it happens. In some ways, I believe using psychic tools like Ouija boards can be as dangerous for kids as taking drugs.

My point is this: Someone may be getting accurate information and still be giving you bad advice, because they are tuning in to a lower level of energy. How can you protect yourself? First, always, always, always use your own intuition and common sense to check any advice you're given. If it doesn't feel right to you, for God's sake, don't follow it. Second, before you get any kind of reading, say a prayer of protection and surround yourself with white light. (I'll tell you how to do this in Chapter 6.) And third, know the person who's giving you the reading. You shouldn't take medical advice from a doctor you don't trust; you shouldn't take financial advice from a guy who approaches you on the street. Why should you take the advice of a psychic you don't know and you have no way of checking up on?

Before I dig myself into a very deep hole, let me say that I'm obviously *not* opposed to people consulting psychics! I'm very proud of the fact that people come to me regularly, and I feel privileged to help my clients communicate with their loved ones, prevent possible problems, and get clear about their life choices. I think most people can benefit from a reading at some point in their lives. I myself go to other psychics from time to time. I also have a few friends who are very intuitive and they frequently get "hits" for me that will confirm what I'm feeling, or take me in a new direction, or give me hope that the situation will be resolved shortly. I believe at certain points we all need an outside perspective. If we're emotionally involved in a situation, it's almost impossible to be objective. We're too close; we get caught up in the emotion and the drama, and we may miss what the universe is giving us. We also may think we're paying attention to our intuition when in fact we're simply indulging in wishful thinking. Good psychics will be able to help you tune in better or give you additional insights on your problem. They can provide information untainted by your own emotions, beliefs, and concerns.

I think it's good to *go* to a psychic but not be *dependent* on a psychic. I believe that before you go to a psychic, you should do some research, just as you would when choosing any other professional. Find someone with a track record, a person you know is credible, through word of mouth or personal experience. If you see someone on TV or hear them on radio and they sound accurate and believable, get their number and call them. Ask for references—a good psychic is happy to have you contact his or her clients (with their permission, of course). If after you've checked references you feel confidence in this psychic's abilities, schedule a reading.

# What a *Good* Reading Is Like

If you've never had a reading with a good psychic, let me tell you what to expect. (This description is based on how I give readings, but the principles should apply to any authentic psychic.) A reading with a psychic is a very confidential, intimate, private experience. I believe it's a privilege to be the intermediary in conversations between my clients and their loved ones who have passed over. When someone trusts what you say and is willing to follow the guidance that comes through you, it's a huge responsibility. Because of that, I am very careful about reading for people without their permission. Even though I am fortunate to be able to read in almost any circumstance (from numerous radio and TV programs to the streets of New York to a chair lift at Aspen), I usually ask, "Is it okay if I do this?" Even when I'm reading in a public arena, such as a TV show, if I believe the information I'm getting is sensitive, I will tell someone to call me later or talk to me afterward. It's not my job to embarrass or discomfit people; I just want to be as clear a channel as possible.

In readings I'm often dealing with fundamental issues in clients' lives. Information may come in about long-hidden family secrets and traumas. Clients may hear things about themselves that they really don't want to know. The reading may be a mirror in which clients see their problems as well as answers to their questions, and it can get uncomfortable at times. While I will always ask permission to be frank with someone, once permission is given I don't pull any punches. What we deal with in this work is the truth—facing it, understanding it—because in truth we are freed. That's why some mental health counselors have told me, "A reading with you can cut six months off the time someone needs therapy, because you can pinpoint the psychological problem, where it comes from and how to deal with it, before we can uncover it."

I do try to be compassionate and understanding while being truthful. I give messages in a positive manner. And I really do care for every single person I read for. That can mean sometimes communicating what I get as gently as possible. If someone's grandmother who has passed over tells me the client's mother is facing health problems, I will say that in a way I believe the client will understand and accept. If I see challenges coming with a job or with finances, I might tell clients to prepare themselves for rough times ahead. But sometimes you have to be blunt to get through. If I see that a client will develop lung cancer in a few years, you'd better believe I'll do my best to get them to stop smoking. If someone's been in an abusive relationship for a long time, I'm not going to be nice about it—I'm going to tell them, "Get out now!" And if someone's behavior is mean or evil or hurting others, you better believe they're going to hear it from me. I'm not here to win friends and influence people. I'm here to help all of us discover our own greatest good. And since my clients are only allowed to call me once or twice a year, I have the responsibility—and the luxury—of being honest with them.

I once heard a story about another psychic. It was during a television program, and audience members were raising their hands to get a reading. A woman stood up and said, "I have no idea where my son is. I haven't heard from him for five years. He had emotional problems but the last we heard he was trying to make his way. We're beside ourselves." She was crying, and her husband sitting next to her was crying. And the psychic said, "Dead. Next!"

I would never be *that* blunt. And let me say right now, if I ever fail to be sensitive and compassionate enough in a reading, I'm sorry. Please know that in my heart I am sincerely trying to help everyone. But that story brings up another point about a psychic reading: as the client, you have to decide whether the psychic is a clear channel, or if his or her ego is getting in the way. That's a huge pitfall in doing this work, especially if you're good at it. People start treating you as if you have a direct channel to complete, total, universal wisdom every single moment of the day. Well, I have news for you: ego will foul up that channel faster than anything I know.

Someone once said to me, "You know what ego stands for? Edging God Out." As soon as you start using your psychic abilities to build up your ego or to control other people, that ego energy causes imbalance. It gets in the way of your being a pure messenger of truth. Ego also attracts (and can make us blind to) lower spirits and spirits that don't wish us well. So if you feel a psychic is on a power trip, don't walk, *run* for the nearest door. You don't need a reading that comes from a place of ego.

# Psychic Etiquette—on Both Sides of the Coin

As I said earlier, I will always ask permission before I read for someone. Unfortunately, some people won't extend the same courtesy to psychics. Once someone hears I'm a psychic, often they will ask me for a reading right then and there. Doing a reading can be very draining for me; usually I don't do more than three a day, preferably in the morning, so I can take it easy for the rest of the day. But it's really hard for me to say no when someone asks for a reading. It's gotten so I won't go to some dinner parties because I know I'll end up being the main entertainment.

I love doing what I do, but I also believe that people need to respect each other's privacy and boundaries. One evening last fall I had a young rabbi and his wife over for dinner, and we started talking about this very issue. When you're in some professions, people always assume that's who you are at every moment of the day. It doesn't occur to them that the doctor or lawyer or clergyman or psychic may not want to hear about your problems in a social situation; they may just want to have dinner or take a walk or hang out with friends. So if you ever meet me or any other professional, please be considerate. Relate to us as a people first, and don't ask for spur-of-the-moment advice. Respect our privacy as we do our best to respect yours.

Setting boundaries is key to anyone who wants to develop his or her own intuition. I tell all my students, "*You* be the one who decides when, where, and how you give information to others. If someone asks you for a reading you can politely tell them no—unless you really feel called to read for them." You see, every now and then I get a message from a very insistent soul who will not shut up until I pass the message along. Even in those cases, though, I always ask permission before I share the information.

The flip side of people asking me for readings on the street are the folks who believe that I can read their innermost thoughts as soon as I come into the room. They'll get fearful and inhibited around me because they think I'm reading their minds and know their deepest, darkest secrets. They expect me to know everything about them, past, present, and future. Oh boy! First of all, I'm good, but I'm not that good. (Heck, I wouldn't *want* to be!) Second, when people have that kind of reaction I believe it's because they're looking inside and seeing the truth about themselves. If they can't deal with the truth or they're hiding something, they become fearful—and I'm not doing anything to cause it! Most psychics I know may pick up certain feelings and impressions, but we usually have to focus to read anything deeper. So if we're at a party together, relax! Your secrets are safe.

Remember I said earlier that a psychic reading is a private, intimate experience? I've noticed with some clients that they can get a little strange or disconcerted after a reading, especially if any truly confidential information came out. (And believe me, it does. I've had readings where the spirits told me a man was seeing a male lover and hiding the relationship from his wife. I've been told of secret pregnancies or abortions . . . health conditions like cancer or AIDS . . . financial difficulties . . . all kinds of very private incidents. The universe has the knowledge, even if no one on this side does.) I guess it's like seeing your therapist out of his or her office—some people tend to think, "Uh-oh, she knows all about me!"

Well, aside from the fact that I would never violate a client's privacy, quite honestly, I rarely remember the details of a reading. I'm kind of like the phone line connecting people to their loved ones, spirit guides, and the universal source of wisdom. The information is not coming from me, it's coming *through* me. The phone line doesn't remember what's said on it; it's none of the phone line's business. And what comes through me is none of my business either. I receive it, I interpret it, and I forget it. That's why you'll see a lot of stories in this book told by my clients rather than me—I can't remember details to save my life!

Now you know a little bit about my story and why I do this work. In the next Section of this book I want to talk about some of the most important aspects of what I do, and try to give some answers to questions that have perplexed humanity for thousands of years. Where do intuitive messages come from? What happens to us when we die? How do spirits manage to break the barrier of death to speak to people on this side? And how can we evaluate these messages to make sure they truly support us in living a life in tune with our wisest self?

# Section One

# People Are Dying *to* Talk *to* You!

What's the biggest, blackest fear that most of us have? It's not just the fear of death—it's death as obliteration, death with nothing beyond it. We fear our loved ones are lost to us forever when they die. Most of all, we fear *we* will vanish when our time comes.

I'm here to tell you *death is not the end.* Almost every time I read for someone I can sense the presence of spirits around them. These spirits are usually the souls of loved ones who are no longer alive on this plane but who still exist and love on another level. Some of the most poignant "thank yous" I receive come from people who, at last, believe in the existence of life after death because they now feel the presence of their loved ones on the other side.

What survives everything—even death itself—is love. My father wrote in a prayer book he gave me, "God is Love, Love is God, We love you, Mom and Dad." Love is the highest energy force in the universe. And when we die, the thing that connects us all—the bridge—is the energy of love.

Our loved ones *want* us to continue to feel their love, to know that they're watching over us no matter how long it's been since they passed over. I feel privileged to be the channel for their messages, and *I want everyone who is open, everyone who is curious, everyone who is ready, to have the same opportunity*—to be able to experience that feeling of connection and closeness, as well as the absolute certainty that we do not die when the body stops breathing. So many people tell me, "I knew it! I knew my grandmother [or father or best friend] was still around me. I could feel it." All I'm doing is confirming what they already know. That certainty of survival is the gift our loved ones are eager to offer us—if we just open our minds and hearts to their presence.

# 4

## What Survives Death?

Philosophy, religion, and science have tried for centuries to answer questions about life and death, with varying degrees of success. What happens when the body dies? What happens to the part of you that is "you"? Does it continue to exist separate from your physical casing? And if so, where and how? What does "life after death" look like—if it exists at all?

I always knew there were spirits around me, but as a young child I didn't identify them as people who had died and were now appearing in another form. Then, when I was eleven, our housekeeper died. Since both my parents worked in the family furniture store, we had always had a housekeeper/nanny—Ruby. Ruby helped raise me. Though she had a daughter of her own, she called me her "other baby." The year I turned eleven, Ruby got very sick from cancer and died.

After her death, I started to feel an energy in our finished basement. It was a nice area, and Ruby had always done the family laundry and ironing down there. But every time I went into the basement, I could sense a familiar feeling, an energy that hadn't been there before but seemed very close to me. I also felt that same energy throughout the house when I was alone, especially in the hour or so after our new housekeeper left and before my parents came home. I didn't understand this energy and thus I was afraid of it. For years I would make my mother stand at the top of the basement stairs and talk to me whenever she sent me down there for any reason. But once I understood that the strange energy I sensed was Ruby's spirit, I wasn't so afraid anymore.

I now know that spirits of our loved ones are around us all the time—looking out for us, checking to see we're all right, keeping watch over us and protecting us as much as they can. It's an amazing feeling to be able to serve as the conduit for messages from those departed loved ones to the living. And since my gift is to be able to give very specific details—to hear names, to see images that have meaning only for the spirit and their loved ones, to feel nuances in relationships that only the departed soul itself would know—I am able to help people move beyond any doubt they may have about our survival after death. Our survival is certain, and not just generalized survival as a bunch of incoherent energy molecules, but survival as the people we are here, as Grandmother Martha or Uncle Frank or Mother or Father or brother Charles or best friend Deborah. Whether they are still here or waiting for us on the other side, we will continue to know and love our dear ones after we leave our bodies.

## Your Own Energy "Thumbprint"

Scientists tell us that everything in the universe is made up of energy, and that energy is never destroyed but simply transmutes into another form. I believe our spirits are made up of a kind of energy, too, and each spirit has its own distinct pattern—an energy "thumbprint" unique to that individual. That's why you can tell the difference between your mother and your father . . . between each of your children . . . even between identical twins. Their energy "thumbprints" are as different as the prints on their fingers. One student of mine describes tuning in to the different energies of her children. "Especially with my two youngest kids, I'll start to get antsy and fidgety, and I'll think, *Okay, one of them is up to something.* And since each child has a different vibration, when I tune in I can tell who it is and what they're doing."

This energy, this life force, is our spiritual body. It is separate from and does not die when the physical body dies, but simply goes to live in another dimension on another level. When someone dies, we may not be able to see that person's life force because it's no longer contained in its physical shell. But the life force goes somewhere. There are many people who have seen this—a lot of nurses tell of seeing an energy, or a "field" of something, leave the body at death. This life force isn't merely a residue or pattern of disembodied energy. It's *us*— coherent spirits with thoughts, memory, emotions, and love. We retain our identities in the spirit world. Your grandmother is still your grandmother, your child is still your child, you will still be you—but on a much more expanded level.

Because we're so familiar with someone's energy "thumbprint," we can sometimes pick up on that energy regardless of whether the shell is there. Can you distinguish between the energy of your spouse and another person? Can you sense which child has entered the room even if he or she is not in your direct line of vision? Can you sometimes tell who's on the phone before a word is spoken? If you've ever had any of these experiences, then doesn't it make sense that you could pick up on the specific energy of someone who has returned in spirit, since the spirit is simply who they truly are?

In recent years one of my students lost both her husband and teenage son, and she tells me she can feel the difference between their spirits. Many of us can feel this spirit energy, even if we can't identify its specific source. Haven't you ever been at your computer or at the kitchen sink and felt somebody near you, and you turned around and there was no one there? Have you ever seen something in your peripheral vision and when you turned your head, there was nothing? Or perhaps you lost a beloved pet, and even now you keep feeling it's still in the next room? (Yes, animals also have spirits and unique energy "paw prints.") Or for no particular reason you have a thought or get a feeling that reminds you strongly of your aunt or grandmother or parent? You're probably picking up on the energy of someone who passed over. People have this kind of experience all the time, especially following the death of a loved one. It's our loved ones' way of communicating with us, letting us know they're around and care for us still.

When I read for someone and connect with the spirits around them, one of the ways I know who I'm speaking to is this "us-ness," this unique energy thumbprint. For example, I'll be giving a reading for a client and different loved ones will come in. Then the client will tell me, "I'd like to hear from my brother," or, "There's someone you haven't talked about yet." And I'll put out a thought, "Okay, calling—" (whoever the client wants to hear from). Then, toward the end of the reading, I'll feel a presence show up, a new energy. And I'll say, "Wait a minute. Was there an N? Is it Nathan? Is that your brother?" The client will say, "Yes," and I'll say, "He just showed up—he must have been busy." Now, I don't know the client's brother from Adam, but I *do* pick up on the fact that a new energy entered the room. That energy will identify itself with a name and, often, a few details, and the connection between the client and the spirit has been made.

It's really important to understand that our loved ones feel our thoughts and good wishes. So many times I'll

give clients a name and say, "Is it your grandmother?"
And they'll say, "Yes—please tell her I love her." I reply,
"You're the one who has the connection. Just feel the love
for your grandmother and think, 'I love you,' and she'll
know it. You don't need me to connect to someone you
love."

## Making the Transition

The moment when someone leaves his or her body is
often sad for all of us who are left behind. Luckily, the
experience is very different for the spirit actually making
the transition. From what I have seen and learned in my
years of speaking with those who have had near-death
experiences, I believe the time of transition is a celebration—sort of like an Irish wake, with our departed loved
ones waiting for us with open arms on the other side.

I'm sure you've read about or heard of the different
elements of the death experience described in almost
every culture around the world: the white light . . . the
feeling of profound peace and joy . . . the sight of familiar faces welcoming us. What better way to help our soul
make its passage than by surrounding us with those we
loved during our lives? I believe this is one of our most
joyous responsibilities as spirits: to serve as a bridge
from this world to the other side for our family and
friends.

However, we are not just surrounded by our own loved
ones. We also may see other beings who mean a great
deal to us, and whom we trust. Some people see Jesus,
Mohammed, the Buddha, or Moses; others see angelic
figures composed of light. Others report seeing a being
they cannot put a name to, but whom they declare is
unconditional love. But whoever and whatever we see at
the time of death, it's clear that we are given these visions
to encourage us to step across the divide.

Once our spirits step fully into the next world, there is

some kind of review of the life we have just completed. I don't believe it's like Judgment Day, with a big bad God condemning some souls and elevating others. I don't experience God like that; the God I know exists at the highest level of absolute goodness, unconditional love, and unlimited wisdom. I believe that instead of being judged by God, we must each judge ourselves in what we imagine to be God's eyes, in line with our own conscience. We are required to account for the use we've made of our lives. Have we grown and progressed? Have we hurt others? Have we allowed ourselves to become victims unnecessarily? Have we helped people? Have we been compassionate to others? Have we loved?

In the twinkling of an eye, everything flashes before us and we see where we have grown and failed to grow. But this is not a judgment to send us to heaven or hell; it shows how this lifetime has helped our soul to progress. You see, I believe that our souls are continuously evolving through many lifetimes. Our whole purpose, the reason we were born and the reason we continue to exist, is to evolve as souls so that we can eventually become part of the universal consciousness—the goodness, love, and wisdom that is God.

We do much of our growing during our lifetimes on earth, but we also continue to grow as spirits on the other side. That's one of the reasons the spirits of our loved ones stay around. They are eager to help us not just because they care, but because it's part of the mission of every soul to help others. And who better to help than the people with whom you are already connected through bonds of love—perhaps a love that has lasted through *several* lifetimes? Remember, you are the captain of an entire team of spirits. You are being watched over and protected and loved by many caring beings on the other side of the divide we call death.

# The World of the Spirits

Where exactly is this other world—what's been called the "astral plane," the "spirit dimension," the "other side," and a lot of other very nonspecific terms? (There's really no way to describe accurately the dimension or plane where our spirits go after death. It's a much greater concept than any term can encompass.) Itzhak Bentov, a great physicist who studied what he called the "mechanics of consciousness" back in the 1970s, believed there was a plane of reality that connects all life—plants, animals, humans, spirits, every single atom of matter and energy in the universe. This reality (which he called the "astral level") is always present even if we cannot always tune into it, but it is where our spirits go when we die. Bentov believed that we tune into this astral level when we sleep; he thought this was nature's way of preparing us to function exclusively on the astral level after death.

Other great thinkers have proposed that when our bodies die our spirits simply move into a parallel dimension or universe, and that multiple dimensions or universes exist for spirits at different levels of evolution. In these dimensions, like energy attracts like energy, and at death you're drawn to the same kind of energy you yourself manifested during your lifetime. I would venture to say when Hitler died, he didn't end up in the same place as Mahatma Gandhi!

In the movie *Ghost,* there were a couple of scenes that showed spirits making the transition to the other side and being drawn to similar energy. Patrick Swayze (the good guy) saw a white light and golden figures beckoning him in welcome. The bad guys saw black shadows with claws, croaking horribly as they tore at the terrified souls they had come to fetch. Simplistic? Sure. Fictional? Of course—but perhaps possessing a grain of truth. (I actually know of someone who had a near-death experience and saw demons. I think it scared her back to life, because it made her realize she had a lot more work to do on the earth plane!)

Perhaps heaven and hell are simply spending eternity in the company of like spirits. Those who have lived at a low level, refusing to evolve, focusing only on causing harm, all end up together, doing the same things to each other and thus creating their own hell. Conversely, spirits that have worked with love to achieve the highest and best on this planet end up with others of the same kind—which could be pretty heavenly indeed! No matter what you believe about the next world and how it operates, however, two principles seem to be at work: 1) what we do here affects us even after we die, and 2) we are in a state of continuous growth and evolution. I believe all dimensions, levels, planes, realities, whatever you want to call them, are part of the same universal consciousness, the same eternal flow of awakened and aware energy. No matter where we end up after this lifetime, we will continually be given opportunities to change, to try again, to make it better the next time—because *that is the nature of the universe.* The goal of every being in every dimension is to grow and evolve until there is no difference between it and that ultimate state of love, goodness, and wisdom. Ending up in "hell" or "heaven" are only different stages of our spiritual evolution.

## Many Lifetimes of Growth

The good news is, we have a lot of chances to grow and evolve right here on earth—not just in one lifetime, but again and again and again. In each lifetime we possess a unique spirit, the energy thumbprint I was talking about earlier. That individual vibration or energy will continue when we enter the spirit world; we will continue to be wife, husband, mother, father, son, daughter, friend. At the same time, everything we have learned and experienced in the lifetime we just completed is added to the record of our soul, which is comprised of all the lifetimes we have experienced over the ages. Our soul is the book, and each lifetime is a different chapter. All the chapters are part of the book, yet each is separate within the greater whole.

I believe the soul level is where we make the decisions about what we need to do in our next lifetime to make amends or grow in a new direction. For instance, in a very early lifetime you might have been a caveman who killed his wife accidentally and then ran off, leaving his children to starve. When you die, your spirit records that pretty bad life in your soul. So you come back in the 1500s as a nun who dedicates her life to healing. The next time you end up as a farmer in the 1800s who raises a family and fights the Indians somewhere in North Dakota. We go through many lifetimes as men and women of all different races and cultures. Each lifetime we're trying to atone for our past misdeeds and continue to grow in wisdom, love, and goodness.

Occasionally we retain some memory of our experiences to carry from lifetime to lifetime. Most of the time we remember our past lives only as vague impressions, or dreams, or that sense of knowing a certain person or place we've never seen before. Sometimes we can retain even more—perhaps child prodigies in fields like music and science are simply remembering what they learned in past lifetimes. But our past lives *can* shape what we do with this life, either consciously or unconsciously. I believe that different sexual orientations may be due to impressions from past lives: women who are influenced by all the lifetimes they've been men, and vice versa. Sometimes I think past-life memories also show up as fears or warnings. Certain people may be afraid of swimming, for example, because they drowned in a past life.

Others may be exceedingly upright and never stray from their marriage vows because they were unfaithful in a previous existence and caused themselves and their loved ones an enormous amount of pain.

I also believe we stay connected with other souls over several lifetimes. That caveman who killed his wife, for example, may end up as the daughter of his wife's spirit the next time, and be abused by her to even out his karmic debt. On a more pleasant note, two lovers on earth may be husband and wife one time, mother and child the next, and best friends the next. When the connection of love is strong enough, spirits can stay linked throughout time and space, lifetime after lifetime.

After each lifetime here on earth, we add those deeds to the record of our soul until it has evolved to a place where we no longer need to come back to earth again. I believe that spirit guides and guardian angels are beings who have evolved to a higher level and are given the task of helping and guiding us. They may have some connection with us from past lifetimes; they may even be people we have known in this life. In my readings several clients have been told that their deceased great-aunt or grandfather or even best friend is now their guardian angel, ready to protect them whenever they need it. It's a nice feeling when someone you already know and love becomes your spiritual protector.

But let me be clear: Spirit guides and guardian angels are *not* God. Some religions and psychics believe that we should regard such beings as infallible and become totally reliant on their advice. But I see great danger in this approach. There is only one highest level of goodness, love, and wisdom that is far beyond any spirit or angel or any other being we can understand. Spirit guides and guardian angels are spirits like us; perhaps they are further along the path of their own growth toward becoming completely united with God. But until they reach that state of union, they should be regarded as advisors and protectors and never relied on exclusively. *We're* the ones responsible for the deeds of our lifetime; we make our own decisions and must live with the consequences, both here and in the hereafter.

That being said, I think that spirit guides and guardian angels are there to help us do the best we can with our lives, mainly by guiding us at certain times and protecting us from negative energies. Like an older brother or sister showing us "the ropes," they grow and evolve by helping us do the same, watching out for us as we walk our own path with God.

It's important to realize how much love and protection surrounds each one of us as we journey through our lives. *We are not alone.* In our darkest despair and our most ecstatic joy, our loved ones, spirit guides, and guardian angels are there to console us and cheer us on. They *want* to see us grow and evolve and learn the lessons of this lifetime to the best of our ability, so we may all come together in the wholeness and glory of the universal love that is God.

# We're in Charge of Our Destiny

One of the things that spirits can do for us here is advise us about the future. But there are a couple of important points to remember. First, spirits have personalities and anything they tell us may be colored by their opinions. (I'll talk more about this in Chapter 6.) Second, not everything is predestined; our lives are not set in stone. A choice, a change by one individual can have enormous effects on the lives of others. What would have happened if your mother had married someone other than your father? What if you were to take a different job, have an unplanned child, or take a different route to the grocery store and run into the back of a truck? Like dominoes, one change can set a whole chain of events in motion. I do believe that some things we are destined to go through, because we have to pay for actions we have taken or not taken in past lives. But a lot more is subject to change than you might think.

Each one of us is being given an opportunity to grow—if we choose to. We always have free will. I would hope that we all can create our own piece of heaven on earth by making life choices that we can live with. It's all about being able to look in the mirror every morning and live with ourselves. I think people who have a hard time acknowledging their faults end up in a hell of their own making, both when they're alive and when they die. We have to take a look at ourselves and see clearly where we have grown, where we have contributed, and where we have failed. We will deal with the truth sooner or later—either now or when we die. Why not do it now so we can continue to grow and evolve the entire time we're blessed to be on this earth?

The most important thing that survives death is love. It's what we are made of, what we communicate with, and what we ultimately return to. Most spirits come to us from love, to let us know they still care, sometimes to warn us or to complete unfinished business, and mostly to connect heart to heart with us again. Love will always be our lifeline—to the spirits around us, the people who are still on this plane, and to the universal unconditional love that is God.

# 5

## Messages from the Other Side

Several years ago I gave a phone reading to a lovely woman named "Jennifer." (While most of my clients are happy to have their names used in this book, a few of them, like "Jennifer," have asked that I respect their privacy by changing their names.) Jennifer had gotten my name from friends, but as usual, I knew nothing about her, and it was her first reading with any psychic.

The messages she received that day healed a very deep hurt from her past. I started by telling her she had three children, but she said no, she only had two. However, I kept picking up on another child. After I got the name Harry, told her it was her father's spirit and that he was her guardian angel ("I knew that," she said), I then picked up on an S, a Sam. "That's my grandfather," Jennifer told me. "But there's another S, a female." Jennifer started to cry. That other S was Samantha, the third child I had talked about. Samantha died when she was a baby.

I said, "Your daughter's fine, she's with your father. I see her, and *she's holding the duck*." Jennifer gasped. "I had put a stuffed animal in the coffin with Samantha when we buried her, but it wasn't a teddy bear or bunny or doll or anything else you might think—it was Jemima

Puddleduck from Beatrix Potter. Only myself, my husband, my son, and the rabbi knew that," Jennifer said.

"Well, it may sound a little hard, but I'm getting that if Samantha hadn't died then, it would have happened before she grew up," I replied. Through her tears, Jennifer told me, "I said almost the exact same thing to my husband when Samantha went."

Later Jennifer called to thank me. "That reading with you gave me such peace," she said. "Knowing that Samantha was all right, that she was with my father, and that my own intuition at the time of her death had been correct—it made such a difference for me. And you were so specific. It wasn't just, 'Your daughter's fine, she's with your father.' Only three other people in the world knew about the duck, but you saw it."

Most of the world's religions teach us the soul lives on, but without evidence it's all too easy to doubt those teachings. Enormous healing can happen when we know that our mother or father, the spouse with whom we raised a family, grandparents whom we remember as sources of unconditional love, friends who passed over through accident or disease, children who left us much too soon, are still there, unseen by our eyes but loving us nonetheless. That's why the details are so important in a reading, why the spirits will tell or show me the little things that only they and their loved ones could know. It's a kind of confirmation that helps most people move from doubting to believing to *knowing* that the soul does survive the body's death.

I did some work about five years ago with a bereavement group of men who were HIV-positive. They had all lost lovers and close friends to AIDS. (This was before the HIV drug "cocktail," so most of these men were walking time bombs.) I picked up so many things about friends of theirs who had already died—like, "So-and-so's with you," (giving the name), or "He gave you a picture and now you have it in your bathroom." Those sessions were very intense, because not only was I letting them know that they, too, would survive the death of the body, but also I was reassuring them that their loved ones were nearby and would be waiting for them on the other side.

Just yesterday I read for a woman and told her, "Your grandmother is showing me a locket. Do you have her locket?" She answered, "No." "Well, she's showing me a picture in a locket," I said, and the woman replied, "Oh my God, I asked my husband to buy me a locket for my birthday so I could put my grandmother's picture in it—and a photo of the other aunt that you just picked up on!"

When my dad was in the hospital several years ago, he shared a semiprivate room with a very elderly retired attorney. One day my father was bragging about "his daughter the psychic" to this gentleman and his wife who was visiting. They both thought it was a lot of bunk. The next day I came to the hospital to visit my dad, and the gentleman's wife was there again. After a few moments, I looked at her and asked, "Who was Gitala?" The woman said, "Oh my gosh. That was my mother." I said, "Gitala's with you now and she's showing me her hands. They're not crippled anymore. She's healthy and well on the other side." The woman started to cry. She said, "My mother had severe arthritis and her hands were completely crippled." Those details completely changed the way this woman thought about life after death.

By the way, it's not only humans who will come through during a reading. Many people are deeply connected to their pets and are devastated when a beloved cat or dog dies. Well, those spirits stay around us, too. Recently a woman came to me because she had just lost her favorite cat. I told her the cat's name and let her know it was fine, and it made all the difference in the world for that woman. I also read for another long-term client whose husband had passed away several years before. During that year's reading, I saw a large black "thing" with her husband's spirit. I said, "Cathy, what is that?" She answered, "Oh, that's Major, our Great Dane. I recently had to put him down. That dog really loved my husband; he would always try to crawl in Tom's lap." "Well, he's with Tom now and they're having a great time," I told her.

For people who have never lost an animal they cared deeply about, those readings can seem trivial; but speaking as someone who has had many beloved animal companions, I always want to know my four-footed loved ones are healthy and happy on the other side.

## Knowing Who's Coming Through

How do we know that our loved ones are truly speaking to us in a reading? How can we tell it's *them,* rather than simply generic information floating through the cosmos? It's not simply the details, the knowledge no one would know but a spouse or child or parent. It's in the way the spirits communicate. We keep our personalities after we pass over, so we continue to talk and feel and react in ways our loved ones here will find very familiar.

Often I'm able to pick up on the language patterns, rhythms and expressions a spirit used while they were alive. For a long time before his death, the great jazz musician Miles Davis was a client and friend of mine. In fact, we were so close that when he went to the hospital during what turned out to be his final illness, he called me before he called the ambulance. Through Miles, I met Gordon Meltzer, who was Miles's manager for several years. Not too long after Miles died, I had dinner with Gordon and his wife in New York City. In the middle of the meal, I told Gordon, "Miles's spirit is here and he has a message for you. He says, 'Don't make my horn sound so tinny.'" Gordon tells me when I said that, my voice got low and raspy, sounding the way Miles used to when he was alive.

The message itself astounded Gordon. Miles had died in the middle of recording material for a very special hip-hop album, designed to make his music more accessible to young people. He had recorded a bunch of tracks with hip-hop sound engineers, who were really familiar only with music generated electronically. As a result, while the studio sessions were great, Miles's trumpet playing sounded very thin, harsh, and metallic on tape. But before they could re-record it, Miles had died. The day we went to dinner, Gordon had decided to go back into the studio and see if he could "warm up" the sound of Miles's trumpet. Only he and a couple of engineers at the recording studio knew about his plans. Gordon told me, "When that message from Miles came through, it felt really good to hear that warming up the sound was the right thing to do. I mean, here was a guy who was my mentor in many ways, who gave me the opportunities to produce records. I missed him. And Miles really wanted this album to succeed. He used to sit in his apartment in summertime with the windows open, listening to the kids on the street with the boom boxes playing hip-hop tracks. Miles wanted his voice heard by those kids. And it was—the album I 'warmed up' that night won a Grammy."

Sandra Messinger has also been a client of mine for several years. At her first reading, she was very upset because her grandmother had died a short time before. "My grandmother had a very distinctive way of talking, and I don't know how you did it, but you sounded exactly like she talked," she told me. "You said my grandmother knew I was putting a lot of effort into taking care of a cat. You said she told you, in a joking way, 'When I wanted something, you didn't do it, but the cat—taking care of the cat is so important to you.' That was exactly what my grandmother would say. I felt it was really my grandmother coming through, and it made me feel that she was okay."

I'm certainly not the only one who can pick up on spirits' voice patterns. A student of mine often has a girlfriend over to play games. One night the two of them were playing Scrabble, and my student said something seemingly innocuous. Her friend turned to her and said, "That's just what my grandmother used to say all the time. At that moment, you sounded and looked just like her." My student laughed and said, "Well then, I guess you'd better listen!"

In many readings people also have the *sense* of a different kind of energy, the feeling that their loved one is standing right next to them. At one reading I asked my client, "Is there a Dora or Devorah?" He said, "Pretty close. My grandmother's name was Doris. She passed away when I was eleven." I said, "She's the one who's communicating with me. She said that she's looking over your baby and everything's going to be fine. She's your baby's guardian." The gentleman told me later this reading meant a lot to him for three reasons. One, his wife was pregnant with their first child at the time, and it was very comforting to know the baby was being watched over. Second, he had very strong feelings arise when his grandmother came through. "I felt kind of tingly, almost as if the hair on the back of my neck was going to stand up," he said. "There was an overwhelming feeling of emotion towards my grandmother—a feeling of closeness, that I'd missed her, almost like I wanted to cry— that just suddenly rushed up and overwhelmed me. I've never felt that before or since." Third, after our reading he spoke with his grandmother's only living sister. It turned out his grandmother's name *was* originally Dora, not Doris—and her Hebrew name was Devorah. "Up to that point I considered myself skeptical but open-minded. *That* made me a believer," he says.

When we speak with those we loved who have passed over, there are also opportunities for unspoken truths to come out, and often I find that expressing those unspoken truths is very freeing. I read for a young man, "Robert," in 1985, right after he had lost his dearest friend in the world to AIDS. Robert had been visiting this man for many months, even though at the time there was still a lot of misunderstanding about AIDS and how it was transmitted. While the friends and family of this man had just about deserted him, Robert kept visiting right to the very end. You see, Robert knew in his heart that he had fallen in love with his dying friend. But, he said later, "I never told a living soul—it was less complicated to keep it to myself."

At our reading, right away I picked up the friend's first name and the fact that he had died of AIDS. "His spirit is around you," I told Robert. "He thought he was in love with you when he passed over." That message absolutely changed Robert's life. "Up until that moment, I had felt judged by God and robbed of my chance of love," he wrote me afterward. "I feared death profoundly. I thought I was alone in life. No more. Now I know the power of love that exists in the universe."

# Being Healed by Forgiveness

Forgiveness and healing are two of the most important messages that come through in readings. Death makes a lot of things clearer; it shows us how trivial many of our quarrels and concerns are, and causes us to focus on the love at the core of our relationships. But so often we feel incomplete when someone passes over. We never had a chance to heal that breach of years past. We could never say the things we wanted to when our loved ones were alive, and now that they're dead it's all too easy to believe we will never have that chance. But you can communicate your love with departed loved ones in an instant—

simply by calling them to memory and using the power of your thoughts to speak to them. Our loved ones hear us when we do that. They are as near as our next breath if we want them to be. And they're often just as eager (if not more) to heal a breach in the family.

I remember a student of mine called me for a reading shortly after her mother had passed over. The mother did come through in our reading, but, as my student said, it wasn't with a welcome message! "You asked me who Helen was, and I had to think about it for a while," my student told me. "Then I remembered and said, 'Yes, I know a Helen but that's not what we call her.' You then hit on her nickname, which was Holly, and said, 'I have a message from your mother. She wants you to let go of the grudge. It's over and done with.' Well, I've had a grudge against my aunt Holly for twenty years. But my mother had just passed over, and since she was bothering to come back and tell me to let it go, I figured I'd better. After all, I was getting it from the 'higher-ups.'"

I believe that forgiveness is very important. I think the truth catches up with us, either here or on the other side, and we have to learn how to face our own faults and face the truth about ourselves and others. We have to learn how to apologize and forgive so that spiritually we can be healed. It's better to handle as much of that as we can before death, of course, because if we don't handle it here, we're going to have to handle it in the hereafter!

Several years ago a movie called *Flatliners* came out. It was about a bunch of medical students who competed with each other to see how long each of them could stay clinically "dead" before being resuscitated by the others. As a result of their sojourns to the "other side," each of the medical students had to deal with people and situations from their past. One fellow had accidentally caused the death of a playmate; another had been part of a bunch of kids who heartlessly teased a little girl who was different from them; another was a sexual predator who seduced every woman he encountered. All of them were haunted by the images of the people they had hurt during their lives.

A fourth student had witnessed the suicide of her father when she was about eight. In one of the climactic moments in the film, this young woman had a vision in which her father came back and asked for her forgiveness. She saw his death was not her fault, and she was able to forgive him and hug him and tell him how much she loved him. Both father and daughter were healed in that moment.

Sometimes the movies can contain the seeds of profound truth. In this case, each of the students in the movie had to atone for the wrongs they had done when they were alive. They had to ask for and be given forgiveness—and also had to forgive in their turn. Unfortunately, when people pass over, we're not always ready to forgive them and be healed. It may take years of therapy for us to understand why a parent was abusive, why a child took his or her own life, why a lover left us for someone else. It can take time until we're ready emotionally to let the hurt go. And that's fine. I believe that healing can always happen when we're ready for it—and our loved ones are accessible to us whether they're still alive, or they've passed over.

So if there's someone you need to forgive, whether they're alive or dead, make sure to do it while you're still here. Every time you think negatively about someone who has hurt you, you're pouring salt into an open wound. As soon as you forgive them sincerely, the wound starts to heal from the inside. Eventually it will form a scar, and then the scar itself will start to fade, to the point you will be able to say, "Yes, I was hurt, but I learned from it. I've let it go. It's just an old, faded scar."

But it's not just important for *us* to heal. It's equally if not more important for those who have passed over that we forgive their actions here on earth. So many times spirits have come through me to tell a loved one, "I'm sorry—I was a terrible father [or mother or spouse] when I walked the earth's plane. Can you please forgive me?" And when the person here can say, "Yes, I forgive you," and really mean it wholeheartedly, it allows them both to "let go and let God." They can start to grow and evolve in the ways they need to, whether they're here or on the other side.

Some of the saddest people who come to me are both the spirits of those who have committed suicide and the loved ones they have left behind. I've seen firsthand the trauma and guilt of the families of those who have chosen to end their own lives. The family members ask why; they wonder if in some way they contributed to their loved one's death; they feel unresolved and incomplete, with anger and grief and guilt all mixed together. And I know for many of them their pain is increased because they believe suicide condemns their loved one forever.

I've had around twenty different readings where spirits of people who took their own lives came through, and almost every single time, an enormous healing takes place. These spirits usually will apologize to their parents or their loved ones for putting them through such grief and aggravation. They will say they killed themselves because they couldn't handle things anymore—most of the time because they couldn't face the truth about themselves—or because they were psychologically or chemically imbalanced. Often they will even say they don't remember actually taking their own lives. But when they got to the other side, they realized that they still had unfinished business on earth. By not seeing their lives through despite all the pain, they didn't fulfill their purpose on earth, and they will have to come back again in another lifetime to finish it. And these spirits need to begin that process by asking forgiveness of their loved ones.

One of the best parts of my work is being a channel for the contact that allows for forgiveness after death. I love helping to bring peace and healing to the world. It's impossible not to be compassionate to these deeply hurting people. I literally will sit and cry with my clients when I see how profoundly they are affected by a message from a loved one whom they thought never to hear from again, or I feel a spirit finally attaining forgiveness. When I give someone indisputable proof of a loved one's survival, it brings incredible peace to them and an amazing sense of satisfaction to me, because I've been able to help.

As my sister Elaine says, "Hearing messages from our loved ones on the other side eliminates the fear of death. Not of dying—I think that all of us don't want to die in pain or of a long, slow, lingering disease. But when you realize that death itself is simply a transition from one place to another, and that we will continue to be connected with and care for the people we now treasure in our lives, then it's not such a fearsome prospect."

Messages from the other side are important because they bring us hope and confirm our faith in life after death. Without faith or hope, it's difficult to move forward. We all want to believe; we want to feel the kind of love that lasts beyond the parting of death. When we get a chance to feel the love and compassion offered so willingly and so completely by our loved ones on the other side, it opens us up to giving that love and compassion to others while we're here, and growing in our own souls as a result.

My client Suzie summed this up perfectly. She wrote, "Before I had my reading with you, I went through life feeling as if I was carrying around a lot of 'extra baggage.' I was terrified of death; I had a lot of losses in my life; and I needed to know that my loved ones were all right. I had a lot of questions that needed to be answered about the direction my life was heading.

"My reading was honestly one of the best experiences of my life. Death no longer scares me. I know that one day I will be reunited with my loved ones, who are at peace and now are my guardian angels. I no longer feel confused or guilty. All my questions and then some were answered! That reading truly gave me peace, and that is something that I will always cherish and remember."

# 6

## Don't Believe Everything You Hear, Even If It's from Your Dead Grandmother

Once a young woman came to me for a reading, and the spirit of her grandmother came through with some very definite suggestions. "Tell my granddaughter she should marry a nice Jewish boy," the grandmother said. Unfortunately, the young woman was in love with somebody very different at the time, and asked me what she should do. "Don't believe everything you hear, even if it comes from your dead grandmother," I said. "Follow your heart and tell your grandmother to take a hike. Just because she's dead, your grandma isn't omniscient. She's entitled to her opinions, but *you're* entitled to live your life the way you want to. You need to go with your gut." My client married her non-Jewish young man, and has been very happy.

We need to remember that spirits are like friends. Some friends give us good advice; some give us bad advice. But it's up to us to decide whether to take the advice we're given. We need to evaluate advice we receive from *any* source with our own logic, common sense, and intuition—the combination that I call your "wisest self."

Many of the stories I've told so far in this book describe speaking with the spirits of departed loved ones. But those

spirits are never my primary source of information. When
I read, I always go first to the highest level of universal
consciousness that is goodness, love, and God. My friend
Mark (an excellent intuitive himself) describes it as going
directly to the *Encyclopedia Britannica* instead of getting
information from the encyclopedia salesman. I believe
that by seeking the highest level of goodness and wisdom
first, I am both protected from evil and also become a
clearer channel for truth for my clients.

Many different spirit guides, guardian angels, and
departed loved ones do come in to help me help others.
But as I said in Chapter 4, spirits inhabit different levels.
There are spirits who are lower-level energy, like poltergeists. Others evolve over time to higher levels; they
become spirit guides, guardian angels, and eventually sit
at the right hand of God. As I frequently remind my
clients, however, "Just because someone's dead doesn't
mean they're wiser than we are."

Each of us on this plane is a spirit in our own right. As
spirits, we are responsible for making our own choices
and decisions. After all, each of us will be held account-
able for our choices when we pass over. We won't be able
to get out of our responsibility by saying (like Flip Wil-
son), "The devil made me do it," or even, "My spirit
guide told me to do it." *We're* the ones who took the
action, and we're the ones who will have to answer for
our actions on the other side. It's our job to choose good
over evil, to do the best we can with the lives we've been
given. Therefore, we should use every single resource we
possess to keep ourselves on track and in alignment with
the highest possible level of goodness and wisdom.

That's one of the reasons I'm so passionate about
teaching people how to use their intuition, because it's
such an underutilized yet supremely valuable tool for living the best life we can. God gave us this sixth sense to go

along with the other five. But God also gave us a seventh sense as well—common sense—along with brains that can think and reason. I believe God expects us to use every sense we have, and our thinking, reasoning brains as well, to the best of our ability. And I also believe God demands that we take responsibility for our own lives every step of the way.

Taking responsibility means first, we must weigh our decisions carefully, using all our faculties to arrive at the best course of action. Second, we must never take advice from *any* source without evaluating it thoroughly. Third, we must realize there is a God/higher consciousness/universal wisdom and seek to align ourselves with that force. And fourth, we must seek to do what's right and be the best person we can.

## Depend on Yourself, Not Your Spirit Guides

When I was first learning to use my psychic abilities, I encountered several people who seemed to elevate spirits to the level of gods. "The spirits will never steer you wrong," they would say to me. They believed spirits were omniscient, always good, always helpful. But I wasn't comfortable with that attitude. I felt it wasn't healthy to give control over to spirits (as many trance mediums do). I thought that people who depended on spirits and prayed to personalities could be misguided far too easily. I couldn't believe that spirits knew everything and I knew nothing. I felt strongly that my spirit was just as valuable as any in God's eyes. I also believed that intuition should be used for our empowerment, not so we could surrender ourselves to someone else's energy, whether it be spirit guide, guardian angel, dead grandmother—or human being.

Then one day I heard a phrase, "Listen to your guides but go with God." That encapsulated exactly what I had been feeling and doing ever since I started to use my psychic abilities. I had automatically gone past individual spirits and touched what I experienced as universal consciousness—where there is only oneness, all individuality drops away and we experience everything as goodness, wisdom, light, and love. I felt that all spirits eventually evolve to merge into that oneness, and I knew I could trust that "God-consciousness" to offer me truth unfiltered by personalities or desires.

To this day, every time I do a reading I say a prayer which asks the universal consciousness to protect me as I communicate with spirits on the other side. When I do that, I know I will be protected from negative energies. I will be tipped off if a spirit wishes harm to myself or a client, and I'll remember to listen to what I call my "wisest self"—that part of me which is always connected to universal consciousness.

## How to Evaluate an Intuitive or Psychic Message

Now, I'm certainly not saying "don't get a reading," or "don't use your intuition." I believe with my whole heart that intuition is a gift from God to help us stay aligned with the universal wisdom and love. I think my readings help my clients to live better lives. But you have to evaluate everything you receive with your own unique psychic radar. Be alert. Keep both your eyes open—and keep your "third eye" open as well.

I tell everyone to check all messages—whether from their own intuition or from someone else, like a psychic—using three criteria. First, *use your common sense*. If you get a message to give all your money to a particular church or individual, would anybody with common sense believe it? I hope not. Second, *use the logical, thinking part of your brain.* Would your departed grandmother come through and tell you to take a gun and shoot someone? Not unless your grandmother was Ma Barker or Bonnie Parker—and logic would tell you it would be a bad idea to act upon that message in any case. If the spirits tell you to do something you would consider stupid, don't do it!

Third, *check the message against your own wisest self.* Put a white light of protection around yourself and say a prayer to be guided by universal love, goodness, and wisdom. So many people tell me, "Char, I got this message from so-and-so or about such-and-such, but when I checked inside, it just didn't feel right." When you use your intuition regularly to tune in to the highest possible level, you'll pick up on subtle changes in energy—what some psychics call "vibrations." You'll be able to tell when something is in alignment with the universe and when it's not. And when you take that sense of rightness or wrongness and put it together with the evaluation of your common sense and logic, you're a lot less likely to be fooled by messages from here or the hereafter.

Remember, you have free will; you have choice. Don't ever let yourself become dependent on the messages you're getting from someone else, whether it be a psychic like me, a friend who can tune in, or even a spirit guide or departed loved one who comes through. You can take or leave any advice you're given. If my clients don't act on the messages I give them, I don't get angry. Frankly, when I read, the messages come *through* me. I give them and walk away, because it's none of my business. I don't have to live with the results of their actions; they do. I'm simply here to help people find their own ways to help themselves.

I will admit, I am very proud of the fact that many of my clients tell me that they have learned to trust their own intuition as a result of the readings they've had with me. One gentleman said, "I tend to call Char when I'm confused and need a better sense of understanding. After a reading, I find I have greater confidence in my own direction. I end up making decisions and going forward, but I'll trust my own intuition a little more. I go my own course with a much greater sense of confidence." Each one of us is always the best evaluator of psychic impressions that pertain to us, whether they come from inside ourselves or from another person. You are more tuned in to your own future, your own path, than anyone else can be. After all, the future can change at any given moment. If you are using your intuition to stay in sync, you will learn to feel the energy of the situation change, which can change the path you will take and the role you will play. That's one of the best reasons I know for developing your intuition as fully as possible.

Intuition often provides us with valuable clues we won't get any other way. But for it to make sense and be applicable to our lives, all information—*all* information—has to be processed and interpreted by the brain. The mind takes what intuition provides (whether it comes from the highest source of wisdom, a spirit guide, a departed loved one, or a guardian angel) and then puts that information in the context of the best course for our lives. The mind is a wonderful "gatekeeper" which can prevent us from making stupid mistakes due to bad information or bad interpretation.

God gave you a brain. God gave you common sense. And God gave you intuition. Use all three and you'll discover how easy it can be to make sense of the guidance the universe is offering you. As one of my students says, "When you know you have intuition and you're comfortable with it and trust it, and at the same time you also use your intellect along with it, you generally will find you can make good judgments."

I have spent the last several years developing my own method for awakening and using your own intuition. The next Section will introduce you to six simple steps that will help unlock your own natural abilities and lead you to discover a whole new world of information and guidance arising from sources other than the logical brain—sources that can make your life easier, happier, and better than ever.

# Section Two

## Tapping *in to* Your Wisest Self

If you want to know what the universe has in store for you . . . if you'd like to communicate with someone you loved who has passed over . . . if you feel it's important to protect yourself from negative energies, both here and on the spirit side . . . if developing your natural abilities to their fullest is one of your goals . . . if you'd like to prevent potential problems in your own life and help others do the same . . . if you'd like to contribute to people and perhaps make this world a better place . . . if your spirit wishes to feel a deep connection with the highest level of goodness, wisdom, and love called God-consciousness . . . or if you'd just like to be able to find your wallet when it's missing . . . then the next section of this book is specifically for you!

Everyone is hungry for answers about their lives, and the universal consciousness has the answers for us. We just need to get out of the way and allow the answers in. Intuition is the primary means the universe uses to contact and connect with us. We all have intuition. We all have the ability to tap in to our wisest self, that part of us which has more knowledge and wisdom than the conscious mind, and which can help guide our lives with greater intelligence. Intuition gives us direct access to the highest levels of universal consciousness, where we join our own spirits to divine goodness, wisdom, and love. When we use our intuition to connect to that level, our lives become easier, simply because we are aligned with destiny rather than fighting it.

Intuition can't eliminate all our problems. We are put on this earth to learn different lessons with each lifetime, and sometimes those lessons require going through difficulties. But when we use our intuition to help guide us, it's like riding a surfboard. We can use the currents of destiny to our advantage, giving us more momentum and a much more pleasant ride than if we had tried to swim through the same patch of ocean. In the same way, tuning in to what the universe has in store for us helps us prevent potential problems and attain the goals we set for ourselves. It enables us to face our fears and live a life grounded in truth—about ourselves, about the people we love, about life, the realities of death, and the life hereafter. And yes, living in tune with our wisest self can make us happier, because we see more clearly how we are surrounded by universal, unconditional love.

After many years of using my own intuition, and now having trained hundreds of people in my method for tapping in to their wisest selves, I can say with confidence that *intuition will take you places logic never could.* The six steps of my method are designed to teach you the fundamentals of discovering and using your own intuitive powers. But before you learn them, we need to get a few old preconceived notions out of the way. We need to answer the question, "Why use your intuition?" and demonstrate that you've already had at least one "psychic" experience, and explode nine common myths that might block your innate intuitive ability. Once we've done this, you're ready to start the journey to your own wisest self. Relax—it's a short trip, filled with wonderful guideposts along the way!

# 7

# Why Use Your Intuition?

Here are two situations that are becoming more and more common: 1) You go on-line, get into an Internet chat room, and meet someone you feel really connected with, who seems to share your ideas, values, background, everything. Over time, you start to develop a serious relationship with this person. Or 2) your company asks you to contact suppliers in Singapore or Abu Dhabi or Warsaw or Bombay. You create a relationship with several business executives via fax, phone, and e-mail. You've never visited their facilities, never even seen the people you've been dealing with. Then your boss comes in and asks, "Okay, which company should we give this multimillion-dollar contract to?"

With the information superhighway, teleconferencing, multinational business, and especially the Internet, the world is becoming so much smaller, and everything seems to be going much faster at the same time. Business deals are created overnight; friendships on the Internet can spring up in minutes. Our logical, analytical left brains are on perpetual information overload—and often it seems the intuitive right brain has been left in the dust.

But what a huge advantage intuition can give you when you use it!

It used to be rare to develop a relationship or do a business deal with someone you hadn't seen in person. But now we create important relationships with people we've never seen and sometimes never even heard. We're talking with them via computer or fax, so we can't even hear the inflections of their voice. One of the few things we can still rely on are our instincts—our sixth sense—our intuition.

When faced with a big decision, most of us try to get as much information from as many sources as possible. But no matter how much information you accumulate and how happy your logical left brain is, there's always a little bit of uncertainty. But what if you could use your *whole* brain in making the decision—including that intuitive part which can sense things that aren't visible on the surface? Most successful business people usually check their "gut feeling" as part of their decision-making. They regard their "gut" as a part of the process equal in value to spreadsheets, sales figures, and consultant reports.

# Intuition: The Mystery Sense We All Possess

A great physicist once described our brains as being like radios receiving several stations simultaneously. One station is a lot louder than the others, therefore it's the one we pay the most attention to. That station is what we define as our physical reality, which is made up of the information we take in through our five senses and process in our brains. Intuition is simply information coming in on a different, quieter channel, so that it's often overshadowed by the other five senses.

We *all* have intuition. It doesn't matter what religion

we are, what color our skin is, what our sexual preference is; in the same way human beings have the senses of sight, hearing, touch, smell, and taste, we also have a sixth sense, intuition. One of my students says, "It's like a mystery sense that everyone has and no one really uses."

I firmly believe my upbringing is one of the reasons I'm able to use my intuition today. My parents gave me roots and wings. There were never any blocks or barriers put on me. I was always told I could become whatever I wanted. Both my parents were also quite intuitive themselves, and they didn't tell me I was crazy or stupid or lying when I would come up with information I couldn't possibly have gotten consciously. And through the years my whole family has been extremely supportive of who I am and what I have chosen to do.

Unfortunately, my experience is not typical. Usually what happens is exactly the opposite: children are told, either by their parents or their peers, they are "acting weird," "imagining things," or "lying." They're taught that they're not supposed to feel, not supposed to love, not supposed to be sensitive to other people. These innocents, who are just using their God-given intuition, are being taught they're wrong and bad. People who suppress a child's natural instincts often mean well, but I can't help but feel it's a crime.

My chiropractor (who has two lovely young daughters) says, "Children have a funny sense about people. When they're very young they either take to someone or they don't—you know, a positive/negative energy type of thing. But as we get older, we learn that's not acceptable behavior, and we stop trusting our instincts. We lose touch with that ability, even though it's still there."

Luckily, intuition isn't something you can destroy easily. *We all retain the ability to use our intuition even if we don't actively put it to work.* Just like our other senses, we continue to retain the *capability* of being intuitive. Think of it this way: say when you were a child you were fed great foods. Your taste buds were stimulated constantly; you got used to tasting all kinds of different flavors. Then, for whatever reason, you were placed in an orphanage where you were fed a very limited diet. For years all you had was bread, milk, meat, and bland vegetables. You were also told, "These are the only kinds of foods people should eat," and you believed it.

Then one day, miracle of miracles, your parents showed up and rescued you from the orphanage. They took you home and prepared a huge welcome feast. There were so many different kinds of foods, you couldn't imagine eating them all. In fact, you were actually afraid it was wrong to enjoy such a varied diet. But your parents encouraged you, and you gingerly started eating. Would your taste buds come back to life? Yes! Would you soon start enjoying all the flavors your sense of taste could perceive? Yes, indeed. Your sense of taste wasn't destroyed; you just 1) weren't offered opportunities to use it and 2) were told it was wrong to really enjoy what it had to offer.

Guess what? Intuition works in the exact same way. Most of us use our intuition very little or none at all, because we're taught to distrust our feelings about things. We're taught to believe only our logical brains and to discount the intuitive side (which, by the way, accounts for at least half of the brain matter God gave us). Well, as a psychotherapist client of mine says, "I believe in the scientific method, but I've learned that logic and intuition work best when they go hand in hand."

## Five Reasons to Use Your Intuition

Now, in the same way that some people have better sight or hearing than others, some people are more attuned to their intuition than others. But that doesn't mean that everyone can't develop their own intuitive abilities to the greatest extent possible. And believe me, the benefits of using intuition can be enormous! Intuition can be used to help you in all aspects of your life, from business situations to romantic encounters, from finding lost papers to saving yourself or your loved ones from potential danger. We can "tune in" intuitively and get hits on our lives and relationships. "Yes, I trust this business deal" or "No, I don't." "Yes, this is a good person I met on the Internet" or "He's not what he seems—watch out."

My friend Mark uses a wonderful analogy about the benefits of intuition—what he calls "our instinctive problem-solving sense." Imagine that life is like a maze, full of twists and turns that prevent you from seeing more than a few feet ahead. Now, what if you could look down at that maze from a point high above it? You'd be able to see where the twists and turns were taking you. You could avoid the pitfalls and dead ends, and take a much easier, more direct path to get where you want to go. Intuition is like being able to see where the maze is going from that loftier perspective. When you use your intuitive powers, you can sense whether a relationship will work out, whether someone is good for you or not, what might happen in this situation or that one, which path you should take. Intuition can help you in almost every area of your life—if you let it.

By the way, you may find that you are more intuitive in certain areas of your life than others. Some people are very good at picking up what's going on with their spouses, for example. Mothers are frequently in sync with their children, able to tell if something's wrong whether they're in the same room with them or not. Business people who use their intuition at work (health care professionals, financial advisors, and so on—I'll give you several examples in Chapter 21) often find they are able to slip into a "groove" because they're so used to tuning in professionally. But in the same way, the financial adviser may not be that sensitive to his or her kids, and the devoted spouse may be a disaster in business.

Even with intuition, practice makes perfect. The more we use our intuition, the better we become. And the wider the range of contexts we choose to exercise our powers, the easier it will be to pick up whatever the universe is telling us. Then, instead of waiting and hoping a flash of intuition will appear, we can use our intuition on demand.

Here are five very important reasons for learning to use your God-given sixth sense.

## 1. Intuition helps us prepare for the future and eliminate worry.

If you knew what your future held—if you had even the merest clue—how would you feel? Intuition can help you and those you love prepare for both the good and bad times. I can't tell you how many people, friends, clients, have come back to me and said, "Thank you for warning me about that particular person." "Thank you for letting me know my grandmother was going to have health problems." "Thank you for telling me to get that medical condition checked."

I once told a client, "Save your money because there's going to be a big problem with finances. You're suddenly going to lose a lot of money. It's like the Bible—you're going to have seven lean years. But it will change just as suddenly, and you'll be back to where you were before." The woman told me later that her family did indeed lose a lot of money, but because I had warned her in advance, they had put something aside to tide them over. It's been almost seven years now, and she says that things are finally beginning to look up: "I'm getting the impression that our lean years will be over very soon."

Because this woman knew in advance that there would be financial difficulties, she and her family could prepare. Equally as important, because she also knew the lean years would not last forever, she was able to face the tough times with a lot more confidence. Another client, "George," puts it this way: "Some people don't want to know about the future, but I think it's great. As an entrepreneur, I've had to deal with a lot of litigation. Once I was in a deposition, and the attorney knew about Char. To make me look bad, he said, 'Is it true you use a psychic for your business decisions?' I replied, 'Yes, I have a good friend who's a psychic and she tells me certain things. In fact, she told me I'm going to win this lawsuit!' Believe me, I went into that deposition with a lot more confidence knowing what Char had said."

We spend so much time thinking and worrying about what's going to happen. For most of us, worrying can consume a huge amount of our time and energy. But when we're able to tune in on the future, we can eliminate some of the *causes* of worry. Even though not everything is predestined and the future can change, intuition will allow you to tune in to whatever the changing circumstances of life will bring. One of my students who is a health care professional tells me how health worries drain her patients. "So many people come in and say, 'Please tell me I don't have a tumor, I don't have cancer.' And most of those people are absolutely fine. The energy we waste worrying doesn't do any good. If something's going to happen, it's going to happen, and those who have it, deal with it. I think that the essence of using your intuition is teaching people to be positive and have faith in themselves."

## 2. Intuition lets us help others, especially our loved ones.

What better gift can we give those we love than tuning in with them, feeling their feelings, being with them on an even deeper level? The feeling of closeness that comes when you're in tune with someone is remarkable. It's a way of connecting that transcends any other kind of sharing you may have experienced, even in your closest relationships. It's like watching two people who have been together for fifty years in a loving relationship—they finish each other's sentences, know each other's needs, feel each other's feelings. That's what intuition can give you from the very first moment when you offer it as a gift to those you love.

Using your intuition around the people you love will also help open them up to their own sixth sense. You can help them understand that there is a universal wisdom they can tap in to, to help them live happier, better lives. Intuition not only connects us here, but also tunes us in to something greater than ourselves—and we are all hungry for that kind of connection. When you use your intuition, you can point people to the light of their own inner wisdom and the universal love which underlies it.

## 3. Intuition lets us know when we're in sync with the universe.

The difference between using your intuition and just going through life is like the difference between swimming with or against the tide. When we're tuned in, things can be just a little bit easier, even when we have to make difficult choices or when misfortunes come our way.

Let's say you're in a relationship and the other person is being abusive or selfish. Although you really love this person, it gets to a point where you've done everything you can and they're not changing. Emotionally and psychologically you're very attached to this person, but your gut's telling you, "I don't deserve to be treated like this. This person isn't who I'm supposed to be with. There is someone better out there for me." So you confront him or her and the relationship ends. Even though there is pain in the breakup, and you may have loved this person very much and now you face the prospect of being without a relationship for a while, the simple fact that your intuition is telling you, "There is someone better out there for me," can help you through the tough times.

Even if it's painful, when you know you've made the right choice, you have the consolation of knowing that you are in sync with what the universe wants for you. Being in sync with the universe and knowing that what we're doing feels right makes the process of living seem to have more continuity, even though the process is changing all the time.

## 4. Intuition teaches us to trust our own inner wisdom.

Sometimes trusting our intuition is the hardest lesson to learn. My student and fellow psychic Hope Grant tells me, "Trusting your intuition is scary. It's a leap of faith. We're so afraid of not being in control. But the most important thing I learned from Char is to listen to our own hearts because they're true, and we can rely on them. And the more we trust that feeling, the more predictable our intuition becomes."

The essence of intuition is learning to listen to and trust yourself. Simply learning that lesson can completely transform the way you live every day. Nancy Newton is a dear soul who took my workshop during a cruise. "As we were leaving the boat," she remembers, "Char said, 'Nancy, I've got two words for you: Trust yourself.' Those two words started me on a path of healing. I discovered that if you trust yourself, you're really trusting the God within you and your God-given gifts. I began to feel worth and value for the very first time."

We all have the gift of God-wisdom within ourselves. We have the ability to tap in to the forces in the universe that shape our lives. We just have to trust our own abilities, our own wisdom, the source of goodness inside ourselves and throughout the universe. And then listen. As one student reminded me, "The essence of intuition is listening to yourself and trusting yourself. When you do that, miracles can happen."

## 5. Finally, intuition helps us grow and develop as souls.

We are all spirits in physical bodies, and the whole purpose for our existence, both here and on the other side, is to grow and evolve to a higher level. Using your intuition to tune in to what the universal wisdom wants for us, to help others, and to make lives better, are all steps that help our spirits grow and evolve.

One way that intuition helps us grow is by helping us face our problems and fears. How many people do you know who are in destructive relationships, or have serious behavioral problems, or who stop themselves from doing what they need to because they're paralyzed by fear? (Maybe you're one of those people yourself.) In so many readings I'll pick up on someone's relationship, or their problem, or their fear, and I'll say, "You need to handle this. Your life is going to be miserable until you get this situation resolved." And I'm amazed at how many people say, "Yeah, I know—I had a feeling that was the problem." Our own inner wisdom often tells us when there's something wrong. Once we're aware, we can make the changes we need, or get help to do so.

You have to be willing to face your fears. You have to be willing to grow and change even if it's difficult. Intuition can help you find the path that will lead you to greater growth—mentally, physically, and most important, spiritually.

Now that you know all the excellent reasons for cultivating your God-given sixth sense, I'll let you in on a little secret: You've been using this ability for years! If you don't believe it, take a look at the list of statements below.

If you can answer "yes" to any one of them, you've used your intuition to tap in to something greater than your own logical brain.

1. I've thought about someone only to have them call me soon afterward.
2. I've felt positive or negative about a particular person and had my feelings proven true.
3. I've bought a stock or made a business decision based on a hunch and been successful.
4. I've sensed something about my health which was verified by a visit to a doctor or the development of a health problem.
5. I've been able to tell what someone else was thinking.
6. I've picked up on the emotions of my spouse or significant other.
7. I've known my child was in distress even though we weren't in the same space.
8. I've felt the presence of or dreamed about a departed loved one.
9. I've had lights or the TV or radio go on inexplicably.
10. I've felt uncomfortable about going down a certain road or stopping in a certain location or taking a trip on an airplane, and listened to the warning.
11. I've been awakened by a dream in the middle of the night that seemed to contain a message for me.
12. I've been thinking of someone and a piece of music associated with them has come on the radio.
13. I've seen something out of the corner of my eye—a person, an object—or simply felt a sense of motion, and when I turned to look at it directly, there was nothing there.

14. I've encountered someone whom I feel I've known before, even though we've never met.
15. I've found myself getting a "hit" on something when I know there is no logical source for the information.
16. I somehow know the right words to say in a situation.
17. I've solved a problem with a solution that came to me out of nowhere.
18. I'm in the car, humming a song. I turn on the radio, and the same song is playing.
19. I ask the universe for a "sign" to help me answer a question and I see a license plate, road sign, TV ad, or something else that pertains to my question and is more than coincidental.

If any of those statements apply to you, congratulations! You're already using your intuition. In the next chapter you'll read more about all the different ways intuition can show up in our lives and bring enormous benefits as a result.

# 8

# You've Already Had
# Your First Psychic Experience!

Have you ever been thinking of someone, only to hear the phone ring and they're on the line? Or had a "funny feeling" about something and it came true? Everyone's had at least one moment where they accessed information they couldn't have gotten consciously. We tend to pass it off as "coincidence," but I believe these are all examples of psychic experiences.

My friend Hope talked to me recently about the experience almost every teenage girl seems to share. "I have a lifelong girlfriend, Shari, and when we were fourteen years old, I'd call her and say, 'Why are you polishing your toenails now? It's so late.' And she'd say, 'How did you know that? Are you outside?' I used to just think it was because we were so close, but those kinds of things happen to everybody. You'll be thinking about somebody you haven't seen in ten years and within the next twenty-four hours you see them or they call you."

My sister Alicia says that when I was very small, I'd say things like, "When is Aunt Rose coming over?" or "When is Aunt Rose calling?" and, sure enough, the phone would ring, or there'd be a knock on the door and there was Aunt Rose. Another client of mine, "Jesse," would be at home in British Columbia and call her mother in Detroit, only to find that the line was busy. (This was twenty-six years ago, long before call waiting.) Jesse would put the phone back on the hook, and it would ring immediately—her mother had been calling her at that exact same moment. Jesse says the same thing would happen when her mom tried to call her grandmother.

Because these things are relatively ordinary, we tend to forget them—unless, of course, the experience is a little more dramatic, like when we're warned about something or get a feeling that something great (or awful) is going to happen. "Matthew" remembers a dream he had when he was about six years old, about a neighbor, Mrs. Buffington, whose backyard adjoined that of Matthew's house. One night Matthew dreamed that Mrs. Buffington passed away. When he told his mother about it the next morning, within minutes there was a knock at the door. It was the person who lived with Mrs. Buffington, coming to tell them she had died suddenly. It was quite a surprise to everyone, because Mrs. Buffington had not been ill at all. No one was more surprised than Matthew—unless it was his mother!

The other kinds of psychic experiences we tend to remember are warnings, especially if we ignore them. I myself got a warning that I failed to heed when I was younger. (Yes, even psychics blow it sometimes.) It was on my wedding day. I was twenty or twenty-one and thought I was an old maid because both my sisters were married by the time they were nineteen. I had wanted a fairy-tale wedding, and it was. My parents went all out: I had a gorgeous wedding gown, the sanctuary was beautiful, all my friends and family and teachers were there. I even made my fiancé take waltz lessons so we could dance the first dance with style.

Finally, the great day arrived. I was standing at the top of the aisle with my father, waiting for the organist to start playing "Here Comes the Bride." I could see my fiancé waiting for me at the altar, and I thought, "This is what every girl dreams of." I was completely happy. Then out of nowhere, a message popped into my head: *This isn't going to work out!*

What did I do? I ignored it. In fact, I was so determined to put it out of my head that I *skipped* the first few steps down the aisle! It was as if I were saying to myself, "Go away, thought!" The guests laughed uproariously, and the wedding went on as planned.

Believe me, this was not a case of bride's nerves. I was completely happy and excited to be marrying this man, and there was nothing that could make me think I wouldn't live a long, happy married life. Nevertheless, out of the blue something told me there was not a happy ending in store for this relationship.

Back then I didn't know I was psychic. I just always got these "feelings" and I thought everybody had them. I didn't think of this as a warning—but, unfortunately, it was. My husband and I were happy for a short while, but then things went awry and we were divorced.

Why don't people pay attention to these feelings? Why don't we acknowledge our own ability to tap into a "knowingness" that has nothing to do with our five senses? Why can't we be more in tune with the information the universe is giving us every moment? I believe it has to do with that four-letter "F" word *fear*—False Evidence Appearing Real. Many of my students tell me they stop trusting their intuition because they're afraid of what other people will say or think. They're afraid to face ridicule, or disapproval. They're afraid to be seen as different. The silly thing is, they're not! We all have intuition; some of us just use it more than others.

By the way, we can also get "good" psychic hints, the ones that tell us, "Go here," and we meet our soul mate. Or we get an inner prompting to call someone, and that call opens doors for us professionally. We all have these kinds of hunches; and if we're smart, we'll pay attention to what the universe is trying to tell us.

My client Jackie has a great example of how the universe will sometimes keep signaling us to take action. She was having lunch in Chicago one day with a friend. When Jackie asked her to have lunch again the next week, her friend said, "I can't do it Tuesday, because I'm going to be talking with a psychic. Her name is Char." Jackie said, "Okay, then we'll do it Wednesday," and thought nothing of it. Two days later, Jackie went to New York for the weekend. She had lunch with another friend, Bobby, who said, "I have to tell you what happened to me in Detroit last week. I was at my sister's store and just as I walked outside, this woman stops me and said, 'I have to talk to you.' Then she tells me about my grandfather and the hereafter. Her name was Char."

The following Sunday, Jackie called her mother in Detroit. Her mother told her, "Jackie, I was walking around my apartment complex and met this lovely woman who says her daughter is staying with her. Her daughter's a psychic and her name is Char." Jackie said, "Mother, stop right there. This is the third time in four days that woman's name has come to me. Give me her number!" A week later, she called me for a reading.

Coincidence? I doubt it. I believe Jackie was being directed to call me because there were spirits that wanted to come through to her. Our reading healed some very old emotional issues that Jackie had been holding onto for a long time. That's one of the miracles that can happen when we take the time to listen to the hints our wisest self is offering.

# Children: The Most Natural Psychics

If you ever doubt that we all have intuition, just take a look at very young children and animals—they're the most intuitive beings on the planet. Every dog and cat I've ever been around can pick up on people's emotions in a heartbeat. And kids—I've heard many stories about children seeing spirits, reading their parents' emotions, even predicting the future.

Ask any parent and they will tell you, children "know" things. They pick up on so much more than most adults. And children are a lot more open to communicating with people who have passed over, especially when they cared for those people before they died. I have heard about several incidents from my students. "Barbara's" daughter Melissa was six months old when her grandfather (Barbara's dad) passed away. Barbara and her dad were in chiropractic practice together, and there was a nursery in their offices where Barbara kept Melissa while she was working. From the day Melissa was born, Barbara's dad would go upstairs every chance he got to see his granddaughter. Right after her father died, Barbara would go into the nursery to find the six-month-old Melissa staring at the wall and giggling—just as if her grandfather were standing there. "It gave me goose bumps," Barbara said. "I feel my father around all the time myself, but for my baby daughter to recognize it—wow."

"Cynthia's" grandson, Jack, also saw someone who wasn't there—the woman everyone called Aunt Frances. Aunt Frances was the mother of Cynthia's ex-husband's second wife. (How's that for a weird connection?) She was like a grandmother to Jack, who was only three years old when Aunt Frances became ill. Because she had had to enter a nursing home, Jack didn't see her at all the month before she died. About a week after Aunt Frances passed over, Cynthia went to her daughter's house to pick up Jack for the day, and her daughter Paula said, "Cynthia, I got up this morning and saw Jack standing at the top of the stairway pointing down into the living room. He was saying, 'Hi, Aunt Frances.' I said, 'Jack, who did you say was there?' And he looked at me and said, 'There's Aunt Frances.' Cynthia, I don't want Jack to be psychic. It frightens me. I don't want him to have that kind of pressure or responsibility." Cynthia replied, "You know what? It'll only be there later on if he wants it to. Just let it go for right now."

Another woman who studied with me remembers her first psychic experience as a child. The night before her ninth birthday, she had a kind of waking dream, where she saw her mother standing in a pool of white light. In the dream her mother handed her a pegboard game. The next day, the mother walked in and handed her a wrapped box. Even before she opened her gift, the girl said, "Thanks, Ma, I really like the pegboard," "How did you know what I got you?" said her mother, completely surprised. "Uhh . . . it was a good guess," the girl answered.

My sister Alicia, a doctor of psychology who does past-life regressions as part of her practice, says that children are naturally psychic and open. It's very common, she reports, for young children to remember past lives. They'll say things like, "Oh yes, I remember when my hair was red," and talk about people and places and events they can't possibly know about. Kids haven't learned yet to put up the walls of fear and doubt that we adults construct so easily and defend no matter what the cost.

# Tuning in to Station WICU ("I See You!")

Fear and doubt can keep us from recognizing our intuition until either we're faced by a "coincidence" that's so outrageous we can't deny it, or the incidents of intuition accumulate to a point where we finally have to admit something's going on. I'll give you a few examples. I have a spirit guide whom I call White Feather. He's been with me for many years now, and as soon as he came to me, I started seeing white feathers in very unlikely places. Recently I had dinner with my business partner in a very upscale Manhattan restaurant. We started talking about spirit guides, and I mentioned White Feather. Then, while we were eating, my business partner saw this enormous white feather come floating down behind me. It had come from a pile of feathers in a pot at the end of the row of booths where we were sitting. But why had it appeared behind me? And why were there no other feathers floating around? My business partner was somewhat taken aback and told me about it. "Don't worry," I said. "I see white feathers all the time. It's just my spirit guide saying hello."

One of my favorite stories about outrageous "coincidences" was told by a client from the Midwest who had gone on a cruise with her husband about four years earlier. On the cruise they had met another couple with whom they really hit it off. The couples had stayed in touch for a while and had even met in New York City for dinner. But over time they had lost touch.

One night my client and her husband were riding in their car, and she said, "You know, I wonder what happened to the so-and-so's?" (mentioning this couple by name). Her husband said, "Yeah, we haven't heard from them for about two years." *The next day* a beautiful card arrived from the couple, with the message, "We've been thinking of you." My client said it had been so long since they had been in touch, she no longer had this couple's address or phone number. She had to ask her husband to go down into the basement, go through their old phone bills and find this couple's number. Then she called them and said, "You'll never believe this—we were talking about you not twenty-four hours before we got your card!"

Larry Jordan, the publisher of *Midwest Today,* is in the process of writing a book about the country-western singer Jim Reeves. Reeves, a contemporary of Patsy Cline, was killed in a plane crash in 1964, but his records continue to sell all over the world. Larry has been a Reeves fan since age thirteen, but recently Larry has developed a strange talent. He says, "I'll be in a conversation or doing any number of things, and I'll interrupt myself, turn on the radio and dial right to where a Jim Reeves song is starting to play. Even when I'm asleep, I'll wake up and turn the radio on. I won't even know the station I'm dialing. It happens in the car, too: I can be driving down the road with someone in the car, we'll be talking about something completely unrelated, and I'll find myself reaching for the radio. And sure enough, I'll turn exactly to where a Jim Reeves song is playing. Thank goodness it doesn't happen all the time or I'd never get any sleep! But I've never been wrong yet. I always tune to a Jim Reeves song."

Coincidence? I don't think so. But remember, we all have these moments of picking up on something else, something that's beyond what we can consciously see, hear, feel, taste or smell. If you've ever . . .

- called someone who says, "I was just thinking of you!"

- felt uneasy about going down a particular street only to discover you avoided an accident
- "knew" something was wrong with a family member or close friend, even though we weren't in physical proximity with them
- been able to tell your child was in distress or danger whether you were close by or not
- been the right person in the right place at the right time in your business
- gotten your car checked because it didn't "feel" safe
- had a bad "vibe" about a person, and discovered you were right

. . . then you, too, have had a psychic experience!

I'd like you to try something. Take a few moments to reflect on your past, and write down at least one similar experience that has happened to you. (Don't worry, you'll remember something.) If you have more than one, write down as many as you can recall. These experiences can be dramatic or subtle, catastrophic warnings or just being able to "tune in" on a beloved sister or brother or spouse or child. I believe you'll find that as you think about those experiences, you'll see how many times you've accessed knowledge provided by your intuition.

Now try taking it one step further. Start keeping track of how many times you "tune in" during the course of a week. I believe the universe tips us off; we just need to learn to listen. So write down all the signals you get from the universe that are more than coincidence. Maybe you need an answer for something and see a license plate or billboard that gives you a clue. Or maybe you're thinking of someone and you hear from them, or from someone who knows them. Or maybe you remember an old flame and immediately "your" song comes on the radio. You'll be surprised how many hints the universe throws your way. However, it's up to us to notice what we're getting, and then apply our common sense to the information. After all, intuition is just another source of information that can improve our lives. But it's also a heck of a party trick!

# 9

## Nine Myths That May
## Be Blocking
## Your Psychic Ability

"All right," you may be saying. "Maybe everyone does have intuition. Then why don't more people use their ability? Why don't we take these messages seriously? Why do most of us keep on blundering through life like we're blindfolded, even though we have perfectly good psychic 'eyes' to see with? Why can't I do what you do?"

Well, first of all I've been doing what I do for twenty-five years, and even with intuition, practice makes perfect! But in several years of teaching people to "do what I do," I've found most of us are held back by one of two factors. First and most powerful is the demon of FEAR. People are usually afraid of what they don't understand. A friend of mine woke up one night hearing a voice calling her name. The voice sounded somehow familiar, but she was terrified because she knew she was alone in the house at the time. "But I was so scared I completely shut myself down," she reported. "And I haven't heard the voice since."

Remember what I said earlier: Fear is only False Evidence Appearing Real. Our fears cause us to ignore the information our intuition gives us every single day. To access your sixth sense, you have to dump your fear about what you will be shown. Now, I'm not saying that there aren't things out there to worry about. I don't believe that there are only good spirits or energies out there, and no one should leave their common sense behind when they use their psychic abilities. But the only way a negative spirit or energy can gain power over you is if you *give* them that power. There are some very specific ways you can protect yourself from negative energy and invite only the highest and best spirits into your life. (I'll be talking a lot about these techniques in Chapter 16.) But don't let fear of the unknown keep you from using your God-given intuitive gift.

The second barrier that keeps most people from accessing their natural sixth sense is the cultural mythology about being psychic. You know what I'm talking about: those things that people say when you mention anything having to do with intuition and psychic abilities. There are nine common "intuition killing" myths floating around, and if you buy into even one of them, they'll block your natural sixth sense completely. Here's a list of those lethal myths, as well as some common-sense information that I hope will make you realize how wrong they are.

## Myth #1: "It's all a fake."

I'd be the last one to say that all psychics are the real thing. Of course there are people out there looking to make a quick buck or giving "readings" from a desperate need for attention. But we tend to let those bad apples poison our confidence in our *own* psychic impressions. And lack of confidence is an absolute intuition-killer.

When a psychic reads for you, or you get a hunch or feeling that just couldn't have come from your conscious mind, you can usually tell if it's real or fake. First, turn on your "radar." I believe we can all sense the truth when we hear it or see it or feel it. Second, when you get a feeling about something in the future, wait to see if it comes true. If it does, file that feeling away as something to pay attention to whenever it comes up. If you're getting a reading from someone, evaluate what you're being told and put it into action only if it makes sense to you. If things happen the way the reading said, then you may have a valid source of information in the person who read for you.

When I read for a client, I usually get so many specific details that it's pretty clear I'm telling the truth. I'm given facts that no one else could possibly know. For example, recently I received a letter from "Christine," who lives in Ontario, Canada:

"You immediately gave me the first names of four people who have passed over and were extremely close to me. You gave the first initial and then the name of two of the parties and their relationship to me, and for the other two, you partially spelled their names and then identified them. All I answered was 'yes' or 'no' and in this particular case, you never received a 'no' from me.

"The most unusual part of the entire reading concerned a young man who had just passed less than one week prior to the reading. The first thing you said was to be patient with you as this boy had just recently passed and wasn't sure about what to do! Not only that, you also said that he was showing you something very symbolic between him and me, and although you couldn't identify the object, he wanted me to know that he had it with him. You then proceeded to ask me if I put something in his casket, which in fact I had.

"You also told me I would be taking a trip overseas . . . at the time I had no intention of going, but now, out of the blue, I am planning a trip for late next month! Your entire reading was astounding and uncanny."

I'm sure there are "psychic debunkers" out there who would say I guessed the names of her relatives, or I could assume she came to see me because someone close to her had just died—but that's not what I do. More important, that's not what *you* do when you pay attention to your own intuition. You don't have to believe all psychics are real. To use your sixth sense, you just have to know that *your own* psychic ability is real.

## Myth #2: "Only certain people are psychic."

How many times have I heard this one! "Only women have intuition." "Gypsies are more psychic than the rest of us." "People who are psychic were born with a caul." "You have to be (Irish, Native American, cross-eyed, left-handed, whatever) in order to be psychic."

I've got news for you: I'm a middle-class Jewish kid from Michigan. I know psychics who came from the South and grew up Baptist. I've known people of every ethnic and socioeconomic background who have developed their intuition and give darn good readings. Almost everyone I meet has *some* level of intuition and could learn to use it if they wanted.

I have a great literary agent, Wendy Keller. At lunch one day we were talking about the fact that we all have this ability to "tune in" psychically, so Wendy decided to give it a try. As we were standing in the parking lot, she gave me the first initial of my ex-husband's name within three letters, then told me his full name. I had never shared any information about my family with Wendy, nor had I taught her any of my method, yet she was able to tap into her own intuition just by deciding to.

So don't ever say, "I can't be psychic, I'm not

_____ [fill in the blank with your own mistaken idea of what a psychic is]." You *are* psychic; *everyone* is psychic. You just have to recognize your own gift.

## Myth #3: "All psychic ability comes from the devil."

Is it from the devil when your grandmother comes in and tells you she loves you? Is it from the devil when your guardian angel warns you about a certain person or event? Look, I'm not naive enough to say there is no evil in this world or the next. There is good *and* evil in the spirit world, but evil will almost always tip you off when you're in tune with your intuition. I always tell students, "Spirits can be good or bad, but there's a level beyond individual spirits where universal love, goodness, and wisdom dwell. When you tune in, always go to that level first. That God-consciousness will never steer you wrong."

Just like our other five senses, our sixth sense can be misused or used for good. It's our responsibility to use it to uplift ourselves and others. So many people I read for find that their faith in God and their certainty about life beyond the grave is greatly strengthened after they hear from loved ones who have passed over. When used correctly, our intuition is a gift from God. And as such, we should honor, appreciate, nurture, and use it to connect to the highest level of goodness, light, and love.

## Myth #4: "People will think you're crazy."

Luckily, this one is disappearing from the mainstream. Granted, if you say you're able to talk to relatives who are dead, you'll still get strange looks. But if you say, "I always check my gut when I do a business deal," nobody will give it a second thought. Intuition, sensing the direction something is going to go before it happens, is considered savvy instead of "woo-woo."

Today more people seem to accept the idea of receiving information from other-than-conscious sources. Years ago when the police consulted me, it felt as if the officers were ashamed of doing something so "weird." But now that I've proved myself by helping the police with several cases, detectives call me as a matter of course to help them locate missing people, find bodies, track down fugitives, and so on. My efforts may not be publicized very much—after all, most police departments still don't want to admit they can't do everything themselves—but what's important is that I can be of help.

As we enter the millennium, we seem to be opening up to our own psychic abilities. I've heard so many people say, "At times I really feel the spirit of my grandmother (or some other loved one) close to me," and then watched as others nodded in agreement. We seem freer to talk about something we've all felt: the presence of our departed loved ones. The key for all of us is to remember that psychic ability is quite natural. It's simply a sense that picks up things the other five don't. And if it picks up the love emanating from our loved ones who have passed on, goodness knows, that's not bad or crazy—that's a gift.

## Myth #5: "It's a sacred ability and you shouldn't use it for little things."

Most people use their intuition *only* for the little things. Say you're driving to somewhere you've never been before—a business or a home. You have a vague idea of where this place is but you're navigating by the seat of your pants. At an intersection, you have a feeling that you should turn right, and in a couple of blocks you see the house or business you're looking for. Didn't you just use your intuition?

That's just one example. Have you ever found your keys . . . called a friend who says, "You're just the person

I needed to speak to!" . . . caught up on a project at work only to find the deadline had been moved forward without your knowledge . . . met someone for the first time and had a definite impression about them that turned out to be accurate . . . went somewhere for no apparent reason and ended up being in the right place at the right time? All of these are evidence of your intuition helping you with the little things.

I'm constantly amazed at the level of practical advice my intuition gives me when I read for people. My friend Peter, a contractor, reminds me that once I told him to check a bill he'd received from a plumber. Sure enough, the plumber had overcharged him. That was just one detail in a reading that included information about Peter's business, his finances, relationships, and so on. But the spirits weren't going to let the details get lost in the big picture!

If we treat intuition as just another sense, and we use our sight or hearing or touch for the little things, why should we only use our intuition when we make major life decisions? So tune in—it'll save you a lot of time spent looking for your health club membership card!

## Myth #6: "You need to study for years and meditate for hours to tap in to your psychic ability."

Culturally we have bought in to the myth that only people who dedicate themselves to years of preparation and study, and deny themselves a life in the world can really use their intuition effectively. If that's the case, why are kids so intuitive? Most children I know are better than almost anyone else at picking up things—and they don't spend hours in meditation or study.

Of course, the more you use your intuition, the better you get at tuning in. Over the years I've discovered a few key elements that will help almost anyone use their inborn psychic ability more easily. When I teach people these elements, I've seen them give readings as accurate as anything I've ever done myself. My teaching sessions are like singing lessons with a good teacher who knows exactly when you're hitting the right note with the right tone and placement. Once students are coached to hit that "note" enough times, they start to recognize what it feels like, and then they can duplicate the note by duplicating the feeling. In the same way, I coach students to distinguish between when they are tuning in (hitting the right note) and when they're guessing. I can teach them this because 1) I've "tuned in" thousands of times myself, and I can tell the difference, and 2) I validate the information they're getting with my own abilities. And since I always go to the highest level of universal consciousness whenever I read, I can tell if something's truthful or not.

Like all abilities, however, intuition gets better with practice. But practice doesn't have to entail meditating for hours, or spending days "communing with the other side." It's about being aware, deliberately getting in touch with your intuition and interpreting the information you're given to the best of your ability. It's simply a shift of awareness. And in this section I'll be showing you exactly how you can activate your intuition more easily.

## Myth #7: "You have to be in a room with someone (or touch their clothes or some other condition) to 'pick up' on them psychically."

Intuition can show up in almost any setting. I have friends who can get a sense about someone just by hearing his or her name. I've done readings for individuals who were sitting in a room with me, and others who were half a world away. I've done readings for people who called in to radio shows. Sometimes information just pops up spontaneously, sometimes I really have to concentrate to get anything. Sometimes I use objects and photos, more often

I don't. The one thing I've learned about intuition over the years is how silly it is to put conditions on it.

Using your intuition may be easier in some circumstances than others. As I said in Chapter 4, I believe each soul has its own particular energy "frequency" and that's what we pick up on. And like tuning in to a particular channel on your radio, there may be certain "frequencies" that are easier for you to receive. That's why we can sense whether the spirit we're communicating with is a brother or great-aunt or lover or grandfather—we know their energy frequency because we've experienced it while they were on earth.

But that doesn't mean the communication isn't coming in on a "wide band" spectrum! Many times we get the most important messages when we're not "tuned in" at all, but just going through our everyday lives—the warnings not to go down a particular street, the overwhelming desire to call a friend immediately, or the irresistible pull to go into a particular restaurant where it turns out that a special someone is waiting. Those messages are a little like the emergency broadcasts you'll hear on the radio: they interrupt our "regularly scheduled programming" to alert us to something important.

But we're receiving more subtle messages from our intuition all the time. We can pick up on that energy anywhere and through many different means—primarily just by paying attention to our thoughts and feelings. Since we communicate to the universe and to spirits through thoughts, that's all we really need. As long as you can think and feel, you can use your intuition. It's that simple!

## Myth #8: "Because their information comes from a 'higher source,' all psychics must be infallible."

Hey, guess what? I make mistakes! And so does everyone. I may misinterpret the cues I'm getting in a reading; you may get a feeling that you believe tells you to make one decision, when it was actually guiding you to do something else. Like our other five senses, intuition or psychic ability provides us with information, but it's up to us to interpret what we're getting. And I believe most of our mistakes occur in the interpretation, not in the reception.

It's always important to evaluate any information using your own, good, solid common sense. Nothing (or no one) is infallible. As I already discussed in Chapter 6, even the spirits on the other side don't know everything—death doesn't automatically make us experts in areas we hadn't a clue about before! So the information you're picking up psychically from your own loved ones or spirit guides may be wise but not infallible. Use the seventh vital sense God gave you: your common sense.

## Myth #9: "This talent can be dangerous. Only professional, trained psychics should be allowed to use their abilities."

Baloney! Remember, I talked a lot in Chapter 3 about how we're being brainwashed by our culture into believing that only "trained" psychics can use their abilities safely. The underlying assumption is that all psychic phenomena is potentially dangerous. It's simply not true.

Most people feel anything psychic is dangerous because their logical brains say, "I don't know what this is. I don't understand this, therefore I'm afraid of it." I once heard about a man who had been deaf his entire life. Then, at age fifty, he had an operation that allowed him to hear. For the first six weeks he would cower in absolute terror every time he heard any sudden noise—a soda pop can being opened, a car backfiring, someone shouting. He had no references for what he was hearing, and so he reacted with fear. Use this man's dilemma as a lesson.

Don't let fear of the unknown keep you from exercising your intuition.

And don't buy into the idea that only a "trained" professional psychic should manipulate these energies. We all have intuition; we all have psychic abilities; and we can all exercise them if we so desire. In fact, I've found that often when people use their own sixth sense, they're far more accurate than I might be. I remember one example of this quite vividly. A woman called me because her daughter had been missing for several days. I tuned in, but all I could say was, "I don't know where your daughter is, but I know you'll find her." Well, two nights later the woman had a dream in which she saw her daughter tied to a chair in a dark room, eating hamburgers. There was a cat with her. The mother thought this was pretty strange and dismissed it from her mind. Luckily, the daughter returned a day or so later. She had been kidnapped and, as she reported to her mother, "I was in a basement. I was tied up. The only company I had was a cat. And they fed me McDonald's every meal." Her mother was far more attuned to the daughter's situation than I was.

You don't need to be trained. You don't need years of practice. You don't have to be scared of what you're going to "unleash," because in dealing with truth we're freed. Believe in your own abilities, be open to what you're getting, and you'll find you're better than 99.9 percent of the "trained" psychics out there when it comes to using your intuition. And just like a muscle, the more you use it, the stronger your intuition will become, and the easier it will be to use it on demand.

# 10

## My Proven Method
## for Accessing
## Your Wisest Self

I always knew that this gift of intuition was something we all shared, and believed part of my mission was to help others become aware of their own abilities. Many people would come to me for readings and I could tell they had a strong intuitive sense. After the reading I would say, "You know, you could do this yourself. I'll bet you've had experiences where you've been tipped off." And they would sheepishly admit they had been warned about something, or felt the presence of a departed loved one, or played a hunch successfully in business.

After twenty-five years of giving readings and developing my own gift, I began to realize that there were very specific steps people could follow to learn to tap into their own wisest selves. To the best of my ability, I wrote down what I was doing and how I was doing it. Then I started to teach this method to individuals and groups a few years ago. It was amazing how quickly people could access their own intuition using the steps I created! In a typical session, I would literally read aloud the steps you'll be learning in the next few chapters, and then I would say, "Okay, I'm thinking of a name. Try to tune in on it." Just yesterday I did this with a gentleman who had never studied with me or anyone else before. First he gave me an initial, and then within three tries gave me my father's name (which is what I was thinking). The guy wasn't just good, he was great!

I believe my method is successful for three reasons. First, it's based on what I've spent the last twenty-five years learning and practicing myself. I have studied with many different teachers and talked with other psychics to discover their techniques for tuning in. I've tried different ways of using intuition and of helping others to use their gifts. I continually refined my method, and I knew from the results my students were getting that this method worked. This is a tried and tested means of developing anyone's intuition.

Second, I believe I'm doing this for the right reasons. This is not about controlling people, or turning anyone into a professional psychic. I want to help people empower themselves to trust their intuition, and then if a deceased loved one decides to come through, to say, "Hi! How're you doing? I love you, and I'm glad you're here. What do you want to say to me?" Third, I believe this method is successful because it teaches people to connect with the highest level of universal consciousness rather than with spirits only. Some psychics advocate letting spirits or spirit guides run our lives, while others do not discriminate about where spirits come from and the level on which those spirits are operating. Remember, some spirits are high, and some are low. Some want to help, and others want to do mischief. You can be fooled if you're not careful. That's why I am absolutely adamant about protecting ourselves from lower forms of energy by putting a white light all around and saying a prayer of protection, which asks that we tap into the highest level of goodness, love, and wisdom we call God.

Developing your own psychic gift frees you from

dependence on others and connects you at the highest level. Knowing that you can look within yourself, make your own spiritual connection, provide your own answers to your questions, and develop your own insights into your life empowers you to live your life with purpose and with meaning.

But where should you start? Start by knowing this.

- You have a psychic/intuitive gift, a gift received from your Creator. You can't just believe; you have to be *certain*.
- Through practice and commitment you can develop this gift.
- Developing this gift requires using it with a conscious sense of responsibility.
- Trust your instincts. Believe in and have confidence in yourself.

You've probably used your intuition without having heard these statements before. I hope you will continue to have many more such experiences in your life. But these simple statements are the foundation for developing your intuitive gift.

# Why Do You Want to Develop Your Intuition?

Developing your intuition brings with it a responsibility, in the same way that developing any ability does. So you should be clear and honest with yourself regarding the reasons why you want to do this. Before you read any further, ask yourself, "Why do I want to develop my intuition?" If you are after money, fame, power, or the ability to manipulate or control others, then read no further. As one of my students says, "Intuition shouldn't be used solely for a self-centered purpose, because if you start doing it that way, you're going to be in big trouble. I've seen a lot of people with great intuition become egotistical, money-oriented, and controlling. I just sit back and laugh, because I know it's going to backfire. Sure enough, pretty soon they can't read accurately anymore. They're reading with their ego and not their true intuition. It's like the universe is giving them a 'time out,' saying, 'You're not going to get any more information until you understand what you're supposed to do with this gift.' You should use your abilities to benefit people."

I believe we are given the gift of intuition to help us grow and develop in the highest possible way in this lifetime. So if you would seek to use your intuition to grow rich, then become rich in kindness, virtue, generosity, love, wisdom, and compassion for others. If you would use it to seek fame, make it a fame born of the good you do for others. If you would use it to gain power, then seek the power to help others become the best they can be. If those are your goals for developing your intuitive powers, then I believe the universe will support your efforts every step of the way.

I ask every new student to tell me why they want to develop their intuition. It's not just so I can hear their answers but for each person to examine his or her own heart, to see exactly why they were drawn to learn my method. Many people come to my class because they want to use their intuition to know more about their own lives. They say things like, "I need to know how to listen when I'm really desperate and impatient because I want something really badly. I want to know the difference between my desire and the ways the universe may be tipping me off. I want to learn to listen to my own intuitive guidance." All that is completely valid, of course. But when people discover the possibilities of using their gift to help others, almost everyone is excited by the prospect. I hope and trust that you, too, fall into that category.

# What Will It Take to Use This Method?

I believe I can teach anyone to use their intuition. But I've also noticed that some students are more successful than others—and often, it has nothing to do with ability! Developing your intuition is just like developing any other personal trait. Yes, some people are more talented than others, but talent won't get you nearly as far as drive and belief. It's like sports: some of the most athletically gifted kids out there make the worst players. That's because innate ability will carry you only so far. The 6'11" well-coordinated kid will sometimes be *less* successful in basketball than the 5'10" kid who has greater mental and emotional drive.

Here are eight "musts" you will need to follow in order to best use my method for developing your intuition.

## 1. You must put aside fear, worry, and doubt.

So many people say they've received intuitive messages, but their fears prevented them from accepting what the universe was providing. Fear can cause you to discount even the strongest intuitive hit—fear of the "abnormal" nature of such warnings, or about what people will think if you act on your hunch. I'm not saying that fear is all bad. It can be a warning that a message we've received is coming from a negative energy or spirit. But if you're letting fear of psychic phenomena in general get in your way, you're unlikely to be very successful in tuning in.

You can't let fear of appearing weird or different hold you back either. You have to be willing to face your fears, check them to see if they're based on feelings of negative or lower-level energy, and if not, put them aside. Say a prayer and believe you are meant to be using your God-given sixth sense.

And above all, you can't let the kind of low-level fear we call "worry" get in your way. If you continually worry about what you will hear from the spirits, what other people will think if you tell them about messages, what happens if you're tuning in to lower spirits and don't know it, or how well you're using your intuition, your confidence in yourself and your abilities will disappear little by little. And without confidence, your intuition will be fighting a losing battle to be heard.

The other demon that will smother intuition is doubt. It takes courage and commitment to use your psychic gifts, and doubts will interfere both in receiving and interpreting the messages you're given. Never doubt that you (along with everyone else) has intuition and can tune in to a higher level of wisdom. If you are given a message, accept it, interpret it to the best of your ability, then act on it if appropriate. Realize that the more you use your gift, the less doubt will arise to interfere.

## 2. You must have the desire.

*Having* intuition is easy; *developing* it will take work. You've got to want to make the most of your own God-given sixth sense. Otherwise, you'll continue to hear what the universe has to tell you in the same old sporadic way. If that's good enough for you, fine. Not everybody has to develop their abilities to the point where they can use their intuition on demand. But I can tell you, the work you put into developing your intuition will definitely help make your life much better. It will also put you in touch with greater love and wisdom than you ever thought possible.

## 3. You must be willing to use your intuition for the benefit of others as well as yourself.

Helping others is one of the greatest gifts of being able to tune in. If you ever have the chance to see someone's eyes light up as you give them a message from a departed loved one, you will know what I mean. But everyone who wants to develop intuition may not aspire to be the bridge between here and the hereafter. Great! You can still help others in many different ways. For example, Nancy Newton is a domestic mediator, helping to empower people to resolve conflicts in their families. She is able intuitively to give the counseling her clients need in that particular moment. What if you could do the same thing in your own relationships? Or perhaps you're in one of the healing professions, like chiropractors Robin Nemeth and Jeffrey Fantich, who use their intuition as part of a rigorous diagnostic process. Intuition helps them pick up on certain conditions they may need to explore more deeply, often revealing problems of which the patient was not consciously aware.

Once you develop your intuition, you will find opportunities to help others appearing all the time. Use your gift to make this world a better place.

## 4. You must face the truth about yourself.

My method is a series of six steps designed to put you in touch with the truth and wisdom of the universe. But before you do that, you have to face the truth about yourself—and sometimes that's the hardest thing of all. Who wants to confront problems? It's so much easier to sweep them under the carpet, deny we have them, or delay dealing with them. How many times have I heard, "I know I'm in an abusive relationship or a dead-end job, but I'll wait until the kids are gone to do anything"? However, one of the essential principles of the universe is, like attracts like. When we are living at a high level, we draw high energy to ourselves, and that high level will not allow anything lower to contaminate it. Therefore, to make the best use of our intuitive gifts, we first have to eliminate anything that does not resonate at the highest level of goodness, love, and God.

Truth demands truth. Wisdom demands wisdom. We must get in touch with who and what we are, and see our own strengths and weaknesses, glories and frailties so we can celebrate the former and repair the latter. We do not have to be perfect, but we do have to be working on ourselves. And if there is some unresolved issue from our past, a relationship that is abusive or damaging, an addiction of any kind, or if we are chemically imbalanced or medicating ourselves with drugs or alcohol—anything that is keeping us from that highest level of truth—then we must get help to heal before we go any further. We owe it to the universal wisdom that wants the best for us and for everyone.

## 5. You must get your ego out of the way.

Don't develop your intuition thinking it will enhance your ego. Ego can warp or even destroy your psychic ability. As soon as you start using your intuition to control other people or to be more powerful, that ego energy causes imbalance. I believe in order to get the truth when we tune in intuitively, we have to be as pure a channel as possible, and that means eliminating ego energy. Ego energy is like a dam in the river of intuition—it diverts the flow of pure information into a power trip rather than loving and helping. When that happens, it's very easy for negative energies to sneak in and take over. Unfortunately, a lot of people use their intuitive abilities to feed their egos. But for me, that's always a danger signal. It's all too easy for the ego to corrupt the information that's being given, or for it to attract the wrong kind of spirit. Whenever ego is involved with intuition, watch out.

We need to check ourselves continuously to make sure our feet are on the ground. We have to learn to be honest with ourselves, check our own motives, ask the hard questions about why we're tuning in and what we're getting. And we have to keep strong our desire to serve as a pure channel of universal love and wisdom.

## 6. You must become a student again.

When you were growing up, did you have any kind of natural ability, like singing, or dancing, or a talent for a particular sport? It felt easy and comfortable when you were using that natural ability, didn't it? But what happened when you started taking lessons or training in that particular area? Perhaps your teacher gave you exercises that felt awkward because you were using your ability in a new or different way. But what happened if you persevered? Your own natural talent was enhanced and improved.

The same thing happens when you develop your intuition. This method will use exercises that may not feel comfortable immediately. You have to be willing to become a student again, to try what the teacher has to offer even though it stretches you. You have to follow the method to the best of your ability and see what happens. And you have to be willing to take someone else's guidance, and benefit from their years of experience in using their own psychic abilities.

## 7. You must be willing to try and fail.

I'll let you in on a secret: even though this method will give almost everyone the basics of developing intuition, there is no exact recipe. Everyone's gift is different (you'll see what I mean as you read more about each step) and I'm sure your intuitive "style" will also be unique.

So you have to be willing to try things and have them fail. Learning to use your intuition is always trial and error. You get a feeling or a thought that is somehow different, and you identify it as a message from your wisest self. Then you have to see how that message plays out in your life. If it was accurate, you say, "Aha! I can trust that particular kind of feeling or thought. I'll follow it next time and see what happens." It's like learning to ride a bicycle. It can take awhile until you learn the feeling of balancing on two wheels, but once you "know" that feeling, you can always ride a bicycle with confidence.

While you're developing your intuition, you're going to make mistakes! You have to learn to forgive yourself for not being perfect while you work to become better. But you have to keep trying; and you have to be confident enough to dissect why you were right or wrong. When I work with someone privately, I can help students figure out when they're in tune. I'll say, "You're guessing— you're not listening. You're being too logical. Make your mind go blank and just feel. Now, I'm going to give you a name. Tell me the first thing that comes to your mind." And usually the first thing is absolutely accurate.

A top hockey player once said, "You miss 100 percent of the shots you don't take." The only way to master your own sense of intuition is to tune in again and again. Take the shots; learn the difference between being absolutely accurate, approximately right, and way off. Use your ability with the idea of getting better each time and I think you'll be amazed at how quickly you'll improve.

## 8. You must be willing to push yourself.

In 1998 America followed the great home run competition between Mark McGwire and Sammy Sosa. That season, the question wasn't, "Would Roger Maris' record of sixty-one home runs be broken?" The question was, "Who would break it first, and who would have the greatest number of home runs—McGwire or Sosa?" Up until the very last weeks, the two players were neck and neck, first one going ahead and then the other. McGwire pulled ahead and ended the season with seventy home runs to

Sosa's sixty-six. But would McGwire have gotten as many homers if Sosa hadn't been pushing him every step of the way? I don't think so. Having something to motivate us to give a little bit more is one of the secrets of success.

I find this is equally true with my students. Whenever I work with people, either individually or in groups, I push them to take whatever messages they're getting and go deeper. (My friend Malcolm says that when I teach someone, I am relentless. And he's right!) But since I won't have the opportunity to work with everyone who reads this book, you have to push yourself.

When you get a thought or a feeling or image that you believe is a message, explore it. Ask yourself, "What else? Is there something more attached to this? Is this connected to someone else?" Keep going until you've traced every connection to its end. You'll be surprised at how much you can pick up simply by asking for more.

Pushing yourself also means practice, practice, practice. I tell my students that they are like athletes who have the capacity to be great tennis players. How far they go and where they end up—whether they are "weekend warriors," regular players, tennis pros, or number one in the world—depends a little bit on natural aptitude and a lot on how much time and effort they're willing to commit. If you put in the time and effort to develop your intuitive ability, you can use it to make your relationships better . . . have an easier time at work . . . grow mentally, emotionally, and spiritually . . . find solace in the presence of departed loved ones . . . be warned of impending danger . . . help those you love . . . feel in sync with the highest good . . . and on and on.

Some of you may already be very good at tuning in, and you may think you can "slide by" with less effort. But believe me, there is no substitute for practice. I had a direct experience of that myself in a different context.

When I was very young, I took piano lessons but I hated practicing—so I didn't. Both my parents were working so they weren't there to see whether or not I was practicing. Well, time came around for the big yearly piano recital, and my whole family attended. I was supposed to play "The Gypsy Song," but there was one small problem: since I hadn't practiced, I only knew the first part of the song. So I went onstage, sat down, and played the first sixteen bars over and over. I had no idea how to stop. Eventually I ended with the worst sour note you could imagine. Everyone was laughing as I stood up and took my bow. My sisters told me afterward they admired my guts. Well, I've always been willing to try anything—but that day I learned the value of practice.

A lot of intuitive people adopt the philosophy that intuition is a God-given gift, and all they have to do is to let go and let God. That's great up to a point—but I also believe that God helps those who help themselves. Rather than waiting for the universe to hit me over the head with a message, I'm willing to meet it halfway by using my gift to its utmost. The more you use your gift, the easier it is for the universe to speak to you clearly, quickly, and easily. So do God a favor—practice!

# Reports from the Field: Students Talk about My Classes

I have taught hundreds of people how to use their intuition. Now, that may not sound like a lot, but I have been very selective about sharing this information. At each workshop or private session, I talk about my philosophy about intuition and psychic ability (basically, what you've read so far in this book). Then I go over the six steps of my method. As you'll see, each step has an exercise attached to it, so people get an experience of that step. After everyone has absorbed the six steps, I either give them a name and ask them to tell me the first thing that pops into their head, or (if it's a group) I pair the students up and have them give readings to each other. It's like teaching a kid the mechanics of swimming—the strokes, breathing, and so on—on land, then having them jump in the water.

I have to tell you, the results are amazing. The people in my workshops are always astonishing me with how well they do—and I love it! I *want* my students to be better than me. I want them to get in touch with their own abilities and excel. Every teacher will tell you, seeing a student succeed is like no other high on earth. I'm thrilled but not surprised, because I don't expect any less from my students than I expect from myself. If I can do it, they can do it.

One year I taught my method to a group on a cruise ship. One student, Margaret, was paired with a woman in her thirties so they could do readings for each other. Margaret kept seeing a little redheaded baby and asked, "Are you going to have a baby?" The other woman replied, "No, we're not having children for a long time because we just started our business." Well, exactly nine months later Margaret received an announcement from her reading partner. The woman had gotten pregnant while on the cruise and had given birth to a redheaded baby girl.

In the course of a group workshop it becomes obvious that everyone's gift is different and everybody reads differently. I'll never forget the afternoon Robin Nemeth and her friend Patti Cimine phoned me for a joint teaching session over the phone. They were standing in a phone booth in a beauty shop! Soon all three of us were laughing and giggling and having a great time. At the end of the session, I gave them a name—Marie—and asked them to tell me the first thing that came into their minds. Robin said something like, "I picture Marie looking like this: she's got blond hair, she's thin and short." Patti, however, didn't get those kind of details. Instead, she got impressions of what Marie was like. She said, "I see Marie like a woman on a throne. She's an older woman, comfortable in her own skin. She has definite ideas about things, she's set in her views, and I see a lot of people coming to her and asking questions." They were both right—they just used their intuition in slightly different ways.

The greatest thing about students doing these readings for each other isn't just the fact they're getting experience tuning in themselves. They're also seeing that intuition is an ability everyone possesses. I once worked with a seasoned financial professional from New York City. After having several readings with me, he took my workshop and said of the experience, "There were all different kinds and levels of ability in that room. There were people in my class who could absolutely see things I couldn't see; there were even people in the room who saw things that *Char* couldn't see! That class taught me that you don't have to be 'psychic' to use your intuition."

Quite honestly, people can make intuition and psychic ability into something bigger than it is. Intuition is not a one-of-a-kind ability that only certain people have. It's something I happen to have an aptitude for, just like other people have an aptitude for history or sailing or mathematics (none of which I have any aptitude for at all!). But when I was first studying to develop my intuition, I was told, "Oh, you have a gift and others don't." That's ridiculous. Everyone has intuition. It's the most natural thing in the world. My purpose is to help people discover their intuition and then use it for their own good and the good of others.

Sometimes it's hard work, breaking through people's preconceived notions and getting them to trust the voice of their own inner wisdom. But seeing my students blossom as they apply these six steps and start to tune in on a deeper level makes it all worthwhile. I get letters like this one from "Tanya":

> "I'm just a normal mother and wife, but I feel so strongly about what Char taught me. I feel so much more spiritual now. It didn't happen overnight, but it did happen after Char's workshop. Every day my intuition is clearer than the day before. And when I get that strong gut feeling, I go with it. I know every day I'll experience some contact from my Dad and/or Grandmother. Thank you, Char, for helping me to be with my loved ones."

## Six Steps to Access Your Wisest Self

In the next six chapters you'll get a chance to delve into each step of my method. You'll learn both the whys and the hows—the reasons each step is important, and how you can implement each step in your life as you develop your own intuitive gift. But let's start here by giving you all six steps in order, with a short description of each.

### Step One: Know You Are Psychic!

It's not enough to "believe" you are psychic, because even the smallest iota of doubt can block your abilities completely. You must develop a sense of inner certainty that will allow you to tap in to your innate intuitive power on demand.

### Step Two: Harness the Power of Your Thoughts

We communicate with the universe and with those on the other side through the power of our thoughts. When we are aware of our thoughts, intuition flows easily. We become more attuned to the highest energy of the universe, and we'll be tipped off when a message comes through.

## Step Three: Use Your Five Senses to Enhance the Sixth

Our intuitive side communicates through our five senses and our emotions. Your intuition may often have a favorite "sense" it uses to get in touch with your conscious mind, but you can learn to use all your senses to tap in to your inner wisdom.

## Step Four: Feeling Other People's Emotions

Have you ever been in a fabulous mood and then walked into a party or group of people, and suddenly your emotions completely changed for no apparent reason? You need to know how to detect and protect yourself from the emotions of others.

## Step Five: How Do You Get Intuitive Information?

Over and over again we're given hints and guidance in many forms, but for them to do any good we must be able to notice and interpret what we're getting. We must learn to develop our own unique intuitive "radar."

## Step Six: Protecting Yourself from Negative Energies

Unfortunately not all energy in the universe is good, and not all spirits have our welfare at heart. You need to protect yourself from energies and personalities who do not wish you well, by going to the highest possible level of goodness, light, love, and wisdom when using your intuition.

Try my method and see what happens. I think you'll discover that a little trust and a little effort will produce amazing results. So let's begin!

# 11

~

Step One

# Know You Are Psychic

Answer this question quickly, without thinking: *Are you psychic?* If you said "No" or "Maybe," or "I'm not sure," or even "I believe so," then at some level you are blocking your own intuition. The first secret to accessing your wisest self is certainty. You have to absolutely *know*, without doubt, that you are psychic.

In the 1970s there were several very popular books with titles like *Inner Tennis, Inner Skiing, Inner Golf,* focusing on the mind-set necessary to excel at these sports. The same thing is true with intuition: your potential for success begins with your mind-set. I could give you tips all day long about tuning in, speaking to spirits, picking up on different energies, and so on—things which absolutely will help you access your intuition more easily—but none of them will work unless your mind tells you, "I know I have intuition."

When people come to me for instruction and say, "I believe I have some psychic ability," I'll tell them to stop right there. You can't just "believe," because belief means we are overcoming doubts. *Knowing* is altogether different. Do you "believe" or "know" the sun will come up tomorrow morning? You must have the same kind of certainty about your own psychic abilities before you can really put them to use. When you "know" you are psychic, it opens you to communicate with the universe.

My student Hank uses a great sports metaphor. "If you were to ask all of the players in the NFL, 'Who's going to the Super Bowl?', every single one of them will say, 'We are!' But there are degrees of belief, and I'll bet the teams that end up in the Super Bowl are the ones that *know* it for certain, in their heart of hearts. There is no substitute for that level of belief. You need that kind of certainty to go on to the next step or it doesn't work."

I love giving seminars because they bring people of like minds together. It's an environment where there is openness and a lack of judgmentalism. There is nobody saying, "This is stupid. This doesn't exist. This is ridiculous." There are no blocks or negativity in the environment to stop someone's growth. And as the students see other people trying—and succeeding—to use their intuition, it gives them more confidence, certainty, and willingness to try it themselves.

But it all starts from knowing that, whether you use it actively or not, you have a powerful sixth sense inside you. If you're still in the belief or doubt stage about your own intuition, ask yourself why. Do you need more examples from your own life of times when you used your intuition? Go back to Chapter 8, "You've Already Had Your First Psychic Experience!" and do the exercises. Do you hesitate to use the word *psychic* to refer to your experiences because of past references? Some of us were brought up in faiths that frown on psychics, or perhaps we are total skeptics as far as anything outside our five senses are concerned. Change the question at the beginning of this chapter to "Are you intuitive?" if that helps. But before you go a step further, you'd better be absolutely certain you have intuitive abilities.

Maybe you've had experiences that can't be explained

but you're not ready to label them "psychic." Or maybe you're afraid of what will happen if you say to yourself, "Yes, I'm psychic." If your enemy is that four-letter "F" word FEAR, or you lack self-confidence because someone in your past hurt your self-esteem or pushed their skeptical beliefs on you, I have three very loving words of advice for you: *Get over it!* It's time to love yourself enough to accept your God-given abilities and know that you are intuitive, sensitive, and psychic.

One of the best things about teaching my students is that they can get instant confirmation that they have these abilities. "Peter," a businessman from Los Angeles, took my class a couple of years ago. He told me later he was amazed at his own abilities during the reading practice at the end of the session. With no prior instruction or intuitive experience, he was able to describe in detail the apartment of the person he was paired with. "I could see the furniture, the carpet, even the view outside the window," he said. "It sure surprised the heck out of me."

Another client asked for instruction because her husband was a professional golfer and she wanted to know how well he would do in an upcoming tournament. Knowing her circumstances, at the end of the session I said, "I'm thinking of something right now and I want you to tune in on it. Tell me, without thinking about it consciously, what comes into your mind." She saw coins and money, nature, and empty spaces in nature. Then I said, "What is the result?" She told me tranquillity and total contentment.

What I *didn't* tell her was, I was tuning in on her husband and asking about his success. The empty spaces in nature were a golf course. The coins and money indicated he would do well in the tournament, creating the feelings of tranquillity and contentment she experienced. She hit it right on the head. When I told her that, she said, "Oh my God, I've got goose bumps." (Goose bumps are a great psychic detector.) She told me later she had known intuitively the answer to her question, but she didn't allow herself to believe it. She was insecure because she wanted so badly for it to be true. "Now I get it," she said. "I know how to go there." (By the way, her husband did very well in his tournament.)

Using your intuition is all about what I call the four C's: *courage, confidence, commitment*, and *conquering*. You have to have the courage to take the chance, you have to have the confidence to go for it 100 percent, you have to commit yourself completely, and only then will you conquer. Doubt is a demon. Doubt backwards is "tabou'd" (or close to it, anyway). Just saying "maybe" will stifle your innate psychic abilities. It's about knowing it, owning it, and using it. If you don't know it, you may as well forget it. Take up needlepoint or some other hobby. At least you can decorate your home with the results.

So here's your exercise: do whatever it takes for you to know you are psychic, that you (along with everybody else) have intuition. If you need to go back to Chapter 8 and add to your list of "intuition incidences," do it. If you have to walk on the treadmill for an hour a day repeating, "I'm intuitive," do it. If you need to meditate and get into a centered space, do it. For extra credit, you might want to go to the library or bookstore and get a copy of *The Little Engine That Could*. Do you remember the story? The engine chugged and puffed up the side of the mountain saying, "I think I can, I think I can, I think I can . . ." And on the other side, he sailed happily downhill, saying, "I thought I could, I thought I could, I thought I could." Be like that little engine on the other side of the mountain, only say to yourself, "I *know* I can, I *know* I can, I *know* I can!" Know you are intuitive, and I guarantee, your wisest self will be right there to support you.

# 12

~

Step Two

# Harness the Power of Your Thoughts

Thought is the most powerful force in the universe. Quantum physicists say we each literally create our reality through our thoughts. That's because nothing in this world has any reality for us *until* we process it through our thoughts. Without the power of thought, our experience of the world would consist of incoherent and random impressions—feelings, sights, and sounds which make no sense.

Unlike the rest of the physical universe, thought has no limits on where it goes, how far it goes, or how fast it goes. It can bridge space and time effortlessly: you can transport yourself over the ocean by visualizing an image of the Eiffel Tower in a split second, or you can take yourself back to your childhood by remembering your fifth birthday party. Thought can create worlds that have never been seen in our physical universe. It can produce visions of what might be and what could have been. It can even reach past the barriers of death to put us in communication with those on the other side. And thought is the way intuition chooses to speak to the conscious mind.

I believe we must harness the power of our thoughts in order to use intuition effectively. We must learn to tell the difference between the thought stream of our logical, conscious mind and the intuitive "nuggets" that appear, like gold, in the water. To spot those nuggets we must make sure that the stream of our thoughts is as clear and clean as possible, free from the muddiness of negativity. And we must learn how to take responsibility for the energy released with every thought we put forth into the universe.

The first step, however, is to figure out just what this thing called "thought" is. What is it made of? Where does it come from? Exactly what are its powers? And how can we use thought to tap in to the world of intuition?

## What Is Thought?

For all its power—and despite the fact that thoughts run through our minds almost every moment—"thought" is one of the most difficult concepts to define or pin down. It's not something you can see or hold in your hand. It's completely intangible, yet its power is immense. Physicists and philosophers have been investigating the mystery of thought for many years, and what they've come up with is amazing.

Remember in Chapter 4 I said everything is made up of energy? Thought is absolutely a form of energy. That's why it is so powerful and so flexible—like Superman, it's "faster than a speeding bullet, more powerful than a locomotive." Biochemists tell us that a thought is created when a series of neurons in the brain fire off, producing an energy current with a particular pattern. But what happens to that energy? If (as physicists tell us) no energy is ever lost in the cosmos, where does that thought energy go? Is it possible that, if our scientific instruments were finely tuned enough, we could literally pick up the energy of our thoughts shooting off into the universe?

Even more important, what happens when we consciously *direct* our thoughts? Some quantum physicists say this is like a radio signal. Usually our thoughts are like static—small pieces and particles shooting off into the universe, their energy weakening as they spread out, lose coherence, and eventually disappear. But when we consciously concentrate and send out a clear thought with intention, it's like a radio signal sent by a strong transmitter. It maintains its coherence and direction for far longer, and has a much greater chance of being picked up by someone.

So if thought is energy, and a directed thought is a more coherent form of energy, then we should be able to harness the power of our thoughts to give and receive energy. After all, what is prayer except a focused thought directed to a particular place with a particular intention? In prayer, our goal is to use the energy of our thoughts to connect us with a higher place (or person, depending on your beliefs)—what I call universal goodness, unconditional love, and wisdom. Now, if our directed thoughts are powerful enough to reach this ultimate level, why shouldn't they be able to touch anything or anyone in the entire universe?

The power of thought is the reason I can read for people over the phone, over the airwaves—anywhere at all. It's how I get in touch with the spirits of departed loved ones. It's how I speak to my own spirit guides and guardian angels. And it's how *you* can do the same, by using the power of your own directed, coherent thoughts, and by learning how the universe sends its directed, coherent thoughts back to your mind. For we are not only transmitters of thought energy but receivers as well. When we clear our minds of the static of undirected thoughts, when we tune in our own mental receiver, we can pick up on the thought signals being sent to us from other people, other places, other levels of reality.

# Thoughts Create Our Reality

Our thoughts have the power not only to send incredible energy off into the universe; I agree with quantum physicists who say that our thoughts actually create our reality. This occurs on several levels. First, as I said above, thought creates our reality because the only way we can perceive reality is *through* our thoughts. Yes, our senses take in impressions, information, and so on, but those impressions must be processed through our minds, and then be turned into thoughts. It's the only way we can make sense of the world.

But I believe the energy of our thoughts interacts with the world around us to create our reality in a very literal sense. Scientists often use the example of someone observing a scientific experiment. In their view, the very fact that there is an observer will affect the outcome of that experiment, because the energy of the observer interferes with or affects the energy waves and particles that make up the experiment itself. Now, I don't understand these theories, but like many people, I have been in a restaurant or at a party talking to someone, and felt something strange—a change in energy, perhaps—only to turn around and see someone staring at me from across the room. Because I was in tune at that moment, I felt the energy of the situation shift due to the change in conditions. For instance, have you ever been at a party that's been a little bit dull, and then a man whom everyone calls "the life of the party" walks in? He's smiling, he's got lots of energy, he starts to say hello to everyone, and within minutes, the atmosphere in the room has changed completely. I believe that's because "the life of the party" has caused the thoughts of many people to become more positive and lively, and the energy of the room has shifted as a result.

Try this experiment. Think of someone you truly love, either on this plane or on the other side. Send them a message that you love and care for them. Don't say anything out loud; simply think whatever it is you would like to communicate to them now. Do you feel the energy created by that one simple thought? If you've ever looked at someone with love, you know how powerful the energy of your thoughts were at that moment. And if anyone has looked at you with that kind of intense emotion, you've felt the power of their thoughts directed toward you as well.

Thoughts are just as powerful as deeds. In fact, no action can take place unless it is preceded by a thought, so in a sense thoughts are even more potent than the actions they produce. If everything is composed of energy, then the energy of a thought can be equally as beneficial or harmful as the energy of an action. Certainly throughout history thoughts have caused as much or more harm than actions. Do you doubt it? Think of the hundreds of millions of people who do not take the actions that will benefit themselves and humankind, simply because either their fears or beliefs held them back—and beliefs and fears are nothing but the result of thoughts. In the same way, thoughts and ideas have also advanced civilization more than any machine or individual ever created. Plato, Einstein, and Descartes were all men whose thoughts and ideas have shaped the world.

Once we put a thought out into the cosmos, it has life. If you think something, consider it the same as an action, because on an energetic level, it is. If you think, "I wish my boss would go jump in the lake," you might as well push her in yourself—not necessarily in terms of the effect of that thought on her, but absolutely in terms of the effect of that thought on *you*. So be careful what you think, because once a thought is out there, it's a reality. If you're thinking something, you'd better own it and accept it as yours, because it will affect you somewhere down the line.

# How the Universe Uses Thought to Speak to Us

Thoughts are also the energy by which the universe communicates to us from places other than the everyday world. Think about it. If thoughts are a powerful form of energy which can instantly transcend boundaries like time and space, wouldn't they be a natural channel for information from other levels of reality? The energy of thought is powerful yet refined, so it can be used by the universe to speak directly to us. It's as if the universe could use our thoughts like radio waves, following their path back to our mental "transmitter." And *intuitive* thoughts are the primary way through which the universe communicates with us.

An intuitive thought is usually not something that we are focusing on consciously. It has nothing to do with our logical, sequential, day-to-day kind of thinking. Instead, it comes from an entirely different place, like a creative idea that pops into your head from nowhere. When a thought pops into your head that's going to help make life easier, tip you off about something, or help prevent a problem for you or for someone else, it's what I call a "God thought," because it is coming from the highest level of goodness, love, and wisdom.

If you pay attention to your thoughts, I believe you'll be surprised how often the universe is tipping you off in different areas of your life. In the second part of this book you'll read many examples of how my students and clients—average, everyday people—have paid attention to their own intuitive thoughts and saved themselves from danger, helped their businesses, deepened their relationships, and much more.

The universe is not alone in using "thought power" to reach us. The spirits of our loved ones, guides, and guardian angels find, in our thoughts, an exceptionally convenient channel for connecting with us as well. Spirits on the astral plane are composed of a kind of energy, so it is easy for them to use the energy of thought to communicate with people on this side.

Do you remember the movie *Ghost?* There was a scene where Patrick Swayze (playing a ghost) was learning to move objects. It took an enormous amount of effort on his part to move a penny or an empty soda can. He found it a lot easier to communicate with Whoopi Goldberg (playing a woman attuned to the spirit world)—he simply spoke directly to her mind, and she could hear him. Of course this was just a movie, but doesn't it make sense that using the energy of thought to speak to us takes very little effort on the part of those who inhabit the level of consciousness/energy which we sometimes call the astral plane? If you've ever had thoughts of departed loved ones occur for no particular reason, it may very well be their way of saying hello!

When I'm reading for people, especially on TV and radio shows when I don't have much time with each individual, the spirits around them communicate to me through thoughts that pop in my head. I'll feel the energy around someone, and then a thought will come out of nowhere, "Joseph, I was a grandfather." So I'll ask, "Did you have a grandfather named Joseph?" and most of the time, I'll be right. Or it may be an initial instead of a full name that comes, or perhaps an image of what the deceased loved one did for a living. It's like I'm turning on a shortwave radio in my mind, and the spirits are sending messages in the form of thoughts.

The great news is, it also takes very little effort for us to use our thoughts to speak to the spirits around us. Our thoughts certainly have enough power to reach our loved ones, and they can feel our positive energy just as surely as they did when they were on this plane. Every time you bring to mind your departed loved ones and send them love and good wishes, their spirits will know it, because their energy will be vibrating with the power of your positive thoughts.

## Becoming Aware of Our Thoughts

While it is true that our thoughts control our actions, we seldom consider just how many thoughts flow through our minds at any given moment. Here's an exercise that will help you begin to develop an awareness of your own thoughts.

1. For twenty minutes, write down (or tape record) every thought that comes into your head. Everything—negative, positive, silly, mundane, profound, whatever.

2. On another sheet of paper, make three columns. Using the list of all the thoughts you had during the last twenty minutes, on the left-hand side, make a list of everything you would consider a negative thought. On the right-hand side, list all the thoughts that were positive. In the middle, write any thought you would consider neutral.

It's amazing how much is going on in our minds, isn't it? To harness the power of our thoughts, we must first become aware of the constant stream of our thoughts. As a child I used to love lying in bed for hours, staring up at the ceiling in my room. I didn't know it at the time, but during those "daydreams" I was actually developing an awareness of my own thoughts—which helped me recognize later that some of the thoughts which showed up were coming from a place other than my own eight-year-old mind!

When we pay attention to our thoughts, we can start to

recognize the flashes of intuition that have nothing to do with our everyday kind of thinking. It is the close attunement to our own thoughts that allows us to recognize psychic thoughts when they appear in our minds. Because I'm very aware of my thoughts, when a thought comes in that's not my own, I can notice it immediately and then really pay attention to it. As another of my students describes it, "I know the way I think, the way I approach things, the words that I use. When something comes in from my intuition, it's different. It's words I wouldn't use, or a picture I've never seen before, or information I couldn't possibly get from my own mind. It comes in, and I know I need to pay close attention."

When I teach people to develop their intuition, I tell them, "When you have time, sit down and get to know your thoughts, because that will help you recognize when those 'different' thoughts show up. You'll realize when you're in sync with the thoughts the universe is putting in your head, and when you're not." You can also practice developing this kind of awareness through any type of meditation or regular period of quiet reflection.

# Shaping Our Reality with Positive and Negative Thoughts

Your intuitive abilities will develop more quickly when the majority of your thoughts arise from a healthy and positive mind. Unfortunately, not *all* our thoughts are that positive! Far too often, our minds are filled with negative, doubting, fearful, mean, worried, even hateful thoughts. Sometimes these thoughts are directed at others; sometimes they are directed at ourselves. It doesn't matter. Negative thoughts of any kind are like a poisonous gas, seeping out of our minds and contaminating the atmosphere around us.

Think I'm overstating the power of negative thoughts? Don't I wish. One negative thought can sometimes cancel out years of positive ones. For instance, imagine you're an Olympic-caliber figure skater at the Winter Games, and it's your turn to do the routine you've done a million times before. One little doubt at the wrong time in that routine can cause you to miss a jump. One negative thought makes the difference between winning and losing.

One negative thought can also stop you from accessing your intuition. Remember I said in the last chapter that you have to *know* you are psychic? The smallest negative thought can block your intuition completely. That's the destructive power of negative thinking. When the mind is filled with confidence and *positive* thoughts, however, intuition flows easily and we become more attuned to the highest energy of the universe.

Both our negative and positive thoughts have the power to create our reality. We are what we think. If our thoughts are positive, we have the ability to heal and help. But if we are thinking negatively and giving power to evil, that's what we will create. And I guarantee, if you're thinking negative thoughts, they will come back to haunt you. Energy always has to go somewhere, and the old saying, "What goes around comes around" is absolutely true.

There's another old saying that applies to our thoughts: "Like attracts like." If you're harping on something that's upsetting you, it's going to make you depressed and bring negative energy around you. Have you ever known people with a really lousy attitude toward life? Aren't they the ones who say, "Bad things are always happening to me"? But here's the question: Do they have a lousy attitude because bad things happen to them, or do bad things happen to them because they have a lousy attitude?

We've got to learn to cultivate positive thoughts. Sometimes this means turning negatives into positives, taking the knocks that fate offers us and figuring out a way to create good from them. Things aren't always going to go our way. Our lives aren't going to be a bed of roses, because that's not how we grow and evolve. But it's up to us to do the absolute best with what we have and create an inner environment of positive thoughts to attract the light and love of the universe to us.

When things aren't going smoothly, it's okay to get depressed and feel sorry for yourself—for a moment. Then you have to learn to say, "You know what? This is the way the universe wants it right now. Okay, so I don't have the job I want, or the person I'm in love with, or the home I want. I'm going to focus on what I have, not on what I don't have." Find the optimistic, positive side to your situation, maybe even laugh at it a little. "Well, I could get the house I want and have lousy neighbors." Or, "I could have the person I'm in love with and they might not really be my soul mate." Or "If I had that job I'd be working twenty-four hours a day because I'd be so worried about having all that responsibility." As long as you've tried everything you can to obtain those things, then you have to let go and put your trust and faith in the universe. Look at the cup as half-full instead of half-empty. Say to yourself, "Okay, I did the best I could. Now I won't feel sorry for myself. I'll learn to enjoy what I have, and keep striving to obtain other things in the future."

I'm not asking you to be naive or live like Pollyanna. I'm simply saying that when we are focused on positive thoughts, we stand a better chance of being balanced emotionally, psychologically, physically, and spiritually. And when we are balanced, our intuitive radar is much more acute, and our ability to send and receive messages is clearer.

Turning negative thoughts to positive thoughts is like changing the TV channel you're watching—you're changing the energy around you so you can bring in the kind you want. This simple yet powerful key can help us become both more in tune with our intuition and psychologically freer at the same time. Make it a habit to turn unnecessary negative energies into positive energies. As one of my students put it, "If you just think positive thoughts and let goodness happen to you, it's going to happen. If you want to bring on bad, be my guest—but I find it a lot easier to bring on the good."

# Tuning in to Intuitive Thoughts

Here are a few simple secrets that will help you tune in to your own intuitive thoughts.

## 1. Go with the first thought that comes into your head.

When you're tuning in to someone or something, clear your mind, ask the question you have, and listen to the first thing that pops into your mind. Just allow the thought to float into your head. If you need to, say it out loud. Don't be logical. The logical brain has nothing to do with intuition; it should only be used when you are interpreting what you receive. Trust the first thought or message that comes to you.

## 2. Get your personal agenda out of the way.

Once I had a phone reading scheduled with a client and right before he called, my secretary told me there was a huge problem with the telephones in her office. I had to get a repair person out immediately if I wanted to keep the office open. Right then, the client called in (on another line). I said, "Please call me back in five minutes. I have to have a clear mind." I can read in almost any situation or setting, but no matter what, during a reading I have to get my own personal "stuff" completely out of the way. It doesn't mean that everything has to be hunky-dory. It just means that, to tap in to your intuition, your mind has to be calm and focused so you can recognize intuitive thoughts when they come in.

It also means you have to dump your personal opinions—anything that might color the messages the universe is giving you through the medium of your thoughts. What we deal with in this work is the truth. That's the beauty of it: dealing with truth, understanding truth, and facing truth, because in truth we are freed. So if there are things that are unsettled in your life, you need to face the truth about yourself first and, at least for the moment, eliminate any personal concerns that may be blocking you.

### 3. Pay attention to everything you're getting.

When I'm reading, I find I have to be aware of my thoughts on many different levels. I'm constantly asking myself, "What thought am I getting, why am I getting it, and what does it mean in the context of this reading?" Sometimes I'll get a thought or image that ordinarily might apply in my life instead of my client's, but on further investigation it turns out there's a message in that thought for the client as well.

For example, I'll be reading for someone and all of a sudden I'll think about a friend of mine, Steve. The logical part of my mind will say, "I'm not focusing on my life right now. Why am I thinking about Steve?" And then I'll say, "Do you know someone named Steve?" and the client will say, "Yeah." Or there will be something about Steve that holds a message for this client. Simply ask yourself, "What is this supposed to mean?" and trust your first answer. It's like a ball of string: you start with one thread and follow it until you unravel yards and yards and yards of information. For example, maybe Steve just went through a job change, or he has to watch his cholesterol because he has high blood pressure. I'll start exploring that thought with my client, and almost always there is some element of commonality. "Steve" was just a kind of shorthand which the universe was using to get its message across.

## 4. Go with the flow.

I know when people are using their intuition and when they're just guessing, so I'll push my students until I can feel they're "in the groove," so to speak. When they tap into that first intuitive thought, however, it's almost like an alternative stream of consciousness happens in the brain, and they can ride that stream of intuition until it plays itself out.

You have to keep pushing yourself, exploring the thought stream further and further. Keep asking, "What does this mean? What more do I want to learn about this? What will it take? What will it be? Where will it be?" Let the stream stop of its own accord—when you're first starting to develop your intuition, it's especially important to let it run. Let the thoughts keep coming, keep asking yourself the questions that will help draw those intuitive flashes out. The more practice you get, the better.

Harnessing the power of your thoughts is easy, once you're aware of them and are committed to keeping them positive and clear of negativities and obstructions. Simply notice the thoughts that come from nowhere and stand out against the stream of your usual consciousness. Then take those intuitive flashes and pursue them until you understand their meaning. It's not rocket science. In fact, it's as easy as clearing your mind and focusing your thoughts!

# 13

⚮

Step Three

# Use Your Five Senses to Enhance the Sixth

How does our wisest self communicate with us? The main avenue is thought, but our five senses and our emotions also play a part. Some people see pictures or words . . . some hear voices . . . some smell aromas . . . some get feelings in their bodies, or emotions that arise for no reason. Our five senses along with our emotional feelings enhance our sixth sense.

Everybody has their own unique radar, and different people will use their senses in different ways. Your intuition may often have a favorite sense it uses to get in touch with your conscious mind, but information can come from each of our senses. As you develop your own intuitive "style," you may notice which sense is your particular favorite. But the spirits who want to communicate with you may choose an entirely different sense, or may come through using several senses. It's not uncommon, for example, for a spirit to show you something that relates to them (a vision of their name, or a possession that meant something) and, at the same time, you'll smell the fragrance associated with that person.

The key is always to *pay attention to what you're getting.* It's like interpreting another language, because when you're getting images and feelings, you first have to try to understand them and then put them in your own terms.

# Sight: Having True Vision

Few people will publicly admit to have seen spirits, but in private it's a different matter—such sightings are a much more common phenomenon than is openly discussed. Have you ever seen something scooting by in your peripheral vision, but when you looked in that direction there was nothing there? Many spirits seem to find it easier to manifest in our peripheral vision rather than directly in front of us.

Visual impressions from spirits can come in a lot of different forms, not just seeing the spirit itself. An image or a still picture of someone may flash through your mind. Sometimes there will be movement or sound with the picture. Some people see full-blown visions, like a movie appearing in front of their eyes. I've heard people who can describe their visions as exactly as if they were watching a TV screen right in front of their eyes. Malcolm Mills, my friend and associate (he's an astrologer and psychic himself), told me recently of seeing a dear friend who had passed over twenty years earlier:

"I was sitting at home one day, all by myself, listening to a Leonard Cohen album, and there was a song that somehow reminded me of my friend Timmy. I looked up and there was Timmy, sitting right in front of me, as solid and real as you and me. He was a little bigger than life, immaculately dressed (which surprised me, because that wasn't his style), smiling and glowing. He maintained his presence for at least thirty seconds, and then he just kind of faded."

Psychic visual impressions don't have to be nearly that elaborate. When I'm doing a reading, for example, sometimes I'll need an answer and I may not know what to say, and all of a sudden something will manifest on the wall. It could be a shadow, it could be the sunlight hitting something in a certain way, forming a kind of figure. A lot of times I'll see an initial or a name, either on the wall or in my mind's eye, and I'll think, "This must be for the person I'm talking to."

Sometimes the spirits will show me the weirdest images, pictures that make absolutely no sense to me but mean something very specific to the person I'm reading for. Usually if I don't understand something, I'll go ahead and say it anyway, because the other person may know what it means. For example, I'll see a hot dog and won't have a clue why, so I'll say, "I see a hot dog. Does that mean anything to you?" Then I might get a name, and ask, "What does that have to do with Peter?" Usually the client will say something like, "Peter was my dad, and hot dogs were his favorite food." Then I may get a feeling of a celebration and I'll say, "Was there a birthday?" The client will respond, "His birthday was yesterday and I was thinking of him, and I had hot dogs!"

Those are the kinds of pictures that flash into the mind. When I'm reading, things happen and they make sense within the context of the communication I'm supposed to give. Sometimes the images make no sense in the moment, but as time goes on, the meaning becomes clear. My friend "Tony" reminds me that I gave him a reading where I saw Sedona, Arizona, an Easter egg, a bell, and a forest. I also told him he would be moving soon. He ended up moving to Sedona, Arizona, to a place called Bell Rock. His home overlooks a large stand of trees. And his moving date was a few days before Easter!

Be aware that, as with everything we receive psychically, how we interpret these visions is the key to our understanding. The Easter egg could have meant Easter time, or it could mean moving to an egg farm. In the same way, a lot of people will see numbers when they get intuitive impressions. But if you see the number 6, for example, it could mean the month of June, a year that ends with a six, within six months, six hours or six days from now, an address that has a "6" in it, and so on. You have to put the number in the context of all the other information and impressions you are getting, and then interpret its meaning to the best of your ability.

# Hearing: Sounds and Voices from Beyond

Some of my students—not many, quite honestly—hear words or voices either inside or outside their heads that give them their psychic information. Sometimes it will be the voice of a loved one who has passed on, or it might be a voice that's not recognizable. Many people will hear voices just before falling asleep, or they'll be awakened by a voice. That's certainly happened to me. But you have to be very sure where the voice is coming from. I tell people to use their instinct and intuition when they hear voices. "Feel whether it's coming from a high or low place," I say. "Then say a quick prayer of protection, and if you're not comfortable with what you're hearing, tell the voice to go away, that it's not welcome. If you are comfortable, then you can ask the spirit what it wants. Don't let it frighten you, because a spirit can only control or harm you if you let it. You control spirits; they don't control you. Surround yourself with white light and go to sleep."

Spirits will use other kinds of sounds to communicate with us. Frequently a loved one will make themselves known by a song. Robin Nemeth told me that one day she was driving around thinking about her dad, who had passed away not too long before. She had the car radio on, and just at that moment the announcer said, "All right, this one's for you—it's from your dad," and "Wind Beneath My Wings," came on. For Robin and her dad, "Wind Beneath My Wings" was "their" song.

Jeannie Starrs-Goldizen was sitting in her kitchen at home with a friend of hers in New Jersey. The friend said, "Did you hear that? I heard a sound like shuffling, either feet shuffling down the hallway or somebody shuffling cards. Is there somebody playing cards in the house?" Jeannie, who knew they were the only people in the house, broke into a fit of laughter. "It was my grandma! She died when she was eighty-nine, and for years the two of us played Old Maid. If you heard cards shuffling, it was granny."

Some people will hear footsteps that come from no physical source. I heard a story from a client whose twelve-year-old daughter, Shannon, was sleeping over at a friend's house. There were four kids sleeping on the living room floor, and about 2:00 in the morning, Keith, who was about nine years old, woke up and heard footsteps. The footsteps came from the front door, down the hall, into the living room, walked straight up to Shannon (who was sound asleep), and stopped. Keith swears he could see no one making the footsteps. The next day he asked Shannon about it. "Oh, that was just my father," she said. "He passed away a few years ago and he just likes to know where I am."

The key to all psychic information is to make sure you sense that what you're hearing comes from a high source, or at least feels familiar. If you hear shuffling and it also "feels" like your grandmother, great. If a voice sounds or feels like your brother or another friend, super. If not, tell it to go away. Just make sure you always say a prayer of protection, and check everything you hear with your own intuitive sense.

# Smell and Taste: Sweet Reminders

Smell is one of the most powerful senses we have. It evokes emotions, situations, and people more strongly than almost anything else. Do you have a particular smell you associate with Christmas or Thanksgiving? Are there certain flowers that were favorites of a loved one? Did someone in your family use a particular perfume or after-shave, so that whenever you smell Chanel No. 5 or Old Spice, you think of them?

I've had people tell me that they were thinking of their mother or their grandmother and then walked into an empty room and smelled roses. While hugging someone, my dear friend Diana Basehart will say, "You smell like my granny." Her grandmother had a special scent that comes out when Diana is with a family member or friend who truly cares for her. A doctor client of mine walks into the office she shared with her father and smells his cologne. I've also heard stories where someone will smell the kind of tobacco a loved one used to smoke. Often there isn't really a specific fragrance per se, but someone can pick up a father or mother or husband or wife by the subtle odor each of us gives off. "I can not only sense when Marty's around, but I also smell the way he used to smell. He has a distinct odor that I'd know anywhere," says one client about her husband of fifteen years who passed away in 1992.

Certain tastes can also be powerful reminders of our loved ones. If you find yourself craving the tuna noodle casserole your mother made, it might very well be your mother saying hello—or at least, telling you to eat better! Every time my friend's grandmother tastes sugar cook-ies, it reminds her of *her* grandmother, and the thought, the memory, and the love connects them forever. At times, certain foods reminds me of my father, who passed several years ago. I'll think, *Hey, daddy, is that you?* Soon after I'll often get an important message to help me with my own life, and I'll know it came from my father.

# Touch: The Goose Bump Factor

Physical sensations can be very startling if they come, from beyond. I've had clients describe the feeling of a hand stroking their hair, accompanied by a strong sensation of love. Other people have the feeling of being held or embraced when no one else is physically present. They'll be thinking of a loved one or be awakened at night feeling that someone just touched them on the shoulder. For example, my student Martha Gresham tells me at night she can actually lie there and feel a soft cheek touch her face, in the same way her grandmother did when Martha was a little girl.

Other very typical physical sensations include changes in temperature. When you walk by a spirit, a lot of times there's a coldness, or a warm or chill breeze will blow through the room for no apparent reason and with no windows or doors open to cause a draft. Sometimes spirits will produce even more tangible physical manifestations. Another client who bought and renovated a house that turned out to have a ghost would occasionally walk down the back steps and feel an unseen foot trip her up.

I remember once a TV producer asked me to go to Maui to investigate a spirit there. A gentleman living on the island insisted that the spirit of a woman would come in at night and lie down next to him in the bed. He would literally see the indentation in the pillow and the mattress. Before arriving on the island, I had envisioned that there was a graveyard adjacent to this man's home. I gave the name of a woman who was buried there and told them I had an impression of a cross connected with her. I also said there was a "John" who was near this woman. When we got to the man's house, there indeed was a cemetery right behind it. In the cemetery we found the tombstone with the woman's name on it. There was a cross carved on her tombstone, and next to her was the grave of a man named John.

There was absolutely a spirit in that house. The problem arose because this man was falling in love with the spirit. He wanted to feel close and connected with someone, and he felt safer falling in love with a spirit rather than a living woman. That's when trouble starts—if we stop living our real lives because we become enamored of the closeness we feel with the spirits.

One of the best indicators of a psychic experience is the physical sensation of goose bumps. I call it a "psychic detector." During a reading I'll get a name and tell the client that a particular spirit is here, and they'll say something like, "I was just thinking about her today and I wrote her name down. Oh my God, I've got goose bumps." So many people I read for (and have interviewed for this book) say that during a reading with me, something will happen—I'll say something that no one but a deceased loved one could possibly know, for example—and the hair will stand up on the back of their neck or on their arms. The body is exceptionally sensitive and will signal us that our intuition is at work.

# Emotions: Your Psychic Early Warning System

Our feelings, our emotions, are one of the best indicators of intuition for almost everyone. How many times have you heard someone say (or said yourself), "That just doesn't feel right to me"? How you describe that feeling of "not rightness" may be very different from the way I describe it, but the result is the same: we know something's wrong.

One of my students told me, "Last year a friend asked if I would like to share a rental house in Southampton, Long Island. We found these people who had a house and my friend already knew she wanted to sign up. But me, I have to get a feeling about the people I'll be sharing a house with. Am I comfortable? Do I think it would be fun? What kind of feeling do I get around them? If I get a good feeling, great. If I get a bad feeling, either around the people or even around the house, I won't do it, because I'll never be comfortable. Sometimes the feeling is physical—I'll get anxious or nauseous or just won't feel so well. It's not so extreme that I can't be in a place, but I'll either be comfortable or not."

Can you see how we can use all our senses to pick up information intuitively? All you have to do is pay attention to what's coming your way. Sometimes you'll get dramatic signs, like visions, voices that come from nowhere, footsteps with no one around, cold drafts, the scent of perfume from long ago, and so on. Much of the time, however, the signs will be far more subtle. The more you practice noticing all the clues the universe is giving you, the more in tune you'll become with your own wisest self. One of my clients told me of many different contacts she's had with her father: "My dad shows up in so many different ways. Sometimes I can be in a room and I'll smell the cologne my father wore, as if he were in the room with me. Sometimes I'll walk outside and see a rainbow that's right over me. Sometimes I'll hear a song that reminds me of him. And sometimes I'll feel a cold or warm breeze blow through the room. I think it's just a matter of tuning in, of listening and accepting and not being scared of it."

Listen to the abundance of clues the universe is giving you through all your senses. You'll be surprised how easy it is to tune in!

# 14

Step Four

# Feeling Other People's Emotions

Have you ever been in a fabulous mood and then walked into a party, and suddenly your emotions changed for no reason at all? If you answered yes, it's because you were unconsciously responding to the emotions of people in the room. I think we all pick up on emotions at one time or another, particularly with those we are close to—spouses, children, parents, best friends, and so on. But picking up on emotions is also a significant part of using your intuition, especially when those emotions lie beneath the surface.

Remember what I said in Chapter 4: everything in the universe is made up of energy, and each of us has our own unique energy "thumbprint." Well, energy also resonates or vibrates at different levels. For example, a happy person's energy vibrates at a different level than someone who is sad. We recognize this all the time. Haven't you ever run into a family member or close friend and, while their outward appearance was either happy or neutral, you felt there was something different going on emotionally? How often have you been right? We know the difference between emotional energy patterns, between the pattern of happiness and the pattern of anger, or the pattern of love and the pattern of despair. When we tune in to someone else, consciously or unconsciously, we are being sensitive to the emotions and energy of others. Understanding this also helps us understand when our own emotions change for no reason at all.

I believe feeling other people's emotions is a part of our fundamental makeup. Look at children and animals—can you think of beings who are more in tune with other people's emotions? One gentleman says of his daughter, Sara Elizabeth, "She's just eight years old, and almost from the time she was born she was more sympathetic toward her fellow human beings than any other child I've been around. She's able to pick up on your mood in a moment. She'll say, 'Dad says such and such but I know he'd really rather say this.' Or 'I don't think Mom feels good right at the moment.' "

About ten years ago, my friend Mark taught me how to "scan" a person's energy. It's sort of like putting up a pair of invisible antenna and feeling what's going on. I let go and let God, and send my awareness in the direction of the person I want to scan, and almost every single time I'll get information. I go from the top of their head to the bottom of their feet and scan the mind, emotions, psychological behavior, health, and so on. I'm especially good at getting emotions. I can tell you someone's mood in a moment, whether they're in the room or three thousand miles away, whether they're still alive or they've passed over.

Now, obviously, being able to pick up on someone's emotions can be extremely valuable in almost any relationship. Knowing when a spouse is in a bad mood has saved many a marriage! But there are some subtler benefits to being emotionally "tuned in." Have you ever heard of the great Eastern philosophy of Zen? One of the key principles of Zen (as I understand it) is the importance of being in the moment, being completely aware of what is happening *right now*. Tuning in emotionally requires that we are completely in the moment, so we can pick up on a very high energy vibration. Operating at that level of awareness allows us to understand who and what we are dealing with much more completely and intelligently. It allows us to respond to changes in someone else with more understanding and compassion. And it opens us up to be more helpful to others because we know where they're *really* coming from in the moment.

# Protecting Yourself from Negative Emotions

I do want to point out a couple of pitfalls in this ability to sense the emotions of others. First, it opens us up to being swept along in emotional highs and lows that have nothing to do with us. Many sensitive people have a bad habit of taking responsibility for the way someone else is feeling. There's a tendency to accept others' emotional reactions on a personal level, thinking that the other person's energy is reflecting their feelings about us. This is rarely the case! Usually what you're picking up is an emotion (sadness, hurt, insecurity, anger, and so on) caused by an event that happened long before this particular moment. Sometimes the feelings are caused by a chemical or hormonal imbalance in the other person, which again has nothing to do with you.

I have a student, Katherine, who is extraordinarily empathic and very good at "reading" people right off the bat. She can tell within a few minutes of meeting someone if they're a person she will be friendly with, or if there's some negativity hidden inside that she doesn't want to be around. She told me about a client who had come to her for several readings. "I finally had to ask her not to call me anymore because she was calling too often, becoming dependent. But every time I spoke to this young woman on the phone, I was overwhelmed with feelings of sadness. There wasn't anything specific in her readings that should cause such pain for her, but speaking with her always made me really, really sad."

If you encounter this kind of painful emotion, unless you've done something to cause it (in which case, please do whatever's needed to make amends), realize it has nothing to do with you. Let it pass, as all emotions pass eventually. If you feel you can help, do so—but do it from a place of knowing you're not the cause of the bad emotion. It's a much freer place from which to act.

Second, feeling other people's negative emotions can actually hurt you if you fail to get rid of those emotions in some way. Unfortunately, many people in the healing and helping professions—nurses, doctors, psychotherapists, as well as psychic healers—can be affected deeply by the negative emotions and energies they have to deal with day after day. When I was putting together the pilot for a TV show, I said to my producers, "Let's get so-and-so," and they told me, "Didn't you hear? She's got colon cancer now" And I said, "How weird is it that so many of the psychics who really care, or are healers, end up with cancer or die young?" Then I realized why: these healers are so busy giving of themselves that they don't take care of their own physical health. They don't protect themselves and thus they become repositories for others' negative energy. Then they don't take the time to clear the energy out of their systems, and they get sick. To stay healthy when we do this work, we have to recharge our batteries with good food, adequate rest, meditation, the company of good friends, and all the other things that help us feel more like ourselves.

Third, being sensitive to the emotions of others means you are more likely to be hurt if someone *is* directing hate, anger, jealousy, and so on, at you. You've got to be vigilant in protecting yourself from any deliberate, destructive energies sent your way. Put a strong white light of protection around yourself and send the negative emotion back where it came from. Now, when I do this, I'm not wishing evil on anyone; I know what goes around, comes around. But I'm not going to allow myself to simply take in someone else's negativity. If I do that, I'm participating in my own victimization.

Despite all the pitfalls, feeling other people's emotions on an intuitive level is one of the most relationship-enriching abilities we have. I'm happy to say that in my student Paula's case, developing that particular kind of intuition opened up an entire new world for her. "Before I started working with my intuition, I had no feelings. None. Not love, not anger, not joy, hate, jealousy, compassion, nothing. I would never even cry. And now everything touches my soul. I feel such incredible freedom—freedom to love people, to feel what they are feeling. It's the freedom to be who I was meant to be all along."

So here's your exercise: Practice tuning in to the emotions of other people. You might want to start with your close friends, family, associates, and so on, then notice the emotions you pick up when you're in the supermarket, at a party, in any situation where you're around people you don't know. Try to get a "hit" on people you meet for the first time. Stay in the present moment of noticing what you're getting right now. If you find you're encountering negative or destructive emotions, shield yourself. And remember, the emotions you're picking up often have nothing to do with you. It's just another way of tuning in to the huge banquet of information the universe is offering you every single moment.

# 15

## Step Five

# How Do You Get Intuitive Information?

Dreams, premonitions, visions, a particular song playing on the radio . . . we're given hints and guidance in many forms, but we have to *notice* what we're getting. Messages are rarely dramatic. When the universe tips us off, it's not like Moses going up to Mount Sinai in the movie *The Ten Commandments.* You're not likely to hear a booming voice coming out of nowhere saying, "I AM THE LORD THY GOD!" It may just be a subtle thought that pops in your head and you say, "Where did that come from?" And since everyone's intuition is unique, there is no exact recipe for communicating with the universe.

Messages come in all shapes, sizes, forms, at any time, night or day. They can come whether you're "tuned in" or not. It could be the busiest time of day and you don't even want to think because you're upset or worried or involved with something, but somehow a thought or feeling pops up saying, "Call so-and-so." Sometimes I'll be having an ordinary conversation with a friend on the phone—not cognizant of my psychic sense or even wanting to use that part of my brain—yet during the conversation I'll get a message that will turn out to be a profound insight for the person at the other end of the line.

My friend Malcolm gets messages all the time from
his best friend Timmy, who passed over in 1976. "They
come through symbols, interesting little coincidences, little inside jokes or memories that had meaning for us all
those years ago," Malcolm says. "For example, before he
died, Timmy and I used to play a card game called 500
rummy a lot. And he was good—I think I won only once
against Timmy in all the years we played. But after he
passed over, my card luck changed completely. Every
time I get in a card game it feels as if Timmy's standing
right behind me, telling me which card to play. Sometimes I think he's wandering around the room, looking at
other people's cards; it almost seems like Timmy's giving
me an unfair advantage! Maybe he's making up for all the
times he beat me at cards when he was alive."

Often messages are not dramatic. Sometimes all you
get is a feeling, or what my student Lisa calls "a gentle
knowing." "There's nothing spooky or scary about it," she
told me. "It's like if you're driving and instead of making
the right turn, something inside you says, ' Go left.' " The
important thing is to pay attention and not to discount
what your intuition is giving you. My client Eleanor says,
"You could easily ignore a message because your phone's
ringing, or it doesn't exactly mean something right then,
or it doesn't seem that important at the time. But when I
get a feeling or a sense of something, I try to stop, take a
little time and see what happens. I've learned from Char
not to ignore these things."

Dreams and daydreams are very common avenues for
messages from your wisest self, because your conscious
mind is not in the way in the dreaming state. You may
spend hours obsessing about a decision you need to make
or a problem you need to solve, and get absolutely
nowhere. And then bang! you'll wake up in the middle of
the night with the solution staring you in the face. Or
you'll turn your attention to something else—another

project, for example, or a phone call, or even making dinner—and all of a sudden something will pop into your head that makes the whole thing come together. That's because your intuition has found a way around all the chatter and interference of the conscious mind to give you a solution from a higher, wiser place.

I get some of the most accurate messages about my own life when I wake up in the middle of a dream that seems very real. In these dreams it's often my father who comes to me to tip me off. Many people have dreams of departed loved ones who come back to warn them. Again, when the conscious mind is asleep or disengaged, our loved ones can communicate with us more easily. I suggest to all my clients and students that they keep pen and paper next to the bed, so they can write down anything that they dream about.

Sometimes it's not a dream but just a thought. If you wake up at three or four in the morning knowing you've gotten a message, or find you can't fall back to sleep because something keeps running through your head, write it down! It may be a message. Many people find that after writing it down, they can fall asleep almost immediately, because the spirits—or their own wisest self—knows an important communication has been received.

When our conscious mind is disengaged or asleep, spirits who do not have our best interests at heart can also come in. That's why it's always best to say a prayer of protection and surround yourself with white light whenever you get those middle-of-the-night messages, especially if they come from spirits you don't recognize. But usually a dream about a loved one is coming from the highest, purest source of love. When I dream about my father, for example, I know I can trust the information he brings.

My friend "Sarah" finds that writing is also a great tool for her to get in touch with her wisest self. "I might be having a funky day and not really know why, so I'll go sit someplace pretty or quiet, write a bit in my journal and just see what comes out. Often what's bothering me becomes really clear, as well as some possible solutions. It's a great way for me to get in touch."

It may sound funny, but another place where a lot of people get messages is in the bathtub or shower. This probably has something to do with the fact that, again, our conscious minds are not especially active at those times, and we tend to be more relaxed. But water is also a very healing and cleansing element. We begin our lives surrounded by water in the womb. In some cultures, water represents the intuitive, softer side of nature. Whatever the reason, if something pops into your head while you're in the bath or shower, pay attention.

## More Than Coincidence

Have you ever had a question about something you should or shouldn't do, and then something happened that seemed to answer your question? People who don't believe in intuition or spirits will tell you it's all coincidence; but I've heard too many stories, and gotten answers too often myself, to believe in "coincidence." In fact, it's more logical to believe in intuition than to say there are that many accidents in the universe!

Here's an example of "coincidence" in action. When I was pulling together a list of possible guests for my TV show, my co-executive producer, Stuart, suggested we do a segment on using magnets for healing. I said, "Great—let me think about it and I'll let you know." The next day, I ran into two different people (one a friend, one a complete stranger) who told me they were wearing magnets in their shoes for healing. Now, Stuart didn't set this up. I didn't ask these people about magnets; they simply told me about it. Needless to say, we scheduled the segment.

A client of mine, a dear woman named Tami, inherited a small amount of money from her father when he passed away. She wanted to use the money to build a pool in her backyard. "I swam competitively all through school, and my Dad was always there to cheer me on," she wrote me. "We even life guarded together. I wanted to build this pool in honor of my Dad, and I also knew my four children would receive such joy from it." But Tami was unsure about putting in the pool; after all, it would take almost the entire sum she had inherited. So she asked her father to give her a sign that this was the right thing to do. "At that exact moment a song I had dedicated to my Dad when he died came on the radio. I knew I had my answer: thumbs up for the pool."

Spirits seem to be able to manipulate energy in many ways to let us know they're around. I've had lights flicker for no apparent reason, or TVs and radios go on all by themselves. There seems to be some kind of affinity between the energy of spirits and the energy of electricity. One client told me that after her father died, her mother kept finding lightbulbs burning out all over the house. And I find it interesting that Thomas Edison, the inventor of the first electric lightbulb, also worked on building a machine to communicate with the dead.

We can use the energy from objects people have used or their photos as means of tuning in. I'm sure you've seen reenactments on TV where a child is missing, and a psychic will take the child's jacket or toothbrush and hold it, and then pick up on what happened or where the child is. That actually does happen. Remember, each of us has our own unique energy "thumbprint" which we leave behind us in places we've been and on objects we've handled (just like the other kind of fingerprints). The difference, of course, is that when I pick up on someone's energy, often I can see where they've been, where they are, and what's happened to them. I can do the same thing with photos. Sometimes I'll be looking at a friend's picture and I'll think, "Gee, I'd better call them today." And when I call, they'll say to me, "How'd you know I wanted to speak to you?"

One of the primary ways I get information is via names and initials of people. Names are basically a conduit bringing someone's energy to me, and then I can scan them. When I pick up on someone's name, it connects me with their soul. That's why we name people after those who have passed over, because the energy of the name links that soul to us.

## Getting Clear

One of the greatest gifts in developing your intuition is being able to help the people you love, to give them guidance and serve as a conduit for messages for them from the other side. But sometimes the toughest thing to do is to read for someone you care about. And it can be even tougher to read for yourself!

I've found over the years that if you try too hard consciously to read for someone, it doesn't work. Let's say you're in love and you want to know if this person is in love with you. Imagine you're obsessing about them; you think about them, wonder if they're going to call, worry how they feel about you, and so on. Is it possible that all those thoughts and emotions might get in the way of your intuition? More often than not, they do. You have to let go a little, relax, and get to a neutral place both mentally and emotionally.

Even when you let go, sometimes it's hard to tell the difference between intuition and wishful thinking. Being emotionally involved in an issue can block or muddy the impressions or messages you're getting, or cause you to put a dubious interpretation on them. You have to learn to listen to the thoughts given to you and not to allow personal opinions or desires to get in the way. One trick to help you get some distance is to ask a question as if you were asking it for someone else. "Is Mike good for

Char?" "Is Suzie going to get this job?" Then "fast forward" that thought into the future and see what you get. Some psychics use tarot cards or astrology or I Ching or runes when reading for themselves, to help them tune in a little more objectively. The key is to do your best to separate yourself from your own feelings about this particular issue. You can be fooled very easily if you want something badly enough. The key is to become neutral.

One common mistake in asking for clarity (or for that matter, in asking anything of the universe) is using an unclear question. When I read for someone and they ask me, "Am I going to move and where?" it produces confusion, because I may get completely different messages about *whether* they're going to move and *where* they might go. I tell people to ask separate questions instead. "Am I going to move?"—that's the first question. You can get a hit on that intuitively. Then, "Where am I going to move?" Questions have to be simple, clean, with no possibility of confusion.

After you've done all this—you've separated yourself from the emotions, you've relaxed and gotten neutral, you're asking specific, one-part questions—if you still don't feel as if you can get clear about a particular issue, find a *real* outside ear and go to see someone else. I have several good friends whom I will consult when I feel I'm not being clear about my personal life. One is a professional astrologer, and the other is just a dear friend who's amazingly intuitive. And sometimes all you have to do is put your desire for clarity out into the universe and the universe will respond. I've had people come up to me and say, "You know what? I have a feeling about you." And I'll almost always listen. But whatever is said to me, I always balance it with my own instincts. I'll say my prayer of protection and then ask, "Is this good advice or bad advice?"

One final point: I think it's very important for anyone

using their intuition to be psychologically and chemically balanced. If you're not balanced I believe you can have a tendency to misinterpret or let your own personal issues get in the way of your messages. When you read for someone else, you have to separate yourself completely from your own life. You can't think about you or what you're doing or your own unresolved stuff that may have nothing to do with this person. If you have unresolved issues, get help to resolve them. I'm a big believer in getting therapy from good, qualified healers; I myself went to therapy when I felt a need for objective guidance. If I believe a client will benefit from therapy, I won't hesitate to tell them so. We create so much of our own destiny—we need to learn balance and self-love so we can create the destiny we want.

# The Key Question: What Does It Mean?

As in everything we receive psychically, *how* we interpret messages is the key to understanding. I believe interpretation is always the most important part of a reading. Whenever I give a message to someone, I'm always extremely careful about the way I interpret it, because it's in the interpretation of the message that the person will get the correct answer. I could pick up on marriage, for example—but is it "yes, marriage," or "no, marriage"? Should they, or shouldn't they?

Many messages come symbolically. For instance, you may tune in and the first thing that comes to mind is a book. What does a book mean? Could it mean writing a book? Going back to school? Watching the financial books, that is, being careful in business? Once I did a reading for a woman named Cheryl Herbeck, who said she and her husband were having trouble with their business. She asked if I thought the business would make it. I said, "Do you and your husband own a restaurant?" "No—we own a medical device company," she answered. "I thought you might be in the restaurant business, because I get that a cook is going to buy your company," I said. About six months later, an investor did come in and buy the Herbecks' business. His name? Dr. Cook.

When I'm interpreting a message for someone, I push myself to get as clear as possible. Let's say a client has met someone and wants to get married. I'll pick up on the name of the person they're considering, then I get nosy. I try to get as much about their lives as I can—if there are any ex-spouses or children involved, their relationship with their parents, and so on. I've found that by understanding this person's relationships with others, I can get a hit on whether he or she is healthy for my client or not.

When you receive a message, keep asking questions about what you're getting and why. Try out several different interpretations; eventually one will make sense. Of course, the more experience you get interpreting messages correctly, the easier it becomes to "home in" on that feeling of rightness. In the beginning, for all of us it's based on trial and error. But if you interpret a message incorrectly, go back and ask yourself, "Why did that come to me? What was I getting? Did I dig deep enough? Did my own personal stuff get in the way?" Sometimes the message itself may have been wrong because it came from trickster spirits or someone who didn't wish you or your client well. Usually, however, I find that if I've gotten a message from a trickster spirit there was also something that should have tipped me off, had I paid attention to it. Evil always tips us off in some way.

As long as you protect yourself with white light, pay attention to what you're getting, and keep digging until it feels right, your ability to interpret messages accurately will continue to grow. When you're in sync, you'll know it. And it's a great feeling when the interpretation makes complete sense and the right message has been delivered! Always keep in mind, however, that what happens after the reading is up to you (or your client). The universe gives us all kinds of signs, and we can interpret messages correctly until the cows come home, but our free will either heeds or ignores them. Sometimes we're even destined to ignore a warning because we need to learn the lesson. Just remember, no message from any psychic or spirit is the last word. We each have to speak that word for ourselves.

## The Importance of Patience

Often I'll get messages that don't seem to make sense in the moment but which play out over time. That's because spirits don't experience time in the same way we do. For them, past, present, and future are all visible at the same moment, so they'll give me a name of someone who won't come into that client's life until a few years from now, for example. I ask my clients to take good notes during our readings, and to consult those notes frequently. They often find that a name or a warning about someone will all of a sudden make sense in a few months.

Patience is one of the most important virtues when it comes to our intuition. Of course, we're the most *impatient* about things that matter the most to us! But when we're emotionally involved, we can't see the forest for the trees. We may be blocking the very signs the universe is giving us. We have to relax, get neutral, trust, and have faith. When we let go, our question goes out into the universe, and if there is an answer, it will come to us eventually.

Some questions do not have immediate answers. Everything is not predestined; sometimes the answer to your question depends on the actions of someone else.

And sometimes we are not meant to know the answer because we have to go through a certain experience for the growth of our own souls. But when we let go and let God, when we have faith, we give the universe the opportunity to respond in its own time. A butterfly when pursued is just beyond our grasp, but if we wait patiently it will alight upon us.

So start keeping track of the messages you receive from your intuition. Pay attention to coincidences, thoughts that come from nowhere, feelings of "rightness" or "wrongness" in a situation, dreams, daydreams, and so on. Maybe start a journal where you record these messages. Notice if there are any particular kinds of messages that show up frequently. Then practice interpreting these messages to the best of your ability. Explore each message as fully as possible. What does it mean? What is it connected to? How many ways could you interpret that particular symbol or vision or thought? Keep track of your own accuracy as you continue to develop your intuitive "antenna." The universe is a twenty-four-hour a-day broadcasting station; it's simply up to us to tune ourselves in!

# 16

~~

## Step Six

# Protecting Yourself From Negative Energies

I was raised in a family where every evening my father would kiss me good night and say, "I love you. Say your prayers." I always said my prayers; I always brought that power of protection around me. I'm a big believer in protecting yourself from any forces, either here or in the hereafter, which do not have your highest good in mind.

Remember I said in Chapter 6 that we take our personalities with us when we die? Unfortunately, that's true of the wicked as well as the good. In the same way there are good and bad people, in the spirit realm there are positive and negative energies. Luckily, there are wonderful spirits around most of us. We're surrounded by our loved ones, by guardian angels, by spirit guides whose job is to help us. However, there are also spirits who operate on lower levels of the other side. Instead of trying to progress and grow there, they're still focusing on manipulating people here.

Some of these spirits are responsible for haunting buildings or appearing as poltergeists (spirits that throw things and make general mischief). I've been in many houses and locations where spirits were lingering. Once I went on the *Queen Mary,* which is filled with spirits.

When I went into the engine room, I said to the people accompanying me, "There's a man in here named——" and I gave them the first name and the first initial of his last name. I told them, "He was killed down here, between iron." Later these people checked the historical records and found the name I had given. It was a man from England who had been killed when he was smashed between the iron doors in the engine room.

I don't believe the man in the engine room was a bad spirit. He may have come back simply to help prove the existence of spirits. Or he may not have known he was dead. Often spirits who are killed suddenly don't realize they're dead—like a soldier running on the battlefield who steps on a land mine and is blown up. He picks himself up, keeps running with his rifle and says to his buddy, "Wow, that was close," but his buddy doesn't see him or hear him. The soldier keeps running and running until he finally notices something that lets him know he's dead. Those are the kind of spirits that stay in the place they were killed, because they haven't quite figured out how to make the transition. It takes someone else—a "rescue" spirit, a departed loved one, sometimes a psychic like myself—to tell these forlorn souls to go to the white light and cross over to the other side.

I believe there are other spirits who just like to come back to their favorite places. On the *Queen Mary,* I saw several spirits dancing in the ballroom, having a grand old time in the place they had enjoyed while they were alive. But often where there's a haunting, the spirits feel dysfunctional to me. There's something wrong, out of kilter, even threatening about their energy.

My student "Stephanie" once ran into that kind of spirit. She and her three young children went to her friend Terry's house, not too far from where Stephanie lived in New Jersey. Stephanie didn't know it at the time, but that house had been occupied by slaves back in the 1700s.

When she arrived at the house, Stephanie saw a man standing in the window, and she asked Terry who the man was. "Didn't I tell you?" Terry said jokingly. "The house is haunted!" That evening, Terry told Stephanie some of the weird things that had happened in the house over the years.

On her way home about 12:30 that night, Stephanie started to feel very uneasy. She kept looking in her rearview mirror to see if anyone else was on the road, but there was no other car. The feeling persisted all the way back to her house. "I knew something was wrong," she told me later.

While her children were getting ready for bed, Stephanie had a strange visitation she had never felt before. "As I was sitting down, the hair on my arms stood straight up, and I felt a cold I can't even describe. It was like a death cold—lifeless and empty. As I felt it, one thought kept running through my head: *Get up and do it now.* Don't ask me why, but I got up, took out the family Bible, got the small vial of holy water I have in the house, and I started to bless each and every room. When I started to go downstairs, into the finished basement, the hand holding the holy water started to shake and I got even colder. I said, 'You S.O.B., you're not beating me!' and I continued blessing the house. I even went into the garage and then blessed the outside of the house as well. After that, everything was fine. But I really do believe that a spirit from my friend Terry's house hitched a ride with me."

These kind of spirits are not there to benefit anyone; they're hanging around because they don't want to progress, or they're tightly attached to a place or a person who's still around. And sometimes *people* keep spirits around through their own desire. I've known individuals who refuse to let the spirit of their departed spouses go, even though the spirit truly wants to progress to the next level. It's a sad thing when it happens. All of us are supposed to keep growing, both here and on the other side, and sometimes the best gift we can give our loved ones is permission for them to move on.

Unfortunately, a lot of techniques people learn to contact spirits tend to put us in touch with lower-level entities or trickster spirits who do not wish us well. I spoke earlier about Ouija boards, which a lot of teenagers play around with. I also heard about someone who had people looking in a black mirror, where they would see faces appear superimposed on their reflection. In some cases, they saw the faces of departed loved ones, which was great. But this kind of technique is a loose cannon. You don't have any control over the kind of spirit that will come in. I am also very leery of trance mediums, people who go into a trance and allow spirits to take their bodies over and speak through them. How do they know who's speaking, and whether that spirit is either telling the truth or wishing them well? I have seen trance mediums who gave helpful advice in one moment, and in the next breath were manipulating people in the wrong direction.

The point is, we can be fooled and taken advantage of by spirits as well as by the living. It's important to use common sense along with our sixth sense. I'll give you some specific ways to protect yourself later in this chapter, but don't ask for trouble by using techniques that attract the wrong kinds of spirits.

## You're in Control, So Protect Yourself

Unfortunately, we can be fooled by spirits who "appear fair and feel foul," as Shakespeare once said. After all, the devil learned all about goodness before being cast out of heaven, and evil spirits can use goodness for their own devices. You can even get good and evil from the same spirit: good that lulls you into a false sense of security, then evil that takes you in another direction. You have to know how to decipher it. You have to learn to check out any message given to you with your own wisest self.

My friend Malcolm puts it this way: "I find most fear-based entities are lower-level spirits. That's one of the tests I use on a conscious level. I'll ask myself, 'Wait a minute. Where is this coming from? Some sacred realm—or somewhere lower?' Over a period of time you learn how to tell when something isn't right."

I can't stress strongly enough, intuition and contacting spirits is not a game or a toy. You have to be smart about it; you have to do your best to tap in to the highest level possible of spirit energy. You really have to know whom you're dealing with and what's going on, and be very, very careful. If you give up your power to spirits they'll take it, just like a controlling living person will take your power if you allow them to. And when you give up your power to any spirit or person, you weaken yourself, because it splits the psyche if you are not totally in control of yourself.

But here's the good news: *We* control spirits, they do not control us—unless we give them the power to do so. *The only time a spirit or person has power over you is when you give it to them.* The only way that evil can overcome goodness is if we allow it to, because goodness ultimately has *much* more power than evil.

By the way, we're not the only ones involved in the job of protecting ourselves. Remember our spirit guides, guardian angels, and loved ones on the other side? One of their jobs is protection. I believe that different spirits come in and look out for us on different levels. One of my guides, White Feather, often shows up to protect me when I'm doing television and radio shows, where basically anyone can call in. But I believe the very best way to shield yourself from any force that does not wish you well is to call on a higher power. Ask for guidance, help, information, and protection from the highest level of goodness, love, and wisdom that we call God, and then tell the unwanted spirit to go away. When we start at the highest level, it's far more difficult for lower-level spirits to come in, and if they do appear, we're able to recognize them more easily.

There are three specific ways I teach my students to connect with their higher power and protect themselves from any negative energy that might come their way.

## 1. *Know* you are protected.

In the same way you must know you are psychic to activate your natural intuition, knowing you are protected will actually protect you. But the slightest fear or doubt can allow a negative energy to enter your life. If you think, "Oh my gosh, I'm afraid an evil spirit is going to come," you might open yourself up to just that. Stand up to a negative spirit. Tell it to buzz off (or something stronger). My feeling is that if your mind is strong and you mean what you say, you can demand that a spirit leave and it should go.

Trust your ability to protect yourself from negative energies, and trust that you'll be tipped off to evil. I've found that evil always slips up somewhere and lets us know who and what it truly is, if we're alert to the clues. All we need to do is know we're protected and stand strong in our connection to the highest level of goodness, love, and wisdom.

## 2. Surround yourself in a blinding white light.

Visualize white light extending from the top of your head to the bottom of your feet. Think of it like electricity. Your intuition is the current flowing through a wire, and putting white light around yourself when you "turn on" the current is like putting insulation around the wire.

## 3. Say a prayer of protection of your choice.

I always say a special prayer of protection that I wrote in 1995, when I was awakened early one morning and guided to write this. I say this prayer before every single reading and teach my students either to say this prayer or another one of their choice.

> We ask the Universal Consciousness
> that holds the highest spiritual power
> of Knowledge, Wisdom and Truth
> to guide and protect us
> as we communicate with our guides
> and angels in the Spirit World
> and tap into the wisdom of the Universe.

> We respect this opportunity and
> take full responsibility to use this
> not for ego or controlling others
> but with the pure intention
> of spreading love and healing life
> on this earth and beyond.

*© 1995 Char*

Many of my students choose to use this prayer; others have their own prayers and rituals of protection. One woman says, "Cancel, cancel" whenever she hears an unnecessary negative thought. "We all say stupid things like, 'You broke my heart,' " she told me recently. "But you don't want anything like that to take root. So I cancel it. And curiously enough, now my husband says it, my kids say it, and all the people at my office say it. I guess it must work!" Another student holds her hand out in front of her and puts an energy barrier up where the hand is.

She believes this barrier will block any negative energy or spirits coming into her presence. When she's working with patients my sister Alicia (the doctor of psychology) says two prayers: one to God for protection for herself and the person she's working with, and one for healing. "I always ask permission of my patients to say two generic prayers because I don't want to offend anybody. But I've never had anybody say, 'No, don't say the prayer.' And if I did, I probably would have to tell them that we can't do this work. That's how strongly I believe in protection."

## Three Levels of Protection

I think we need to protect ourselves on three different levels. First, we must protect ourselves from negative spirits, using the steps I described above. Second, we must protect ourselves from negative thoughts, either our own or those directed at us. As I said in Chapter 12, thoughts have power. We have to learn to control our own negative thoughts by focusing on the highest good and staying out of judgment. But we also have to protect ourselves from negative thoughts and actions directed at us from others.

Remember, bad people can do just as much damage as bad spirits. Let's say you're alone in your apartment and you see or feel the presence of an unfamiliar spirit. Most people would feel a little bit of fear, right? But what if in the next moment you see somebody come through your window with a nylon mask on his face and a weapon in his hand? Who should you be more afraid of—the unfamiliar spirit or the living guy coming through the window?

Most of the time (thank goodness) we don't have masked men breaking into our houses. But we do have to deal with the thoughts and emotions of those who do not wish us well. It's unfortunate that everyone doesn't always have our best interests at heart. And if the universe is tipping you off about some negative energy being directed your way, you'd better protect yourself.

When I say, "Protect yourself," I'm not talking about revenge or retaliation. I'm not interested in "getting back" at someone who doesn't like me. To my mind, that puts me on the same level as the person who is wishing me harm. I don't wish evil on anyone; I trust that the universe will take care of them because I have seen in my own life that what comes around, goes around. But I also feel it's important to come from a nonjudgmental place when dealing with negative energy that's directed at you. When I have a bad feeling about someone, the first thing I do is check inside my own soul. Is this feeling coming from my own jealousies or insecurities? If not, and if I truly believe the negativity is coming at me from someone else, I put a blinding white light of protection around me from head to toe, so bright that anyone looking at it would hurt their eyes. Then I send the negative energy back whence it came. It's not welcome in my head or in my heart.

The third level at which we must protect ourselves is from what I call "psychic debris"—the negative energy that others can release and then leave behind. People who work in the healing professions know exactly what I mean. When we're being healed of a physical, emotional, spiritual, or psychological problem, the negative energy of that old injury or trauma has to go somewhere. Usually it ends up staying in the atmosphere of the area where the person has been healed—or worse, it flows into the energy field of the healer. Perhaps that's why some of the sweetest, dearest souls I know in the healing professions get sick and even die young. These people are such caring, loving human beings that they take the illness into themselves. They don't know how to process the negative energy that's being released by those they've healed, but they want to heal others so much that they don't care what happens to them personally.

The same thing can happen when you use your intuitive abilities with others. When I first started reading professionally, I would read for clients all day long, then occasionally do a radio call-in show in the evenings. I found myself getting sick to my stomach, becoming exhausted, feeling like I was surrounded by negative energy. I was draining my battery, and I had to stop. I quickly learned how to take care of myself. Now I limit the number of readings I'll do in a day, and I make sure to protect myself before each session.

There are several ways to clear negative energy out of your environment. Always start with a prayer of protection and the white light. Different kinds of incense or lighting a candle can help also. For hundreds of years the Native Americans have burned sage. Others find having living plants in a room will help keep the atmosphere clean and healthy. As you saw earlier, Stephanie used holy water to clear her house when she felt a particularly bad spirit around. Once your house has wholesome energy, however, you'll find that negativity can't stick around. Stephanie knows very well how this works. "Anybody who is a negative or nasty type of person won't stay in this house more than five minutes," she tells me. "They get fidgety and nervous; you can see them shifting in their seats. One girl actually got sick to her stomach. She said, 'I gotta go, I don't feel good.' I smiled and said, 'Yeah, I guess you'd better.'"

When we keep ourselves consciously protected—with prayer, with the white light of protection, and with our thoughts—it's very tough for negative spirits to get through. And if they do show up they won't stay, as long as we let them know in no uncertain terms they are unwelcome. The best protection is to stay away from any technique that is likely to put you in touch with lower-level spirits.

Remember always that other spirits are protecting you. We all have guardian angels and spirit guides that walk with us. Most important, we have the greatest energy that is known as goodness, love, and God protecting us. Always, always go to the highest level whenever you use your intuition. Be conscious of your thoughts, and say your prayers. Your best protection against any energy that may wish you harm is to stay firmly connected to the source of ultimate goodness, love, and wisdom. I love the way my friend Hope puts it: "I ask to be protected all the time. Before a reading, or even just in the course of the day, I ask God to love and protect me, and to be there for me and the people I love and care about. And I ask that people will also be good and loving to each other. That's my quiet little prayer."

# Take Control of Your Intuition

I want to end this chapter by putting negative energies into perspective. In the same way there are negative people in the world and you need to take sensible precautions to protect yourself (like door locks, car alarms, and so on), you need to protect yourself from any negative energies you may encounter. But *there is no spirit which can make you do something you don't want to*. You are always and forever the one in control of your own life and actions.

Most important, using your intuition will *not* open you to negative energies or spirits. Instead, it's like going to the shopping mall. When you walk inside the mall, you're going to encounter all kinds of different people and stores, right? There will be hundreds of opportunities to shop, talk, eat, rest, maybe see a movie, depending on what's in the mall. But you're the one who decides which opportunities to take. If someone you don't like comes up to you, you can walk away. If you don't like the merchandise in a store, you can leave. If you don't want to eat Mexican food in the food court, you can have Chinese or Italian or not eat anything. Working with your intuition is just like that. You are always in control of who you associate with and how you use your gift. So go ahead—enter the world of your intuition with confidence, knowing that you can protect yourself from any negative energies that may come your way. And know that your best and ultimate protection will come from your power to choose how you use the sixth sense God gave you.

# Section Three

## Intuition *in* Action

You've just learned my six steps to awaken and use your own intuitive gift. If you were in class with me, at this point I'd ask you to pair up with someone and do your first reading. And if you had done the exercises listed for each step, you'd probably be amazed at how good you were at picking up things intuitively from your partner.

Unfortunately, I can't give you that experience. But what I will do instead is give you scores of examples of intuition in action—stories of how I and my students use our intuitive gifts to connect with spirits and guardian angels, create closer relationships, monitor health, find things, help the police, tune in at work, and make the time of passing easier for ourselves and our loved ones. I'm giving you lots of examples of intuition in action so you can develop the confidence and certainty you need right from the start. I will guarantee you that every single story you read is a true account of people *just like you* using intuition to make their own lives and the lives of others better.

When you acknowledge your own abilities, have confidence in yourself, consistently go to the level of universal wisdom for your information, and learn to trust what you're getting because you've evaluated it with common sense, then you're ready to make the most of the intuitive talents you possess. I hope these stories will give you even more certainty as you start using your own intuitive gifts. I know you will find these "intuitive tales" informative, eye-opening—and inspiring.

# 17

## Tuning in to Loved Ones, Guardian Angels, and Spirit Guides

*"Dear Char:* One night as I slept my daughter climbed into bed with me and I awoke. At the foot of my bed I saw two glowing figures as if they had white Christmas lights around them. At first I thought it was my younger son sleepwalking, but he was lying beside me. One of the glowing figures was doing something with his hands—I couldn't quite figure it out.

"A calm came over me. I felt such peace and happiness. I wasn't scared; I just lay there watching the two figures. I knew these were guardian angels watching over us, and I went back to sleep with serenity"—*"Judith."*

*"Dear Char:* I had just come home after being in the hospital for ten days. It was the first time I was totally alone. I was resting in bed when the phone rang. I answered it—and my deceased grandmother's voice was on the other end! I sat straight up in bed. In her broken English, she kept asking how I was. I kept saying, 'Nana, Nana, this can't be you, you're dead!' She said, 'Never mind, how are

you?' I said I was sick, and she said, 'I know.' Then her voice faded. I fell back to sleep. When I awoke the telephone was sitting at the foot of my bed. Before I fell asleep the first time it had been on the dresser (where it always was). So I knew it was not a dream, because the phone had been moved from the dresser to the bed.

"When I was a little girl, my grandmother always said that dead people knew everything that happened here on earth. Now I believe her"—*Nancy Spinelli.*

*"Dear Char:* After a particularly stressful time in my life, I went to a place called Moonstone Lodge outside of Phoenix for a kind of spiritual retreat/rest cure. As part of the program, all of the people there would sit around in a big circle, and the retreat leader would ask us to talk about things in our lives. On the last day I was looking at the reflection of light on a large table in the center of the room. All of a sudden something inside the reflection started moving and I saw a series of different images. I saw my face being older and then it moved around and looked younger. (Shortly after I returned home I had a face lift, which I had not planned prior to my trip.) I saw a new man entering my life. (At the time, I was married to someone else—in fact, my husband was at the retreat with me. But we were divorced within the year.)

"Then all of a sudden I started feeling as if my body had become very, very old. I had become an old Indian chief who was blind in his left eye. Standing in front of him was another Indian warrior in a beautiful headdress, holding a staff. I knew it was the old man's son. And then I saw a little girl with a feather and she was tickling the old man. He

called the child Wildflower. I was very aware that I
had been the little girl in another lifetime, and the
old man and his son were my spirit guides. Since
then these spirits show up at different times in my
life, always to protect me and let me know what I
need to do next"—*"Margaret."*

We are surrounded by spirits who love us and want to
communicate with us. When we tap in to our own natural
psychic ability, we are opening a channel that can allow
us to connect more deeply with the people we love who
have passed on, as well as with spirits who are there to
guide and protect us. It's always so gratifying to hear the
stories from students who have awakened their intuition
and are hearing messages from the other side. These messages take many different forms, as you can see from the
three letters I just quoted. It is my sincere hope that some
of the examples you'll read in this chapter will open you
to connecting with your personal guides, guardian angels,
and departed loved ones.

Of course, remember what I said earlier: our guardian
angels and spirit guides are not God. Spirits do not know
everything, and you are just as much of a spirit as they
are. You have free will and do not have to follow their
advice. Always make sure to protect yourself whenever
you receive a message from the other side by saying a
prayer and surrounding yourself with white light. And
evaluate every message by checking it with your wisest
self: your intuition, common sense, and logic. With these
precautions, you can enjoy all the love and connection the
universe is offering you through your guides, angels, and
loved ones.

# Hearing from the Newly Departed

Death is almost always a difficult time for those of us who are left behind. But it is also the most common time for our loved ones to communicate with us from the other side. It's as if their spirits wanted to reassure us they are all right and still love us very much. These communications can come in the form of feelings, noises, strange experiences, "coincidences" that are too striking to be accidental, and so on. One woman was in her laundry room shortly after her father passed away. She said out loud, "All right, Dad, it's me. You can come back now. I'm ready." Just at that moment, a bottle of detergent fell off a shelf. The woman dropped all the folded laundry she was holding and said, "I take it back, Dad, I'm not ready!" But even so, she says to this day she feels his spirit around her all the time.

Many years ago my friend and fellow psychic Malcolm studied tarot with a wonderful lady named Jacqueline Murray. They developed an amazing rapport and talked on the phone two or three times a week for twenty years, until her death in 1996. Her passing was very sudden and of course saddened Malcolm a great deal. He decided he wanted to send flowers to the funeral (which was being held on the other side of the country), but he was taken aback to realize he had no idea what Jacqueline's favorite flower was.

Malcolm called Jacqueline's daughter (who's also his goddaughter) and asked her about her mom's favorite flower. "Gee, I don't know," she replied. "Let me call my grandmother and ask her." "I was sitting in my house waiting for her call when all of a sudden from out of nowhere this 1950s song, 'Hi Lili, Hi Lili, Hi Lo,' started floating through my head," Malcolm told me later. "I thought to myself, 'Lilies!' Just then, the phone rang. It was my goddaughter, and of course her grandmother had just told her that lilies were Jacqueline's favorite flower."

My student Patti Cimine lost her grandmother a few years ago. The night of the funeral, Patti had an extraordinary experience that she firmly believes was her grandmother making contact. "I had gone to bed and my dog was sleeping on the bed with me," she said. "I was lying there in a deep sleep when I heard a large thud. Both the dog and I sat up. I said aloud, 'What fell?' I looked around my room, but there was nothing.

"I turned out the light and went back to sleep. Maybe ten minutes later, I heard the exact same noise again. I turned on the light and looked around—still nothing. The dog ran down to the foot of the bed and started barking at thin air. I said to her, 'Get down!'—but she absolutely refused to get off the bed. I tried to push her off, but she wouldn't go.

"We heard that same thud three times that night. And even though I slept with the light on, I wasn't scared by the spirit as much as by the strangeness of it. The next morning I checked with everyone else who was sleeping in that part of the house, and no one else had heard the thuds or seen anything that might have fallen during the night. I thought, 'All right, Grandma. I know you're here. Maybe you're just new at this and don't know how to come to me any other way.'"

That time between waking and sleep often is a time when spirits choose to communicate with us—perhaps because the chatter of our conscious mind isn't in the way. Another client told me that about six months after her father passed, she had just gone to bed but was not yet asleep and out of the blue, she could see her father's face in the corner of the room. "He wasn't on my mind, so I didn't believe it could be wishful thinking," she told me. "I remember saying to myself, 'Don't be afraid, don't be afraid,' because it was so real. And then the face vanished. Afterwards I felt very comfortable with the appearance. It's as if he's still here watching over me."

Once I was the vehicle for a very specific message that had been set up before the gentleman actually died. The following letter tells the story.

> "*Dear Char:* In November 1997 I saw you on the Cleveland morning show. As you attempted to do a reading for the first caller, you spoke my father's name, then you apologized to the caller, saying that you'd been interrupted by that spirit. I spun around and glared at the TV; I KNEW it was my father. He'd just passed over, and days before he did, I had said to him, 'If there is a way to reach me from the other side, please do so. There's a great psychic intuitive I remember hearing about, named Char. See if you can contact her.' You probably didn't know at the time what a vital role you would play in confirming my belief in life after death"—*Tarrah Sterling*.

I also received a very touching letter from another client about one of those "coincidences" that is far too perfect to be the product of mere accident. In 1998, "Terry" lost her beloved father. Terry describes herself as a "busy stay-at-home mom" with four kids, a husband, and a house to look after, and so she very seldom gets a chance to read the newspaper. But exactly four months to the day following her father's death, she sat down with the paper, and the words, "Love, Robert" caught her eye. Robert was her father's name and so she felt she had to read the letter. It was a beautiful note from someone who had passed on. It said:

> When I am gone, release me, let me go, I have so many things to see & do. You mustn't tie yourself to

me with tears, be happy that we had so many years. I gave you my love, you can only guess how much you gave me happiness. I thank you for the love you have shown, but now it's time I traveled on alone. So grieve a while for me if you must, then let your grief be comforted by trust. It's only for a while that we must part, so bless the memories with your heart. I won't be far away for life goes on, so if you need me call & I will come. Though you can't see or touch me, I'll be next to you & if you listen with your heart you'll hear all of my love around you soft & clear and then when you must come this way alone I'll greet you with a smile.
*Love, Robert*
*Sept. 5, 1964 • Feb. 17, 1998*

"When I read the date at the bottom of the letter, my whole body felt chills," Terry wrote me. "February 17th was my father's birthday. I have to believe that my Dad meant for me to read that letter and get the message it contained."

When a loved one passes over, take a few moments to send them blessings and the white light of protection after they're gone. Let them know you love them still—and if you want, ask them to give you a sign of their presence. If they choose to come through to you with a sign, you'll almost certainly be able to tell it's them; remember, every spirit has its own energy thumbprint and we do not lose our personalities when we pass to the other side. As long as you keep the white light of protection around you, you can use your intuition to open a "channel" for your departed loved ones to keep in touch.

But don't hold on to your loved ones too tightly. Your need can tie them to the earth and keep them from progressing on the other side. Let go and let God, and trust that you will have their love always, no matter where they may be. Then they may come to visit when you least expect it.

## "Who Pushed Those Doughnuts onto the Floor?"

Sometimes I think the spirits have a pretty warped sense of humor, because they can choose some pretty strange methods for making their presence known! "Patricia," a student of mine, once told me about an evening when she went out for drinks, leaving a good friend, Lala, to baby-sit for her three children. Several other kids came over and it turned into a sleep-over party. About midnight Lala was in the kitchen doing the dishes. The sink was next to a cabinet, which was next to the refrigerator. It was a calm winter night, and all the windows were closed and locked.

Just as Lala finished rinsing all the cups and putting them in a rack to drain, whoosh! all of a sudden the cups fell out of the rack and onto the floor. There was nothing anywhere near the cups to make them fall, but Lala figured, "Oh well," picked them up, and started rinsing them again. Bam! the cups fell out of the rack a second time, again for no reason. Now Lala was getting suspicious, but she picked up the cups and once more started rinsing and stacking them in the rack. But then a box of doughnuts flew off the top of the refrigerator and landed on the kitchen floor!

When Patricia came back that night, Lala told her what happened. "Oh, it was probably my husband," Patricia said. "He's such a practical joker, always fooling around. You remember—we even buried him with his Super-Soaker water gun." "Yeah, well, tell him I don't need any of his jokes from beyond the grave," Lala retorted.

"Rebecca's" dad had had a lot of health problems and

one day, half-jokingly, her mother said to him, "Well, if you decide to let us hear from you after you go, how will we know it's you?" This was around the time the movie *Ghost* was released, and I suppose because he remembered the scene where the ghost moves a penny, Rebecca's dad said, "I'll send dimes." Well, ever since he passed, Rebecca and her family find dimes in the strangest places. "I'll get in my car and there will be a dime," Rebecca says. "I'll go to work in the morning and sitting on my chair will be a dime. Even my husband, who used to be the world's biggest skeptic, can't explain the fact that we keep finding dimes. It's gotta be my dad."

Physical manifestations of a spirit's presence take many different forms. Since spirits are composed of energy, often they find it easy to manipulate electricity. One client told me that for a month or two after her father's death, the doors of her car would lock by themselves. She took the car in to get the locks inspected, but there was nothing wrong with them. By the way, the car was an older model Nissan with locks that had to be depressed manually! "I figured that it was just my dad making sure I was safe," she said.

Another woman who lost her husband noticed some changes occurring in a painting she had hanging in her house. She showed the painting to several friends, and asked them, "Do you see what I see?" They answered, "We thought you had noticed it—it's been like that for two weeks." The face of the woman's husband had appeared in the picture. "I would have thought I was going crazy, except for the fact that other people saw it, too," she told me.

Most of the communications we get from spirits aren't quite that uncanny, thank goodness. One client told me that she had visited Disney World with her family the summer after her father passed over. "My Dad loved nature, and he had a pond on his property where ducks would nest every year. Well, when we stayed at Disney World a couple of months after he died, every single day ducks would come to visit us. We were quite a ways from the duck pond, and there were a lot of other ground-floor rooms that were closer to the pond than ours. But the ducks came to visit us every day for eight days. (No, we didn't feed them.) I strongly felt it was a visit from my Dad."

Ducks continue to pop up in this woman's life. A couple of months ago she received in the mail a magazine called *Ducks Unlimited.* When she called the company to let them know she hadn't ordered the magazine, they said the subscription was paid for—but they had no record of who had purchased it for her. The same day the magazine arrived her youngest son won a drawing for a Beanie Baby toy. You guessed it: it was a duck.

Children and animals seem to find it easier to see spirits than the rest of us. Sheba is a mixed-breed dog with a lot of Sheltie in her. She's a small dog and was fiercely devoted to her master, "Kevin." After Kevin passed away, his wife noticed that at certain moments Sheba would sit up for no reason and stare at empty space. Now, that's not an uncommon occurrence with a lot of dogs, but Sheba would then turn her head as if she were watching someone crossing the room, even though there was no one present to human eyes. Then she'd stand up and, with her tail wagging, walk over to the spot where she had been looking. "I know Kevin's in the room when she does that—he's the only one Sheba would ever go to," reports his wife.

After Jeannie Starrs lost her son, Clint, she promptly adopted C.J., Clint's two-year-old child and her grandson. "C.J. sees his dad all the time and talks to him, too,"

Jeannie tells me. "We were at dinner one time and I got a hit that Clint's spirit was around. I told my friend Jimmy, 'Watch C.J.' Well, C.J. rolled up his napkin in exactly the way his dad used to. He looked to his right where there was an empty chair, just like he was looking at someone for instructions, then he grinned and threw his napkin in my direction. That's exactly the kind of thing Clint would tell his son to do."

## Coming Back for a Reason

Sometimes the spirits of our loved ones come to us for a reason other than simply letting us know they're around. When "Helen" was engaged, for example, there was a lot of conflict between her father and her future mother-in-law about the wedding. They were always fighting about who was going to be invited, who would do what, and so on. Helen's fiancé Stewart had lost his father when he was a teenager, but he had told Helen what a wonderful man his dad was, what a peacemaker. Helen kept thinking, "I wish Stewart's dad was alive right now—he's probably the only one who could straighten out this mess." The situation got so bad that Helen took to praying every night, "Please, God, if you're there, please ask Stewart's dad to help me handle this."

One night Helen was drifting off to sleep when she got an uncanny feeling that Stewart's dad was in the room with her. She was afraid to turn over and look up because she didn't know what she would do if she actually saw his spirit. "I remember so clearly talking to him and hearing him tell me he loved me and approved of my marrying his son, and that everything would be okay," she says. "I told my fiancé later, 'If I heard tapes of the voices of twenty different men, I would be able to pick out your dad's voice—that's how sure I am that he spoke to me.' And he was right about the wedding. Somehow our parents calmed down enough for everything to come off beautifully. I'm positive that Stewart's dad exercised some kind of positive influence over our families."

Shortly after she passed to the other side, one mother sent a very sweet message to her new daughter-in-law. Three weeks prior to their wedding, Chantale Bruno and her fiancé found out that his mother had only a few days to live. They decided to get married before she died, and they had the ceremony the next day in the hospital chapel. The mother's last words to the couple were to ask them to start a family right away.

The couple were married again three weeks later, in the ceremony they had originally scheduled. After the honeymoon, they moved into the house which Chantale's mother-in-law had left to them—the house where Chantale's husband had grown up. One evening shortly afterward, Chantale got a very strong urge to play Monopoly®, which was rather strange since she normally disliked board games. Rooting around a closet looking for the Monopoly board, she found something else: an antique christening gown wrapped in paper that said "Baby Girl" on it. "My husband is an only child so we knew it wasn't his, and he couldn't remember ever seeing the dress before," Chantale says. "At the time I told my husband it was his mother sending us a message. A week later I found out I was pregnant, and we did have a baby girl, whom we named in honor of my mother-in-law. I really believe the dress was a message from her to expect a baby girl soon."

Isn't that exactly the kind of thing you'd expect from a grandmother-to-be? But since this grandmother was in spirit, she could see into the future. She could let her daughter-in-law know what to expect, while providing a sweet gift for the coming grandchild. We're very lucky that love isn't changed, even by an untimely death.

# Spirits Watching over Us—Guides and Guardians

When a loved one comes in, it's nice to know they're there, they're okay, and they still love you. It's also a wonderful feeling to know that you're being protected on a spiritual level by the people you knew while they were on the earth plane. And, as I discussed in Chapter 4, we have spirit guides and guardian angels helping us as well.

Sometimes we know who these guides and guardian angels are, because these spirits were related to us in their last earthly form. The first time I met Gordon Meltzer in person was at St. John's Hospital in Santa Monica, California. Gordon was Miles Davis's manager, and Miles was in the hospital for what turned out to be his final illness. Gordon had never believed in any kind of psychic phenomena, and even though Miles consulted me frequently over the years, Gordon always rationalized every prediction I made which came true.

Gordon had been asked by Miles's family to keep all visitors away from the hospital. So when I called and told him I wanted to come to the hospital and bring a healer friend with me, Gordon was less than enthusiastic, but he agreed to check with the family. They said yes, and requested that Gordon stay in the room while I was with Miles.

That day in the hospital, Gordon remembers that I sat by Miles's bed, said a prayer and then told Miles (who was in a coma), "Don't worry, because your mother and father are here in the room with you." Since Miles's parents had died forty years earlier, Gordon was somewhat surprised by this. But he stayed in the room for the healing session, which took about a half hour, and then he walked me to the front door of the hospital. As we reached the door, he said to me, "You know, that was all very interesting, what you and your friend did in there. But what was the bit about Miles's mom and dad? They've been dead for a long time."

"Don't you know?" I replied. "Everyone has a guardian angel watching over them. Miles's parents are his guardian angels. Yours is your dead grandmother Anna, from Russia." You've rarely seen someone straighten up as quickly as Gordon did when he heard that! But it was true—his grandmother was his guardian angel on the other side. And being given a specific name and relation (which I had no way of knowing other than psychically) opened Gordon's eyes to a whole new perspective on life and death and spirits.

Another client of mine, Julie Krull, was tipped off when she acquired a new guardian angel. "I had a dream about a co-worker who had passed away a few months earlier," she wrote me. "I was fond of him, but because he was married I did not tell him or anyone else. In the dream, he said he would never leave me. It seemed so real, and nothing like that had ever happened to me before, but I still just assumed it was just a dream. When I had my reading with you, however, even though I had never mentioned it to you, the first thing you brought up was my dream. You said that this man's spirit will never leave me and he would be my guardian angel."

We have guardian spirits around us everywhere. Sometimes they also show up on earth in physical form. I think a lot of firefighters are absolutely guardian angels who decided to incarnate so they can protect people here. Many dogs and cats that protect their owners are also forms of guardian spirits living on the earth.

It's great to know your guardian angels. If you sense the presence of a spirit guide or guardian angel around you, just say a prayer of protection and then say, "I'd like to know who you are" or something similar. Often you'll get the answer as a thought popping into your head.

Spirit guides are there specifically to guide us when we connect with the astral plane, and also to keep us pointed in the right direction while we're on earth. Often we were associated with our spirit guides in an earlier incarnation, like the Indian figures in "Margaret's" story which you read earlier in this chapter. Another student of mine who was born Irish-Catholic also has Native American spirit guides. "All my friends tell me I could pass for a full-blooded Native American, so it's not surprising that my spirit guides would be Native as well," she says. (Many spirit guides seem to be Native American—possibly due to the strong tradition of honoring spirits in many of those cultures.)

Any energy we come in contact with is there for a reason. Many of our spirit guides and guardian angels come to us because they are working off karma they have accumulated with us in the past. There may even be some unfinished business between us and them lingering from a former life, and in order for these spirits to progress any further they have to help us out. As one of my clients said, "When we leave this earth, our work isn't done. We have to keep learning and growing—and helping others do the same." Remember, the goal of every spirit is to reach the highest level of consciousness, merging with the goodness, wisdom, and love that is God. Spirits have to be willing to put in a lot of work both here and in the hereafter in order to keep progressing.

We also have different guardian angels and spirit guides for different needs. They come in at certain times in our lives to help us with certain things, and some stay and some go. For example, if you're embarking on a speaking career and you haven't done a lot of public speaking before, you may be loaned a spirit who was a great speaker. These "task-specific" guides are there to help you out when you take on a new field of endeavor. Then there are other highly developed spirits who remain with us for our entire lifetime on earth, helping us to progress.

On the astral plane, spirit guides and guardian angels protect our energy fields. If you've ever read anything about auras, you know that we project energy all around ourselves. Some of that energy is in this dimension, and some is in the astral dimension. But because of physical and emotional trauma, our energy field can be diminished or damaged. Sometimes it can even develop serious "holes" or places where it is coming apart. When that happens, it's all too easy for negative energies and negative spirits to gain access. However, the spirits around us can protect us from those negative energies, holding them at bay until we can repair the field ourselves.

I believe that many children's "imaginary playmates" are actually their guardian angels, spirit guides, and departed loved ones. "Watch a child carefully," someone once told me. "You can tell when they're playing with a make-believe friend, and when they're talking to someone we can't see but they can. Watch their faces, watch where their eyes go, listen to how they talk and respond to voices we can't hear. Watch the way they interact physically with these beings. You can tell the difference between a make-believe playmate and a being that's simply invisible to our eyes."

Even though most of us grown-ups can't see these beings, we can often sense their presence around us as a feeling of being protected. This feeling has nothing to do with confidence; an insecure person can have it as easily as a confident person. And it doesn't always have anything to do with bad or good things happening to us. After all, everyone has to go through their lessons. But if you put out your intuitive antenna, you'll be able to tell when you're being protected by spirits either here or in the astral plane.

# A Few Words of Caution

I want to offer one caution about being strongly connected with spirits: I've seen people who substitute spirit relationships for life on this plane. I knew one woman who was so dependent on her spirit guide that she almost didn't live in reality. She would wake up in the morning and say to her guide, "Hi there—what are we going to do today?" Psychologically, her guide replaced anyone else with whom she might have developed an intimate relationship. Obviously, that wasn't healthy. It's never healthy to become dependent on a personality, either on earth or in the afterlife.

The other tendency I've sometimes seen is for people to blame their spirit guides or even God when bad things happen in their lives. They'll say, "Why wasn't I warned? Why didn't my guides tell me? Why didn't my guardian angel tip me off?" We can't use our guides as excuses. We have to take responsibility for our own lives. All of us are here to learn the earthly and spiritual lessons this dimension has to teach us. Some lessons we have to live through without knowing about them in advance. We have to trust our own intuition and guidance first and foremost.

All spirits have limits. They're not God and neither are we, even if we're all part of God's divine energy. Remember, your guides are also working to raise themselves to higher and higher levels in the spirit realm. They're certainly *not* infallible. We need to recognize that there is a level of energy that is goodness, love, and God, and we don't need spirits to get us there. When we have confidence in our own spirit, our own intuition, we can tap directly in to that God energy.

Using intuition to communicate with our loved ones, spirit guides, and guardian angels can bring us consolation, advice, and a feeling of being protected and loved unconditionally. The most healing energy and the most powerful force in the universe is love, and we are surrounded by the love of our own personal guiding spirits. When we tune in to the presence of love in our lives, and offer it in return to others, we and our guardian spirits can continue on the path to our ultimate union with God.

# 18

## Intuitive Warnings: Predicting Danger and Averting Disaster

Take a moment right now and think of a time you wanted something. Perhaps it was someone you were attracted to, or a person you wanted to do business with. Maybe it was moving to another location. It probably was a very simple desire—but at the same time something was warning you off. You tried everything in your power to make this intuitive feeling or thought go away, but you succeed only in going into denial. Time proves that you made a poor choice. *Then* you remember the warning you received, and say, "I knew I shouldn't have done [whatever it was]."

That warning was the universe looking out for you. Whenever your intuition tips you off about danger, learn from it. Remember the feeling when it happened, and obey your first instincts. This is a time when logic can get in your way rather than helping you. When danger is near, the universe will warn you. You just need to learn to listen.

Often our first experiences with intuition are warnings. As my friend Mark says, "Animals sense danger instinctively—and so do we. We just bury that instinct under layers and layers of logic. But when it comes to warnings, the instinctive, intuitive response is the one to respect."

Stuart Krasnow is the co-executive producer of my TV show, and he is learning to respect his own intuition, especially when it comes to warnings. "I think we have built-in sensors and we have to listen to them. A few days ago I went out for breakfast with some friends in L.A. We were all in the same car, driving on a quiet street, and my friend who was driving went to make a U-turn. But even though many people make harmless U-turns every day, I had a funny feeling and said, 'You know what? Let's take the extra minute and go around the block instead.' Maybe there was a cop nearby, maybe something would have happened—it just didn't feel safe to me to make that U-turn."

When I was in New York City recently, I found myself waiting for an elevator in the lobby of the hotel where I was staying. I noticed a young guy hanging around the lobby, and somehow I felt wary of him. When the elevator arrived and I stepped inside, he followed me. Now, the logical part of my brain was saying, "Big deal—he got in the elevator with you," but my instinctive side was screaming, "Watch out!" Right before the doors closed, I said, "Oh! I forgot something!" I jumped out of the elevator and went up to the front desk. When I came back to the elevator about thirty seconds later, the young man was back in the lobby. As soon as he saw me looking at him, he dashed into another elevator and disappeared.

I talked earlier about fear being something that can hold us back and stop us from using our God-given intuition. Well, sometimes fear can be a friend. It can be a signal to you that something's wrong, that danger is close by. Sometimes fear is the only thing that will get through to people, getting them to protect themselves and prevent a disaster from happening.

Not too long ago I received a letter from a client,

Debby White. I want to quote the entire letter because her story about heeding an intuitive warning is so powerful.

"It was December 19, 1997 and my family of six were getting ready to leave for Vail, Colorado the next morning. My youngest daughter, Cassie, was out riding bikes with a friend and had told me where they were going. Our home was very busy and my son ordered pizzas for dinner.

"We order pizza a lot and I was used to seeing the same delivery man. That night, however, when I opened the door to get the pizzas, there was a new delivery man standing there. I looked in his eyes and I got chills up and down my body. I knew somehow that he had done something terrible. I paid for the pizzas and slammed the door. Immediately the words came out of my mouth, "Where is Cassie?" Frantic, I grabbed my car keys and drove to where she'd said she would be biking, and I was scared when I couldn't find her there. I then returned home and my body relaxed when I saw Cassie through our windows. I wondered what was going on because the feeling I had had earlier was so strong.

"When I got inside I learned a neighbor had brought Cassie home. She had run to the neighbor's house because a man had tried to get her into his car. My husband had already called the police, as the neighbor lady had gotten the car's license number. Within an hour the police called back and said we were lucky to have a daughter who was smart enough to stay out of that car: the license plate was registered to an ex-sex offender recently released from the penitentiary, where he had served time for child molestation.

"But I still could not shake my feeling about the

pizza delivery man. I called the pizza place and told the owner a little fib. I said I wasn't sure, but I thought one of his delivery men said something inappropriate to my daughter. I asked him not to say anything to his employees but to check and see if one of his drivers had this license number (the number of the car owned by the man who had tried to abduct my daughter) and to please call me back. Naturally the owner was concerned, so he agreed to check it out. A little later he called me back and said it was the same license number. I was then able to warn my friends, neighbors and our community. We would never have found out that the man who accosted my daughter was the pizza delivery man if my intuition had not told me."

This ability to pick up on danger is something we should make sure to cultivate in our children, because it will offer them protection when we're not around. A good friend of mine will always check with her young son when they're out driving somewhere, to see if they're getting the same kind of "hit" on their surroundings. "One night we were going to visit an aunt of mine who lived in a suburb not too far away," she told me. "We drove by the house and I couldn't tell if my aunt was there, so I said, 'Let's find a phone and call her.' We drove into a gas station that was very dark, and I had a strange feeling about it. I looked at my son and asked, 'Do you think it's a good idea to get out of the car and call from here?' He said, 'No—if somebody bad was around we wouldn't know it.' 'Great,' I told him. 'I agree with you. Remember, Brian, if something doesn't feel right, most of the time it's not.' I want to make sure my son knows to pay attention when his intuition warns him of danger."

Obviously, you have to take a good look at fear when it arises, and make sure to identify where it's coming from.

Hope Grant tells me, "Occasionally I'm invited some-where and I get a feeling I shouldn't be going. For the most part I follow my feeling, but first I check in my own mind that I don't feel this way just because this particular invitation is something I want to get out of. Intuition means you have to be very honest with yourself."

But ultimately, I believe it's to our benefit to pay close attention to those feelings of warning and unfounded fear that may arise. I know of too many instances when people were warned and then regretted it when they didn't fol-low through. Several years ago one of my students was a brand-new doctor, unmarried, making good money, with-out a care in the world. She and her current boyfriend were going to visit friends who lived in Forest Hills, New York. They were riding in her brand-new Mercedes con-vertible. It was during the U.S. Open, and there were people all over the streets of Forest Hills. As they parked the car, she saw a bunch of kids up the street. She said to her boyfriend, "Vince, those kids are up to no good." Vince told her, "You're being neurotic. Stop it." The woman replied, "All right, but the kid is wearing a blue shirt, red Nike sneakers, and a green bandanna, and I'm getting a weird feeling about him."

Vince (who is 6' 4") answered, "Honey, they're ten years old, half my size and half my weight. Give me a break." As the two of them got out of the car, Vince said, "Look, they're leaving. They're probably going home to bed." But the kids walked past the car, turned—and the kid with the green bandanna pulled a gun and pointed it right at Vince's head. They stole the car at gunpoint and drove off.

Luckily, the story has a happy ending. All six of the kids involved in the robbery were caught because my stu-dent was able to provide such a good description of them. When the district attorney asked how she could be so accurate, she said, "I knew they were up to something, but I was talked out of listening to myself." My student told me later, "I will never fail to listen to that warning voice again."

# Helping Others Avoid Danger

When we're highly attuned to our intuition, the warnings we receive aren't just for ourselves but will often include our loved ones as well. Several years ago, before my dad passed away, both my parents were planning to visit me for the fourth of July. It would be a five-hour drive for them, and before leaving the house Mom called and asked if I needed anything. Without thinking, I said, "Tell Daddy to stay in the righthand lane."

That day, the holiday traffic was miserable; the freeway was wall-to-wall cars. My father did the driving, and my mother kept telling him, "Stay to the right. Get in the right lane." Luckily, my dad stayed over to the right—because a couple of hours into the trip he fell asleep at the wheel. The car veered to the right and went onto the shoulder, at which point my father woke up. If the car had been in any other lane, it would have run into someone and caused an accident. I was very grateful my mother paid attention to her daughter's intuitive warning!

The spirits give me warnings for my clients all the time. Of course, it often takes awhile for those warnings to play themselves out. My client George tells me, "In a reading you would mention a name and say, 'Be careful of this person.' It wouldn't be a name I'd recognize, but I'd make a note of it. A few months later I'd review my notes and often I'd notice that someone with that name had indeed entered my life. Occasionally I'd think, *Wait a minute—that couldn't be the person she warned me about. This Wanda is a good person. It must be someone else.* But sure enough, I'd do business with Wanda and it would turn out to be exactly the way you predicted. If I'd taken your advice about certain people, I would have saved myself hundreds of thousands of dollars."

My friend Mark swears I helped him prevent a burglary. "Char warned me that I needed to put a security guard on my house because someone was going to try to break in and take something," he says. "As it happened, a friend of mine called that day and, because he needed a little extra money and I was leaving town, I asked if he would house-sit for a day or two. The very next day, while he was in my house, someone tried to break in. His being there prevented the burglary, and I have Char's warning to thank for it."

One of my students once got a "hit" while she was on the phone. "I was chatting with a friend of mine, and I knew she was going on a trip of some kind. And I kept getting a car. So finally I asked her, 'Does your car have a problem with the front end?' Then her husband came on and I told him, 'This is going to sound strange, but get the car checked. The left front wheel is going to come flying off and there'll be a major accident if your wife drives the car.'

"The husband was silent for a minute, then said, 'You just described the work we had done on my wife's car. She was driving the car and it felt wobbly, so she took it to the garage. On the left front side, the frame had broken and the wheel almost came off. If she had driven it a mile further, she would have been killed.'"

## Warnings of Many Kinds

As I said in Chapter 15, psychic information can come in many different ways, and that's true of warnings as well. Chantale, a client of mine, heard a voice out of nowhere. At the time Chantale's daughter Virginia was a year old. One day Chantale was dozing on the couch while her daughter played in the next room. All of a sudden Chantale heard a man's voice say, 'No, Virginia, don't touch that!' She jumped up, thinking that her husband was home early (it was only midafternoon). But when she went looking for her daughter, she found her sitting on the bedroom floor playing with a pair of very sharp scissors. Her husband was nowhere to be seen, and his car wasn't in the driveway, so the voice couldn't have been his. Chantale told me, "We live in the house where my husband was raised, and both his parents are deceased. I believe it was my father-in-law's voice I heard, warning me that my daughter was putting herself in danger."

Of all the people I know, Larry seems to be the star of disaster predictions. It's not a distinction he enjoys, and luckily, it's not something that occurs often. But when it does happen, his warnings are exceptionally memorable. The night before Richard Nixon died, for example, Larry dreamed the entire scene in vivid detail. "I saw him sitting on a porch, being stricken, going to his knees," Larry remembers. "In the dream I was there to assist him. I was summoning help as we were trying to get him sitting up in a chair, I was right there giving medical assistance as ambulance arrived, and so forth. It was such a powerful dream that the next morning I asked my wife, 'Did Richard Nixon die or is he ill?' And she said, 'Not that I've heard.'

"All that day I kept checking CNN, but it wasn't until around nine o'clock that night that the bulletin came on. When I read the details of his death, they confirmed exactly what I had seen. Nixon had been sitting on the porch in his home in New Jersey and he had summoned his housekeeper when he was stricken. In fact, he had fallen down to his knees and she helped him up and then called the ambulance."

Larry also predicted the death of Princess Diana. "I don't know where that one came from," Larry admits. "The Tuesday before her tragic accident, I had been sorting through a pile of papers in my office and came upon a tabloid with pictures of Diana and Dodi el-Fayed on the front page. I glanced at the photos—and found I couldn't let go of that newspaper. As I held it in my hand, I thought, *This woman is going to die soon. It's going to be a dramatic, quick, violent death, and the worldwide reaction is going to be cataclysmic.* I somehow thought it was going to be a helicopter crash, so I was wrong in that regard; but I didn't envision her drowning, I didn't envision her having a skiing mishap or becoming ill. I envisioned her dying a violent death in some kind of crash.

"Then I forgot all about it. I heard nothing until my sister-in-law called us with the news. When my wife told me, 'Something's happened to Diana,' my first thought was, 'Oh, she's getting married to that boyfriend of hers.' Then I remembered my premonition. I looked at my wife and said, 'Remember what I was telling you just a few days ago?' Even though I didn't want to believe that I could foresee things like that, it all came back to me at that moment."

Before we leave the subject of warnings, I want to add a lighter note. Sometimes the fact that we're *not* feeling fear or any other warning signal can be a confirmation of what the universe wants us to do, even though it's not necessarily logical. My friend Annie swears that she is the best person in the world to fly with because she knows she will not die in a plane crash. Another friend was roped into going tandem skydiving with a group of people, even though she was terrified of heights and had never even been up in a small plane before. She went through all the training and signed up on the list (in the last possible slot). She was praying that it would get too late in the day for her to go. Finally, it was her turn to get into a suit and take the next plane. "I could have chickened out at the last moment, but somehow as I got into the flight suit, my fear left me," she said. "I knew that I was going to make a successful jump. If I had felt even the slightest hint of fear and doubt, I would have taken the suit off and said 'no' quite firmly—but I didn't. All the way up in the plane, I was amazed at how calm I was. When the time came I got out on the wing with the jump master, let go, and screamed with delight the entire way down."

Martha Gresham had a similar experience of going from absolute fear to absolute calm. She had always been deathly afraid of flying, but several years ago she had to make a quick airplane trip due to a family emergency. When she looked out of the window of the plane, she saw her spirit guide on his horse, riding in the air alongside the wing. In that moment her fear was gone forever. Now she flies in small planes through storms, fog, you name it. She says she knows she is protected by her spirit guides whenever she flies.

## Warnings We're *Supposed* to Ignore

Here's the interesting part about all these warnings: sometimes we're *not* supposed to heed them. Sometimes we're supposed to live out the event because it's an important life lesson, painful though it may be. It's kind of like putting your finger on a hot stove when you're a child—you learn an important lesson because of the pain. I believe that many of us are warned intuitively about certain relationships, but there's something that must be played out in those interactions—a karmic connection, perhaps—which causes us to ignore our instincts and forge ahead.

Remember, just because you get a warning it doesn't mean you're necessarily supposed to act on it right away. It may be a tip-off for dealing with your life in the future, helping you cope with the end result. You may have a funny feeling about a certain business deal, go through with it anyway, and end up cheated. But if that encounter taught you how to read people better and evaluate a business offer more accurately, might that experience of being warned and then being cheated actually benefit you as you get involved with bigger and better deals?

I was warned on the day of my wedding that my marriage wouldn't work out. I ignored the warning—but years later, remembering that warning helped me cope with getting divorced. It taught me the important lesson of listening more closely to my intuition about myself as well as others. It also showed me how strong I could be when I relied on every aspect of my wisest self—intuition, logic, and common sense. Because of that experience, I feel I'm prepared to cope with many different situations that might arise in my life.

So be alert to that twinge at the back of your neck alerting you that something is not quite right. Pay attention to your first, instinctive response to someone you meet. There's a reason for the importance of first impressions: they're often correct! If fear comes up, check it out. Did the fear arise for no good reason? If so, it's usually your intuition warning you of possible danger. Here's the key: PAY ATTENTION. It's up to all of us to be aware. And the more we pay attention the more the universe will bring to light, because we're in sync with our own instincts.

# 19

## Using Intuition in Your Close Relationships

Gazing into a loved one's eyes, you feel a deep sense of connection. You both find yourself finishing each other's sentences. You almost feel as if you can read their thoughts, and they can read yours. Or perhaps you're a new mother, with the baby you've always wanted sleeping peacefully in the next room, and you feel as connected to that child as if you were still carrying him or her in your womb. Or perhaps you meet someone for the first time and there's an instant bond between you. It feels as if you've known this person all your life, or perhaps over many lifetimes. There's no logic to it, but you can't deny the feeling of not just familiarity, but intimacy with this stranger.

Almost all relationships cross over the boundaries of logic, reason, and shared experiences, and enter the territory of intuition. That unexplained sense of connection is a universal feature of our deepest and most profound friendships, romances, and familial bonds. Some of the best uses of intuition occur in relationships: anticipating and eliminating conflicts, touching those we love in as many ways as possible, and helping ourselves and our loved ones become more fulfilled as we grow together.

Strangely enough, our intuition can both blossom *and* become blocked within our intimate relationships. We're more likely to feel intuitively linked to those we love, yet at times that emotional connection can block certain aspects of our intuition, especially when it comes to "tuning in" for them in the context of a reading, for example. As a friend of mine says, "When you're too close to something or someone, you're blinded by how you want things to be." Your intimate knowledge of someone combined with your own emotions about them can muddy certain intuitive communications.

But most of the time intuition adds greater richness to relationships. One man commented to me recently, "I can walk into a room and my wife will say, 'All right, what's on your mind? Something is bothering you.' Or sometimes she'll hang up from talking to someone, I'll walk in and she'll ask, 'Do you have a bad feeling about this person?' She knows without my telling her when something's up, and vice versa."

A friend of mine once described how she picked up on something that was worrying her young daughter. "When my daughter was twelve, she came in and said, 'Mom, all the kids are going over to Sandy's house for a sleep-over Friday, and I've been invited.' And as soon as I heard her, I knew she didn't want to go. So I told her, 'If it really won't disappoint you, I'd rather you didn't. I'm not comfortable with that crowd.' She said, 'Okay, I'll tell them'—and she wasn't upset at all. When you really know your kids, you can tell what's up with them without anything being said."

Small instances? Of course. Could they be the result of simply knowing a loved one well enough to be able to read their moods and emotions? Perhaps. But what is being able to "read" someone if not the ability to connect with them on a deeper, more subtle level, to be able to discern things using more than just our five ordinary senses? And that's what intuition is all about.

# Finding Someone to Love

Long ago, all marital relationships were arranged by the families of the parties concerned. (In certain cultures it's still traditional for the bride and groom to meet for the very first time on their wedding day.) Later, our romantic partners were almost always either someone we knew from the community, or else they were known by someone we knew. But that's no longer true in our modern world. We are consistently meeting potential partners through anonymous sources like the Internet, the job, personal ads, and so on. I believe for both our happiness and safety, it's more important than ever that we check people out using our wisest self. Whether we're chatting on-line, asking someone at work for a date, or getting "fixed up" by a friend, if we're smart we'll use our intuitive "antenna" to get a sense of whether this person is right for us.

Of course, sometimes we're lucky. Sometimes it's as if the universe puts up a neon sign saying "THIS ONE," with a large arrow pointing to a certain man or woman. When Robin Nemeth met her husband-to-be, it was like that. One evening she and a friend went to a karate school close to where Robin lived. Darrell, the owner of the school, asked Robin why she wanted to learn karate.

"I need to lose weight," she said.

"That's the wrong reason," he replied. "What do you do?"

"I'm a chiropractor."

"I don't believe in chiropractic," he said.

*What a jerk,* thought Robin. But over the course of the evening she noticed he was walking as if his foot hurt. After the class, she said to Darrell, "When you're ready to get your foot fixed, come and see me."

"I told you, I don't believe in chiropractic," he said, and they left it at that.

Two weeks later, Darrell was sitting in Robin's waiting room, filling out the physical questionnaire. They had one session (during which he was still argumentative) and he was scheduled to come back the next day. But that night Robin's father was brutally mugged, and she went to the hospital to be with him. For some reason, Robin called the nurse at her clinic and asked her to contact Darrell and make sure he knew why she had to miss his appointment. In turn, he sent her a card signed, "Fondly, D. Schulze"—"not exactly the stuff of hot romance," she remembers.

The day Robin's dad left the hospital, she called her girlfriend and said, "I have this feeling I really need to go to karate." Afterward, she walked into Darrell's office and said, "Do you want to go to dinner with us?"

"I don't socialize with students," he said.

"I don't socialize with patients, either," Robin replied. "But do you want to come anyway?"

He agreed—and that did it. Robin remembers, "You know how in the movies the world stops? That night as we sat in the diner, the world stopped. When Darrell drove me home he stopped the car at my house, turned to me and said, 'I know this is going to sound crazy, but do you want to marry me?' I said, 'You know what? I do! But I have to know first, do you want to have a baby?' 'I never did until this minute,' he told me. 'Well, if it's a girl, do you want to name her Brittany?' I said. And that was it.

"Talk about following your instincts—he couldn't marry a student and I couldn't marry a patient, but we did. All my friends thought I was crazy to marry someone I barely knew. We were married two months later and we've been together eleven years. We have two beautiful daughters (the oldest is named Brittany) and it's absolutely the best marriage. We both felt this relationship was meant to be."

"Meant to be"—in other words, the pull between

Robin and Darrell was so strong that it didn't matter whether they knew each other for a long or short time, if they weren't "supposed" to be dating, or even if they were involved with other people. (Robin was actually seeing someone else at the time.) Their intuition about their love for and connection with each other overcame all the conventional obstacles.

I believe we're always getting tipped off by the universe about our relationships. For instance, let's say you're thinking about getting involved with someone romantically, and within days you end up talking to a friend or even a stranger who knows that person. Or you invite someone over to your house and as soon as this person walks in the door, your dog starts barking and baring its teeth. Information from the universe can come from many avenues. It could be your dog barking at your date, or several different people saying, "You have to meet this woman!" and it turns out to be the same woman each time, or even just your own intuitive feeling that says, "Yes!" or "Watch out."

Sometimes, of course, the information we get about a relationship is very, very specific. In the summer of 1975, shortly after my sister Elaine was divorced, I called her and said, "I want you to circle the date February 3rd on your calendar. You're going to be married again by that date. I see a man with brown curly hair and three sons and I think he's the right man for you." "You're crazy," she told me. "I've got to get my life put together. I don't need another relationship right away, and I'm certainly not going to rush into another marriage by February. That's only six months from now." I said, "I'm not telling you it has to happen. We all have free will. But if it does happen, it's right."

Of course, I promptly forgot the phone call. (I don't remember the details of my predictions, even for my own family!) But that fall, Elaine met David, the gentleman with the brown curly hair and three sons. (Talk about "meant to be"—David was the cousin of a friend of one of Elaine's girlfriends, who set up the meeting. Not exactly a direct connection!) By December, both of them had realized this was a special relationship and they were talking about getting married, perhaps in the summer of the following year. However, the universe had other plans. In January, one of David's sons broke both legs in a skiing accident, forcing the family to cancel a planned vacation trip to California. David called Elaine and said, "You know, it's silly for us to wait to get married. Why don't we do it now?"

"Don't ask me what possessed me to say, 'You're right!'" Elaine remembers. "We started looking through the calendar at possible dates, and that's when I saw 'February 3,' with a huge red circle around it. I gasped and said, 'Oh my God!' I had forgotten all about Char's prediction. I called her and started screeching on the phone, 'You predicted this! You predicted I'd be married by February 3rd and David and I are getting married February 1st. He's the man with the curly brown hair!'"

I'm happy to say that twenty-four years later, David and Elaine are still happily married. "If I drew a picture of the perfect husband and put a list of his qualities next to it and said, 'Okay, someone find me this man,' David would be it," Elaine says. "I'm so glad he's in my life. And I'm so glad my sister told me about him in advance!"

When you take the time to tune in intuitively, you'll have a lot more certainty about finding the right partner, whether it makes logical sense or not. After all, Martha Gresham is absolutely confident that her intuition says she's going to meet someone and get married again—and she's seventy-one years old!

# Many Lifetimes, Many
# Relationships—in
# Many Forms

Frequently people come to me for a reading with one burning question: "Will I ever meet my soul mate?" Well, I believe we have more than one soul mate, because I think a soul mate is simply someone who helps our soul to grow. Your greatest enemy could be your soul mate, because you both have things you need to work out karmically, and until you handle those issues, you will keep running into each other, lifetime after lifetime.

As far as a soul mate in the way most people think—an eternal connection between two souls—I have certainly known people who have met their soul mates and occasionally even married them. But I believe sometimes our soul mates are born as our children. Sometimes they appear as our best friends. Sometimes they're a parent or trusted advisor. Whatever the lesson we're supposed to be working out in this lifetime, that's where a soul mate will appear.

A young mother I know once answered a knock on her door to find a little boy, about four years old, standing there. He said, "My mommy told me that a little boy lives here. Can I come in and play?" The mother was startled. She did, indeed, have a two-year-old son, but she had never seen the little boy at her front door before. She asked his name and if he knew his phone number, and then called his mother. It turned out the child lived a short distance away, but the two families had never met. "It was strange," my friend said, "But as soon as I saw this little boy, I knew he would be a very special friend to my son. Well, they hit it off immediately, and they have remained friends for almost thirty years. Each was best man at the other's wedding. I really believe there was some kind of connection there from the very start."

Could this kind of friendship be a kind of "soul mate" connection? Why not? I believe that we live many different lifetimes on this earth, in many different bodies of both sexes. There's nothing to stop us from being born male in the same time a soul mate is born male as well. In fact, I often wonder if people are attracted to others of the same sex because they feel a karmic connection to this person from past lifetimes. There's an attraction of souls that transcends whatever gender we happen to be this time around.

It's also possible we retain the masculine or feminine energy we had in a past lifetime and bring it into our new body. The last time around someone might have been female, for example, and even though the spirit is born into a male body this time, it still has the feminine sexual energy and desires that attracts it to men. Sexual energy is such a driving force in the human spirit. It controls a lot of our actions—look at what it did to President Clinton. And we pull from that energy more than we know. It wouldn't be surprising if we carried the residue of sexual preference from lifetime to lifetime, reincarnation to reincarnation.

Sometimes a soul mate will appear and the relationship will still be blocked—by fear. One of my students swears she knows the gentleman who is her soul mate, but he is about twenty years younger than she is. He, too, feels the connection, but he's unwilling to pursue a romantic relationship with her. "That's okay," my student says. "We're linked on so many levels it doesn't matter that we're not lovers this time around. We have been lovers in other lifetimes, and I believe we will be again."

I don't want you to think that all relationships are pre-ordained. Remember, we live in a universe where both

free will and destiny are operating. Yes, sometimes we're
meant to be in a certain relationship. Yes, sometimes that
relationship can cross perceived barriers and restrictions.
But something can be destined to occur and then the decisions we make can change the course of that future. If
two people were soul mates and they were supposed to
live their lives together, and then one of them got scared,
or got married to someone else before they met their soul
mate, or even stepped off a curb and got hit by a truck,
how do we know which fate was really their destiny? We
don't know when something is predestined or not. All we
can do is use our intuition to keep as attuned to the universe as possible.

We have to be careful, however, when using our intuition to discern whether to enter into a relationship. The
fact that we're attracted to someone and we can't figure
out why doesn't necessarily mean that the universe has
selected that person for us! We may be attracted to a
familiar energy that's not good for us at all—a lot of abusive relationships fall into this category. Someone is
abused in childhood by a parent who never gave them
approval and perhaps even beat them. The child then
grows up looking for approval, but at the same time they
may be attracted to the same kind of abusive energy they
experienced from their parents. We will often keep making the same mistake over and over again until we deal
with the past, understand it, and grow in self-love from it.

Each lifetime we are learning different lessons, and
sometimes those lessons are focused on our sexual
energy. It's also possible that our lesson this time around
is *not* to act on our attraction to someone. For those
people unfortunate enough to be attracted sexually to
children or who are abusers, I have to think that their lesson is either to get help and eliminate the desire, or to
resist the temptation of a relationship that creates harm.
We all have free will. We can choose to stay out of rela-

tionships that are destructive. If you feel a relationship is not totally right or will hurt the other person, you shouldn't enter into it, because relationships are supposed to help us grow. That's the only reason the universe puts us into relationships—so we can help each other become more in touch with our own greatest selves.

# Growing through Our Relationships

At their best, relationships are the greatest place for learning and growing in this world, and our loved ones are our greatest teachers. One of my clients adopted a daughter shortly after her own daughter had died. I told this woman, "Your adopted daughter is connected psychically to you, your husband, and your son. You've been with her in other lifetimes and this time around she's chosen you. "I knew exactly what you meant," my client told me afterwards. "*The Mountains of Tibet,* a book for children on death and reincarnation, talks a lot about how children choose who their parents will be, and adopted children doubly so. My adopted daughter is only eight years old and she has already taught me so many lessons."

Not too long before I gave a reading for a journalist, he had followed his intuition and gotten in touch with his older half-brother. "My father had two boys and a girl, then divorced his first wife and married my mother," he said. "When I was growing up I was very close to my oldest half-brother, but we had lost touch over the years. One day out of the blue I wrote him a letter for no reason I could articulate. Well, it must have struck a chord, because he sent me back a handwritten letter, several pages long. My brother always dictates letters to his secretary, so it was a big thing for him to write me himself. It was the beginning of a complete renewal of our relationship. I took my family to meet him at Christmas that year, and now we e-mail back and forth all the time."

How we nurture our relationships is so important. If

you love someone, let them know today, because no one knows what will happen tomorrow. Make sure you give 100 percent of your love and affection. Even if things don't work out and you have to move on, if you've given your all you can leave with a clear conscience. And while your relationships last—whether it's for days or for lifetimes—you will have gotten the most because you have given everything you are.

Strangely enough, however, the way we learn the most in our relationships is *not* to allow our emotions to override the truth of who we are and who we are meant to become. Far too many people let themselves be drawn into bad relationships because they are so hungry for love and affection. If someone is very lonely and really wants to be in love, he or she might let their hopes and desires and needs outweigh their intuition and even their good old common sense about a particular partner. Instead of seeking a partner who is truly right for them, they will let their fantasies draw them into a bad relationship.

"Do you know who always asks me if they'll ever meet their soul mate?" one of my students told me recently. "The people who are in relationships that aren't right for them! They keep asking why, how come, what's going on, while they keep doing the exact same thing with the exact same partner. You'd think they'd figure out by now that they'd better start learning something pretty quick so that both people can move on."

Often the universe will let you know when it's time to move on from a particular relationship. A young woman I know had been dating the same man for ten years, since she was in high school. He was going to school in another state and they both had been trying to figure out what the next step for the relationship should be. Should she move to be with him? Should he move back home? Should they get engaged? Then the young woman's grandfather was injured in a severe accident. He was hospitalized for several months before he ultimately passed away. The young woman ended up being the person who went to the hospital almost every day and took responsibility for the decisions about her grandfather's care. "I really missed my boyfriend at that time, but whenever he came down, we ended up fighting," she remembers. "One day I went to church with my parents. I was feeling really bad about my grandfather and disappointed in my boyfriend. I thought, *If he's not here for the bad times, why have this relationship?* And then came to me suddenly, *This relationship is over.* As soon as I thought that, I felt as if a huge weight had lifted off me—certainly not what I expected to feel.

"The next day my grandfather passed away. My boyfriend called and couldn't make it down until the actual day of the funeral. But the first day of my grandfather's wake, everyone was asking me where my boyfriend was. (At that point I hadn't told anyone, including him, that I wanted to break up.) Well, one of the young surgeons who had worked on my grandfather came to the wake. We were all surprised that he showed up, because usually hospital doctors don't do that for their patients. He sat down next to me and started talking. To make a long story short, we dated for several months. It was an important relationship for me because I needed someone to help me make the transition away from my long-term boyfriend. I believe that the universe was telling me to end the first relationship, and because I listened, it put this doctor in my path at the right time."

Sometimes you have to love someone enough to get them out of your life. A time could come where you know the two of you love each other as much as you can possibly love someone, yet you get to a crossroads where something must change. Maybe your partner has been cheating on you. Maybe he or she has a drinking or substance problem. Maybe this person is abusive to your children. If you continue in the relationship in its present form, both you and others will be hurt. To keep growing, the relationship has to change. At that point, free will comes into play. If you both are able to face the truth and work things out, the relationship can continue; if not, however, you'd better love yourself and your partner enough to break it off.

A woman named Annie once came to me for a reading because she was worried about her boyfriend. At the time, he was on a vacation in Australia and he had not invited her along, which had prompted her request for a reading. Annie didn't mention anything about her boyfriend, but I immediately picked up that she was having problems with him. "He's on a trip out of the country," I told her. "I'm sorry, but he's not thinking about you at all. In fact, I'm picking up that he's with someone else." I suggested strongly that she get some therapy and work on developing more self-love.

Instead of being agitated by what most people would consider bad news, the reading actually calmed Annie down, because it confirmed what she already knew instinctively. When the boyfriend returned two weeks later, however, he was very affectionate and attentive to her, so she pushed the reading to the back of her mind—until she found a hotel receipt for "Mr. and Mrs. So-And-So" on her boyfriend's chest of drawers. When she confronted him, he admitted he had met someone on the plane going to Australia and had spent his entire vacation with her.

Annie was smart. She dumped the boyfriend and went in for some short-term therapy to help her work on her self-love issues. She tells me she's much more focused and settled now that this man is out of her life. She is glad that she was able to see that the relationship wasn't doing her any good and that she chose to end it when she did.

You've got to make sure that you stay true to your own

truth, your instincts about your own soul and what it needs. Don't let the desires or neediness of a moment keep you from living with integrity, which is living in sync with what the highest level of consciousness wants for you and for all of us. When we know we're in alignment with the universe, even though we may be hurting emotionally in the moment we will be able to take the steps we need to become whole again.

When your intuition speaks up, you have to tell the truth to yourself and your partner. You have to confront them. Yes, you may be risking the relationship. Yes, you may end up alone again. But if your intuition is telling you, "I don't deserve to be treated like this," and you don't have the guts to do something about it, then you will never grow as a human being. Now, if your loved one cares enough, then hopefully he or she will rise to the occasion. They'll see the confrontation as an opportunity for them to be honest and grow with you. But regardless of the outcome, you must take the risk. If the relationship ends, so be it. If it was a relationship built on dishonesty and inequity, it wasn't doing either of you much good. Remember, sometimes the greatest gift we can give ourselves is to learn to be kind to ourselves—and that's often a lesson learned best when we are alone.

## Love beyond the Grave

We can have many marvelous relationships in the course of our lives, relationships that help us get in touch with our wisest selves while they deepen our sense of love and connection with the universe. And those relationships do not disappear with death. One of the primary reasons people come to me for readings is to hear from those loved ones who have passed over. I'm here to tell you, your loved ones want to keep that connection just as much as you do.

Love is the bridge that connects us to each other—

across the miles, across the years, across the barrier of death. And love isn't exclusive. A man or woman who loses a spouse and then remarries isn't being unfaithful to the dead. (Certainly the dead don't regard it as infidelity.) Life is for the living. When you love somebody, you love them for who and what they are. You love their soul which is unique. If the person you love dies, the love can continue—but that doesn't mean you can't have a different love for someone else.

The important thing is to remember that love exists regardless of circumstances. As Shakespeare wrote in one of his most famous sonnets, "Love is not love/Which alters when it alteration finds,/Or bends with the remover to remove." Our circumstances may change, yet love remains. The form of love may change, yet love remains. The body that love shows up in may change from lifetime to lifetime, yet love remains.

One of my students said it beautifully: "The best gift we have is each other. And the bigger your circle of life, the more people you know and the more people whose lives you touch and who touch you back, that's what will make you rich in the truest sense of the word. You'll be rich in the love you give and receive."

# 20

## An Intuitive Health Checkup

Almost everyone I know has had this experience: You're getting ready to go to bed and you sense there's something not quite right with your body. No specific symptoms, no runny nose or sore head or muscle ache—just a feeling that physically you're "off" somehow. You dismiss it and go to bed, and the next morning you wake up with a raging cold or fever or stomachache or headache.

If we pay attention, we can "tune in" to even the smallest differences in our health and well-being. And sometimes we can be tipped off before the changes actually show up. A good friend of mine went to his doctor for a checkup, asking specifically about a particular mole on his back. The doctor said everything was okay. But six months later my friend was awakened from a dream in the middle of the night. In the dream he had seen a white picket fence, and painted in red on the fence was the word "cancer." He immediately went to his doctor and had the same mole checked again. This time the diagnosis was stage four melanoma—skin cancer. The man had been tipped off in his dream. He knew intuitively what was wrong with him before the doctors did.

One of my chiropractor clients sees this all the time in

her practice. "Patients can almost always tell you just exactly what's going on with them, even though they may not know it on a conscious level," she tells me. "That's why I believe one of our best diagnostic tools is often the patient's case history, and the most important diagnostic skill is listening. Yes, you still need X-rays or MRIs or CAT scans or blood tests, but you also have to listen to what that patient is telling you, because often they will know exactly what's wrong.

"A patient's nonverbal speech is just as important as the verbal. After all, you can sit in a room with a friend and before she says anything you know what's going on, right? As doctors, we need to be able to shut up and listen to what the patient is telling us, both verbally and nonverbally."

Over the years I've gotten very, very good at picking up on health issues for my loved ones and clients. My mother, God bless her, has had a lot of health problems during the last few years. And every time she's been sick, I've been tipped off in advance. For example, last year something told me to go by my mother's house, and when I arrived, they were just taking her to the hospital. When I was living in Los Angeles, every time my mom was ill, I knew to come home to Michigan ahead of time. I believe that when we truly, purely, unconditionally love someone, it opens a door for us to connect to them on every level, including that of intuition.

Many mothers have this kind of intuitive connection with their children. Chris Blackman once told me a story about a time when her six-week-old daughter was ill. Chris took her to the pediatrician, who prescribed oral antibiotics. The next day the little girl's fever was getting worse. Chris called the doctor's office and reached the nurse, who said, "Don't worry—the antibiotics take a full twenty-four hours to work." "After I hung up the phone, I said to myself, 'That's not right,' " Chris told me. "I called back and said, 'Let me speak to the doctor,' but the nurse refused. I said, 'Okay, we're going to come down to your office and sit there until we can see the doctor.'"

At that point the nurse got really angry, but she put the doctor on the phone. Chris described her daughter's symptoms and the doctor said, "Meet me at the hospital as soon as you can." It turned out Chris's daughter had bacterial meningitis, and if she hadn't gotten to the hospital quickly, the little girl might have died. "Something told me, 'Don't listen to the nurse. You have to be proactive; you have to talk to the doctor,'" Chris says. "I didn't call it intuition then; I thought it was just mother's instinct. Now I know they're the same thing."

One of my students has an intuitive link with her current boyfriend, which includes picking up on physical ailments. "If Ned's left shoulder bothers him, all of a sudden my shoulder will start to bother me, too, even if I haven't seen or talked to him in a while. Then I'll see him two days later and I'll say, 'Man, my shoulder's killing me!' and he'll ask, 'Which one?' When I tell him 'the left,' he'll just smile at me."

## Discerning Specific Conditions

The famous psychic Edgar Cayce had an ability to go "inside" someone's body and tell them what their health problems were. I can do that too sometimes. I'll scan the person's body and a health issue will come to me. I'll see or feel the poor circulation or diabetes or migraine or whatever. And while I will never diagnose a medical condition, I will tell clients about what I'm picking up on for themselves or their loved ones. I'll recommend they go to a doctor and get checked out just in case. Quite honestly, I'm rarely wrong. A client, Cheryl Herbeck, wrote me recently to remind me about a reading we had a few years ago. "You asked me how my father was and if he was in good health. You said that you didn't want to alarm me but that you felt as though something was wrong with his blood. When I got home that night, I called my Dad to tell him how fantastic our reading had been. When I told him that you said there might be something wrong with his blood, he confessed that he had kept a secret from me so that I wouldn't worry—he had leukemia!"

When Mike's mother had to have bypass surgery in her leg, everything went fine, except the incision wasn't healing properly. Eventually the leg started turning gangrenous and the doctors recommended immediate amputation. But Mike refused to act in haste. "I called Char to get her take on the situation before we did anything. She said she saw my mother leaving the hospital with her leg intact, and suggested we find some solution other than amputation, perhaps changing doctors. So I spent a fair amount of time finding another doctor at the same HMO but in a different location. He operated on my mother's leg twice. The first operation didn't work but the second one did. Today my mother is doing just fine; she's walking and, of course, she still has her leg."

Sometimes we can pick up very specific things intuitively; sometimes we just get a sense that things are all right or not. My student Joanna gets a kick out of doing what she calls "instant readings" for people. Someone will come in and ask about so-and-so, and Joanna will say, "Well, tell him he'd better get his high blood pressure checked, number one. Two, he'd better watch his diabetes. And three, he'd better watch what he's eating, because he's pigging out as usual." All this for someone she's never even met! On the other hand, my friend "Agnes" doesn't necessarily get specific diagnostic information, but she can pick up on the ultimate outcome. "I have a friend who has had fibroids for a long time and finally decided to have them out," Agnes told me. "This woman was so concerned that the doctors would find something worse, possibly cancer. She kept asking me,

'What do you think? Do you think it's bad?' Intuitively I felt absolutely certain she was going to be fine. I knew the outcome of the surgery was going to be positive, and I told her so. And she came through with flying colors. She had a twelve-pound fibroid tumor removed, but there was no cancer, and she recovered quickly."

# Intuition and Healing

I believe the best physicians and healers all use intuition or instinct or whatever you want to call it, as part of their healing repertoire. Of course, intuition can't take the place of good, scientific diagnosis—nor should it. But in the same way a human being is a lot more than a collection of biochemical processes, a doctor should be more than a machine that looks at symptoms and spits out a diagnosis and a treatment regimen. If that were all we needed to be healed, computers could do our doctoring for us!

I've had several conversations about this with doctors, especially chiropractors, and they agree there is something more going on than simply A + B = C, "symptoms plus knowledge equals diagnosis." As one chiropractor reminded me, it's not just about symptoms. Healing must take the whole patient into account. "Whenever you meet a new patient, you have to really trust your instincts, because what the book may tell you to do and what really is needed may be two totally different things," she said. "Sometimes people are sick for physical reasons, sometimes for emotional reasons, and sometimes for spiritual reasons. I think part of healing is being able to tune in to that patient and find out what they truly need. You have to discover what will really help that patient get well."

She adds, "Sure, you go to school and you learn all the techniques, but I find that when you put your hands on somebody's spine, you have to know where to go. I've had students come in to be mentored by me, and they'll say, 'How'd you know it hurts over there?' And I'll tell them, 'It's those bionic things I had implanted in my thumbs. They work great.' But when you put your hands on somebody's spine, if you're in tune with them you'll know where to go."

"Peggy" is an excellent massage therapist, and she has the exact same experience when she massages her clients. "Half the time clients don't know which muscle hurts, so I try intuitively to find the spot where the pain is," she says. "You have to listen to the patient *and* get a sense or hunch or feeling as well. I find that the more I practice massage therapy, the better I am at getting in tune with my patients."

I'm lucky to have a truly great chiropractor in Michigan, Dr. Jeffrey Fantich. He's one of the most intuitive healers I know, although he isn't completely sure of that himself. "I know there's something going on, but I'm not comfortable calling it intuition," he said recently. "However, as I talk to people who are very, very good in the healing professions—and that means everybody from top heart surgeons to massage therapists—I think that all of them are going to tell you that it's not just experience or training; there's something else going on.

"I know that when I'm working with patients, I'll find myself beginning to examine an area that may seem unrelated to a particular complaint. But something pulls me to look in that direction a little deeper. I don't know if that comes from my experience or training or instinct— perhaps it's all three.

"I'm a firm believer in training and expertise. I'm a physician, and I confirm every diagnosis with everything I know to do—standard orthopedic and neurological tests, diagnostic imaging, whatever's indicated. But I also think that being in tune with that instinctive side is what separates some doctors from others in terms of their ability to get to the core of things. Obviously, I think it would be wrong from a medical standpoint to rely on intuition exclusively. But especially in more difficult cases—when things may not be going as they should and you know there's something else going on—aside from ordering the appropriate tests, sometimes doctors rely upon what they call their 'experience.' But another term for that might be gut instinct. I think that part of being a good doctor is being able to draw upon and trust both your experience *and* intuition."

When a doctor is a true healer, I believe intuition plays a part in their ability to help patients at the highest level possible. It's not just about sensing what's going on medically with someone; it's also important to be in tune mentally and emotionally as well. When you're consulting a doctor for your own health, make sure you're in tune with him or her on every level. And don't be afraid to stand up for what your own intuition is telling you about your physical well-being. After all, no one knows your body better than you do, because no one else lives inside it every single minute. You simply have to trust what you're getting, then find yourself a good doctor who will listen to your concerns without judging.

Your intuition can be an important part of keeping yourself healthy while you're here. Chiropractor Robin Nemeth sums it up this way: "The best doctor we have is the one inside ourselves, but so many times we ignore it and shut it off because we think we can't possibly know what we're talking about. But we do. And that's really the essence of our intuitive gift: to listen and trust ourselves."

# 21

## Intuition at Work

Almost all successful business people will tell you that intuition—or "gut instinct," or some other name for the same thing—has played a large part in their accomplishments. The career choice that just "feels" right . . . the new employee you somehow know will do great things . . . the business deal you avoid even though it looks great on paper . . . the leap of creativity that produces a new industry or technology or scientific discovery . . . all of these are examples of intuition in the workplace.

Even people who don't believe in psychics or intuition can see the value of knowing more than what's on the surface in business. I'll never forget when Gary Hughes sent his business partner to me for a reading. "The guy had been ribbing me for a long time about the fact that I consult a psychic," Gary said. "I said, 'Look, I'm going to get you a reading with Char. I won't say a thing about you to her, but I guarantee she'll tell you things that you never told me and I couldn't find out.'

"Well, I was in the next room when he had his reading, and when he came out, he looked at me kind of funny. He told me Char had described details about his father's death which he had never shared with anyone. She had given him advice about his mother's illness, talked about his relationship with his sisters, and a lot more. Then he said, 'Gary, we need to put Char on payroll. We'll make a fortune with her in the business.' I agreed with him—even though I knew she'd never do it."

A lot of my clients come to me for advice on their careers or businesses. After our sessions, I often tell them, "Look, you can do this for yourself. Tuning in is simple. Take a moment to separate yourself from the situation, let your mind get quiet, and then ask a question about the deal or the person or the next move in your career and see what comes up. Trust your instincts—they'll rarely steer you wrong."

## Choosing a Career Intuitively

Are you in the right career? Does your current profession "feel" like it's what you're supposed to be doing? If we're lucky, we end up in careers that somehow match our talents and our instincts. Martha Gresham knew from an early age she wanted to be an interior designer. "Even though I've never had any formal training, I'm very well known in my profession, and I've received awards from the American Society of Interior Designers (ASID) for my work. I've always used my intuitive talent when it comes to interior design—I'm able to walk into a house and see exactly what it will look like finished. If I can't, I won't take the job." Nancy Newton came to her profession as a mediator after several years working in state government. "I knew intuitively that it was time to leave for reasons of personal growth," she said. "I've always been able to counsel, even as early as junior high school. So I founded "Partners for Youth" in an attempt to get youth organizations from across the state to network with each other and empower young people to come together to solve their own problems."

Sometimes, however, we need a little nudge from the universe to discover exactly what we should be doing. The first time I read for Patti Cimine in New York, she was working as an office manager in a chiropractor's office. It really wasn't what she wanted to do, but she was uncertain of her next step. Patti had a degree in finance and economics, but she wasn't interested in going back to school for an MBA. Then a friend gave her a reading with me as a birthday present.

In the reading I asked Patti, "Are you a chiropractor? Are you in the healing field?" When she told me she simply worked in a chiropractor's office, I said, "You have healing hands and you have a good head for business. You should be a massage therapist. You could have your own business, work your own hours, and it would give you the freedom that you want."

"The thought of being a massage therapist had never even entered my mind before that reading," Patti told me later. "But two days later I started calling some schools, and the more I found out about the profession, the more interested I was. I ended up doing really well in massage school, and my time in the chiropractic office helped a lot, too—I knew how to deal with patients, handle insurance paperwork, workers comp cases, and so on. The year or so I've been doing this has been the best year I could ever imagine. I own my own business, and I have a very flexible work schedule. When I have kids I'll be able to plan my work week around them. I'll be able to spend as much time with them as possible."

Years ago I also gave some unexpected career advice to my sister, Alicia. When she was thirty-three years old, Alicia decided to go back to school and get a master's degree in psychology. It was an exhausting project. For a while she was going to school at night, teaching kindergarten in the daytime, and taking care of her husband and two children. But she managed it. She got the degree, completed an internship, received her license, and even got certified to become a school psychologist. The school where she was teaching offered to create a psychologist position for her if she continued to teach there as well. Everything seemed set for Alicia—until I called her.

I told her I had seen her in the Ph.D. program at the University of Michigan. She told me I was nuts. (That's sisters for you.) "Number one, I'm exhausted," she said. "Number two, I've got quite enough on my plate already. Number three, U. of M. accepts only two or three people a year out of 400 applicants. There's no way I could get in." I said, "Well, it's there for you if you want it."

Alicia decided she would apply just to prove me wrong. (Thanks, Sis!) She and a girlfriend applied for the program together—and both of them were turned down. Alicia called me and said, "See? You're not always right." But I told her, "You just need more experience under your belt. Open up a practice, and in a few years apply again." At that time, Alicia didn't have any clinical experience other than the internship, so she started taking patients. Within four years she had built a successful practice "almost without trying," she says. Then I called her and said, "It's time. You have enough experience. Reapply now, and you'll get in." Today Alicia has her Ph.D. in psychology from the University of Michigan and she is a well-respected, well-liked professional with a thriving practice. "Once again, you were right, Char," she admits. "In my experience, you have never been wrong."

So often I find that when we start working at the profession the universe wants for us, all sorts of "coincidences" arise to help us along that path. I read for a woman who worked as a television producer and I told her she should explore her writing talents. I said she should go off and write in the place where she spent her summers. Within a very few months the woman happened upon a course called "Writing from the Heart," and took it. Now she's enrolled in a memoir writing program at Northwestern University, has plans for two different books, and she and her husband are planning a move to Martha's Vineyard, where they used to spend their summers.

A successful businessman whom I consult with told me, "I try to teach people how to use their intuition to discover what it is they truly want to do, so I can see if the jobs we put them in here are a match. This has nothing to do with altruism on my part—I've noticed that when people are doing what they want and they're in jobs they like, they have endless energy and drive. And that's the kind of employees every business owner wants."

## Using Intuition with People

Someone once said, "All business is nothing but relationships." I find that intuition helps me in my own business relationships every minute. Whenever I walk into a business meeting, I scan the energy of every person in the room. I get their name, and I feel their energy from the top of their head to the bottom of their feet. I scan their mind, their emotions, their psychological behavior, their health. I get an immediate "hit" about who these people are, whether they're honest or not, what their own agendas are, and whether I think we can work together. And I'm not unique in being able to do this. Time after time my clients and students describe their own ability to assess people instantly and correctly. "It's not that I'm real opinionated—I think most of my friends or people who know me would not describe me that way at all," one student told me. "But I do form a yea or nay about people immediately, and time usually proves that I was right on the money. I think my instincts are good as far as people go."

I know someone who is a partner at an investment banking firm, heading up a group of stockbrokers. He deals with money and finances all day long, yet he says that intuition about people is one of the most important abilities he possesses. "Contrary to what the public would believe, 80 percent of the decisions that I make in our business are all people decisions. And I think intuition plays an important part in that arena. I use my intuition at least a million times a day, in practically every decision I make."

I once told a friend of mine that a man with the initials J.S. would be very good for him for a time and then that would change. (My friend told me later that was some of the best advice I have ever given him, because he was able to benefit from the relationship when it was good and get out before it went sour.) In another reading I said that he was dealing with a Bob in a business context. My friend replied, "I'm dealing with two or three Bobs. Which one are you talking about?" "It doesn't matter," I answered. "All Bobs are good for you." "And you know it's really funny," he admits. "All the Bobs that I've dealt with since that reading have been very good for me indeed."

Whenever you meet someone in a business context, do what I do: Take a moment to "scan" their energy and see what kind of intuitive "hit" you get on them. Those first moments before the logical, analytical part of our brain kicks in can provide some of the most valuable information we can have in developing profitable business relationships.

## Using Intuition on the Job

As I said, successful business people use intuition on the job constantly. It's not just in terms of getting a "hit" on the right decision to make. Often, the most important thing our intuition can do is to alert us to potential problems that haven't yet surfaced. Larry Jordan, who publishes and edits a monthly magazine as well as producing his own radio news show in Wisconsin, says, "I play hunches all the time with my work. I've always got a lot of irons in the fire, coordinating a lot of different free-lancers, managing all the production details of the maga-zine, and so on. Sometimes my wife (who works with me) gets very exasperated because I seem to procrasti-nate, but if something doesn't feel right I don't move on it. And nine times out of ten it turns out to be a good thing I didn't.

"Just last week my wife was going to wire transfer a large sum of money to the printer who was supposed to be producing this month's issue of our magazine. I told her not to do it. 'What are you thinking?' she said. 'We've got to get it there so the magazine will be printed on time.' I said, 'Just don't do it.' Thank goodness she lis-tened. You see, we had switched printers for this issue because our regular printer couldn't get us on press. On paper the deal with the new printer looked great, but I had one of those gut hunches and told my wife, 'This is not going to come together.' Sure enough, the whole deal fell apart over the weekend and we had to go back to our old printer. But if we had wire transferred the money to the new printer on Friday, we would have been in deep trou-ble. We would have had a heck of a time getting that money back in a timely enough fashion to get the maga-zine printed by our old printer.

"Something told me the deal was going to go sour. The new printer was saying all the right things and giving us all the right assurances on paper, but I just felt that some-thing wasn't right. Because I listened to my intuition, I held onto the funds and even had a back-up plan ready for getting the magazine over to the old printer.

"I heard somebody say once that in business we often operate on what are called 'pre-logical insight experi-ences.' We have assimilated a lot of information that's stored in our minds, and we have an ability at times to cull from that and to put things together. We don't know why we believe or think something, but we just do. I don't know how it works—all I know is, I'm glad that it does."

Once Martha Gresham didn't listen to her intuition about an important job, and paid a very high price as a result. Martha's interior design business had grown to the point where she had several other designers working with her on staff. One staff member was given the assignment of redecorating the home of a famous movie star. As the founder of the design firm, Martha always supervised the work of her staff, but this particular woman hadn't been sharing information about the project, and Martha kept getting uneasy feelings about it. "I knew the furniture wouldn't fit and the client would hate the draperies," Martha said. "I told this woman on my staff that the project would be a failure, but she told me that she was doing what the client wanted. Eventually I had to let her go. Unfortunately, she took the project with her. I heard later that the client absolutely hated the finished project and wouldn't even allow the draperies to be put up in the house. I learned from that experience to trust my intuition, not only when it comes to design but also when it comes to people."

# Making Decisions Intuitively

Occasionally our intuition will point us to business decisions that make no sense at the time, but which prove to be very beneficial in the long term. The husband of one of my students once bought a house in an unpromising area of town as an investment. His brother-in-law told him, "You're never going to be able to sell that house, especially for a profit." But the man replied, "That's what you think." A year and a half later, he sold the house and made $25,000. As the brother-in-law remarked ruefully,

"Whenever Jack made a decision, there never seemed to be any logic or rationale behind it, but everything always came out on the money."

Obviously, I'm not advocating being stupid with your money or your business. You have to use logic and reason as well when making important decisions. But intuition can give you information and direction from a whole other source, and very possibly help you to succeed in unexpected ways. For example, a woman I know bought a restaurant with her husband eleven years ago. At the time, it was a very illogical choice, as neither of them had ever been in the restaurant business before and both of them continued their work at other professions. Nevertheless, the restaurant prospered and they were happy they had gone with their instincts.

They didn't realize how important those instincts were until about a year and a half ago. The couple's adopted son (who had never liked school or done particularly well academically) was in his early twenties and trying to figure out what he wanted to do with his life. To keep him busy, the couple suggested that he work in the restaurant. It turns out the young man is an extremely gifted cook. Today he's the operating partner of the restaurant, on his way to buying an interest in the business. "At the time we bought the restaurant, our son was only fourteen and had never demonstrated any talent with cooking," the woman told me. "He made pancakes and things like that, just as most kids will do. But because we followed our intuition and went into the restaurant business, our son has a career he loves. He has blossomed into a confident, successful young man—what every parent hopes for."

Intuition can be one of our best advisors when it comes to making business decisions. The universe is constantly tipping us off as to the right road to take and the pitfalls to avoid. Let's say you're thinking about getting involved in a business deal. When you're tuned in intuitively, you'll find that something will happen to clue you in about the wisdom of taking the offer. You'll end up talking to someone who knows the person you're dealing with and who can offer you insights as to their honesty. Or maybe your car breaks down on the way to a crucial meeting—the universe's way of saying, "Stop!" As one of my entrepreneurial friends puts it, "When I'm doing a business deal, if it's not working I back out. Every time I force something, it turns out badly because it's not supposed to happen. So I do the deals that go smoothly, even if they seem like the most impossible deals at the start. By going with the flow, I've made a lot of things happen that have amazed my colleagues."

When we take the time to "tune in" to our careers, we can keep ourselves in alignment with what the universe wants for us. Intuition can also help us avoid career situations that might cause us harm. Once I advised a man who was selling his business. The group buying it wanted to pay over time, but I said no, take less money and get the cash up front, because they won't make the payments. So the man took less money and sure enough, the buyers went out of business in a year or two.

Another student of mine went to a hairstylist friend of hers and said, "Tracy, why are you staying in this salon? The vibes in this place are so bad it makes me sick to my stomach." And it was true—Tracy admitted that she would come into work every day feeling happy, and by the end of the day she would have a headache, feel nauseated and completely drained of energy. "She was picking up on all the negative energy in that salon," my student told me. "I told her to move on and find another salon and everything would be just fine. She's working in a completely different place now and it's like somebody took a thousand-pound weight off her shoulders. But honestly, I think she would have been a long time realizing what the problem was if she hadn't listened to me—and I hadn't listened to my intuition about the problems with the other salon."

Ultimately, using intuition to help make decisions in business can also give us greater peace of mind. When we feel we're in alignment with what the universe has in store for us, there's a new level of confidence. It can help us face the pressures of difficult times with a lot more equanimity. "You gave me a reading several years ago in which you told me my business was going to be successful," a client wrote me recently. "Since that time there have been a lot of crisis points, times where I could have given up and succumbed to the pressures of a multimillion-dollar business. But because you had said I was going to be successful, I was able to stick with it and come out ahead. Instead of losing $100 million, I sold the business and made a handsome profit."

## Inspiration and Intuition

Intuition can also help us make the kind of "leaps" from logic to insight that characterize geniuses, Nobel prize–winning scientists, and pioneers in every field of endeavor. Where did Steve Jobs get the idea for the personal computer? How did the vision of the structure of DNA appear in the heads of Crick and Watson? From what place did Einstein pull the letters $E=MC^2$, revolutionizing modern physics? And how in the world does it happen that two artists on opposite sides of the world come up with almost identical melodies at the same time?

My chiropractor, Dr. Fantich, is an expert in a special kind of allergy elimination technique called N.A.E.T. This treatment was developed by a doctor with numerous degrees—R.N., doctor of chiropractic, Ph.D., and O.M.D. (Oriental medicine doctor). Suffering from allergies herself, she tried combinations of techniques to help pull her out of acute allergic reactions, and over time she discovered several solutions that worked dramatically.

She later researched these combinations and developed the N.A.E.T. speciality over a period of years. But were the combinations truly accidental, or was she tapping into intuitive knowledge? Yes, her skills and training gave her the tools to use in creating this allergy elimination regimen—but what led her to the particular combinations that proved successful?

This is the question for all researchers, entrepreneurs, and artists. How much of the newest ideas comes from the accumulation of logical knowledge and experience, and how much is due to instinct, intuition, a source of inspiration far beyond our own limited resources? Are the people who produce the most inspiring artworks, the most innovative technology, the most astounding scientific breakthroughs simply tuning in to the universal consciousness? Many successful people will always tell you that yes, they put in a lot of hard work—but at some point there was a spark, a "hit," a bit of intuition that helped them skip a few steps along the path to success.

As a student of mine says, "Intuition can simply make you better at whatever it is you do." So use this vital tool as part of your own professional skill set. Take those few extra moments to "tune in" when you meet someone, when you're offered a new project or new opportunity, when you come into a new situation or are faced with a change in your current circumstances. Pay attention to those "twinges" of caution that arise with no apparent cause. Don't discard those ideas and notions that may seem crazy in the moment—they may pay off big in the long term. You'll find that your "on the job" intuition can dramatically increase your success!

# 22

# Helping the Police and Finding Things (and People!)

In January 1993 I had just appeared on Larry King's radio show, where I talked about intuition and read for people who called in. Late that night, I got a message from my secretary: "Please call Chief Joel Dobis of the Zilwaukee, Michigan, Police Department."

Now, like most people who get a message from the police, I quickly ran through the past several weeks in my mind. No, I hadn't run any red lights or broken the speed limit . . . my taxes were all paid up . . . I hadn't even been near Zilwaukee. There wasn't any reason for a chief of police to be calling me—unless he needed my help.

That was it. On the show, I had mentioned working with police detectives in California, and that had caught Chief Dobis's ear. He told me later, calling a psychic was the last thing he ever thought he would do. "I'm a realist," he said. "I graduated from the Northeastern Regional Police Academy when I was only twenty-two, and at age twenty-seven I was made Chief of Police in Zilwaukee. I've been involved in just about every kind of case and every aspect of law enforcement, and I've never personally witnessed anything I couldn't explain. And I'd certainly never been involved with psychics. But after I heard that show while I was riding around in my patrol car, I drove to this tavern where I knew my sergeant was relaxing after work. I pulled him aside and said, 'Sarge, don't think I'm whacked, but I listened to a psychic on Larry King and I'm going to call her to see if she can help us on the Michele Lalonde homicide.'"

I called Chief Dobis at the police station later that night. He told me he was sitting with the file open in front of him, and, after a few "Hello, how are you" remarks, I started giving him information about his case. The facts, as he summarized them for me later, were these: In 1992 a passing fisherman had found an abandoned, burned car under a bridge, on the banks of the Saginaw River. He called the police to report he had seen what appeared to be bones in the backseat. Chief Dobis picked up the fisherman and they drove down to the spot where the car had been abandoned. The vehicle had been so completely torched, even the tires had melted. But just visible in the backseat were what looked like the ribs of a small child. The body had been so completely destroyed by the fire that the only way the police could even begin to find out who had died was by tracing the car's license plate.

The car belonged to Michele Lalonde, a twenty-one-year-old nude dancer at a local strip club. (The police made a positive ID on Michele based on two teeth—all that was left of her skull after the fire.) She had last been seen three days earlier, when she and a girlfriend had gone to a dance in nearby Lansing. Michele had driven both of them and dropped the girlfriend off when they returned from the dance. After that, no one had seen Michele alive.

Chief Dobis obtained a warrant to search Michele's apartment. There were no signs of struggle anywhere. The police did find a travel bag, which the girlfriend confirmed Michele had taken to the dance, so the police knew she had made it home that night. However, what had happened after that was a mystery.

The police started investigating Michele's background and associates, and pretty quickly they focused on her boyfriend, Robert Brisbee. He didn't have a solid alibi for that night (he had been at a large fraternity party), and he was known to have been dating both Michele and another woman (who was extremely evasive when answering the police's questions). Robert had been heard to argue with Michele at the apartment before she left that night. Robert had no vehicle, so Michele had given him a ride home and then came back, picked up her dance things, and went to Lansing.

Robert had previously dated other women from the club where Michele worked, and had taken them to that same spot under the bridge where Michele's car was burned. There was also a witness who told a story about seeing a young black male walking away from the bridge (an area of town that was predominantly white) on Saturday morning. But she couldn't identify the man, and failed to pick Brisbee out in a lineup. The car was so totally destroyed, and the evidence against Brisbee so circumstantial, that Chief Dobis despaired of ever getting an arrest, much less a conviction, on Michele's case. But, as he said later, "Some cases take on a special and personal meaning for officers, and I really wanted closure for both Michele and her parents." That's what led him to me.

"What you did that first night was uncanny," Chief Dobis told me later. "You were in California, I was in Michigan, and for twenty-five minutes you told me everything about my case. You mentioned the bridge, the fire, you came up with the name of my victim and the name of my suspect, as well as the names of other people involved in the case. There's no way you could have found any of that information out, even if you'd been able to research the case before I called you, because we had withheld most facts from the press due to the ongoing investigation and the fact we hadn't made an arrest."

Chief Dobis was excited, and so was I. He asked if I could take time out of my schedule to come out to Zilwaukee. I said yes—I was heading back to New York from California anyway, so it would be easy to stop over. Chief Dobis managed to pull several (very large) strings and got the county to pay for my stopover ticket and a hotel room. He told me later it took a lot of nerve to walk into the city manager's office and say, "Listen, I want to bring in a psychic, pay for her plane ticket and put her up at the Sheraton on the city's dime." Chief Dobis must have made a really good case, because the city manager said okay immediately. (I still wonder how those expenses were listed in the city's year-end report.)

So a few days later I flew into the Tri-Cities Airport. Chief Dobis picked me up ("I knew who you were as soon as I saw you," he remembers) and we drove to Zilwaukee. At my insistence, instead of going to the hotel we went straight to the crime scene. As we sat in Chief Dobis's car, I started conversing with Michele, the young woman whose body had been found there. She told me there had been a pregnancy and an abortion having to do with her relationship with Robert Brisbee. (Chief Dobis said that only one other person besides himself knew that particular fact.)

After a while, we went on to my hotel. We were planning a "sting" operation for the next day, where I would be wired with a microphone and go in to talk with Robert Brisbee's girlfriend, Beth. I hoped I would be able to get her to say something to break the case open, or perhaps even get her to introduce me to Brisbee himself. The sting came off flawlessly (even though I still remember going into the ladies' room and worrying that the police in the van could hear me over the microphone). I met Beth, and she agreed to have a reading and to bring Brisbee with her. But unfortunately, Brisbee refused to have anything to do with me. Both Chief Dobis and I were disappointed, but I promised him I would be available if he needed my help at any time.

As he drove me down to the airport, however, I started picking up what would be the most important aspect of this case. "You're going to get this guy," I told Chief Dobis, "But it's going to take you awhile. *And he's either going to kill or attempt to kill again within six months.* You've got to do everything you can to get him. I feel he has the makings of a serial killer if he's not stopped."

Through the next several months Chief Dobis and I kept in touch over the phone. One day he called me, enormously excited. "Char? You'll never guess what happened. I was sitting at my desk today and heard a call come in from another jurisdiction about an attempted murder. They mentioned Robert Brisbee by name as the suspect. Char—*it's six months to the day since you said he would kill again!*"

The crime was truly bizarre. Beth, Brisbee's girlfriend, shared an apartment with a girl named Sherry Desempler. That night Beth had been over at Brisbee's place, visiting him. Brisbee, who had no car of his own, told Beth he wanted to go out for some fast food. So he took Beth's car and drove to her apartment, knowing that Sherry would be there. He let himself into the apartment (using a key Beth had had made for him) and went into the bedroom where Sherry was sleeping.

Sherry awoke in her pitch-black room with someone on top of her. He had one hand over her mouth and one around her neck, and he was attempting to assault her sexually. Sherry struggled, tried to scream, and bit her assailant on the hand several times. Somehow her foot hit the light switch, and she saw her assailant's face—it was Robert Brisbee, her roommate's boyfriend.

Brisbee ran as Sherry started to scream. He headed for a local grocery store, where he intentionally broke a bottle of juice and cut his hand to hide Sherry's bite marks.

He even made a report to the grocery store people to cover his tracks. But the cover-up did him no good. Sherry identified Brisbee as her assailant, and the case went to trial shortly afterward. Brisbee was convicted and sentenced to fifty years in prison, which he is serving today. Chief Dobis has gone to speak with Brisbee repeatedly, asking him again and again about the Michele Lalonde case, but he refuses to talk.

Chief Dobis also tried once more to put me in contact with Brisbee. Before the trial for the attack on Sherry Desempler, I flew out and we went to the prison where Brisbee was being held. I was still hoping I could talk to Brisbee and get him to confess. Dobis had me wait outside the interview room until Brisbee was brought in. Then Chief Dobis excused himself for a moment and opened the door. Well, as soon as Brisbee saw me, he bolted from the room, before anyone could say a single word. As Chief Dobis went after him, I was saying, "Robert, talk to me," but he wouldn't come back in for anything. Brisbee wanted nothing to do with me—even though there was no way he could know who I am. All I can think is, he somehow knew I was a threat to him because I had recognized who he was and what he had done. I'm certain Brisbee killed Michele Lalonde, and if he's not brought to justice for that crime on earth, I know he will be on the other side.

To this day, Chief Dobis and I talk occasionally. He's such a dedicated police chief and a good man, willing to go beyond his own doubts and prejudices and call me up about this case. "We brought in all the best people we could—including the forensic pathologist who worked on the Jeffrey Dahmer case," he says. "I called Char because she was the best. I hoped she would be able to pick up on something that I'd overlooked—like a lighter, or a piece of paper with a fingerprint on it—something at the scene that she could tell me about that I could go retrieve. Instead, she gave me a whole range of specific information, and, more important, told me that Brisbee was going to attempt to kill again. I've had several other officers that were involved in this case and none of them can explain the details that Char was able to pick up."

While I don't publicize it a lot, I have helped the police on a number of occasions. They've consulted me on several cases of murder and missing persons. Quite honestly, it takes a secure police officer or detective to work with me because of the attitude of most law enforcement officials toward psychics. But when we all can put our egos aside and focus totally on solving the case, the results can be amazing.

I've also been called in by the families of the victims, to see if I can pick up any information that will help the police. These cases are often so sad, because there is such a need for closure, anything that might bring the loved one back or put the kidnapper or murderer behind bars. I often request to see an object belonging to the person in question—a toothbrush, an article of clothing, a treasured toy if it's a child, and so on. These objects keep a residue of their owner's individual energy "thumbprint," and I can use them to tune in to the owner's whereabouts. A picture also helps; if I'm looking at someone's picture, I can often pick up details about them. In the case of Kim LaVallee, his mother brought both a jacket belonging to her son and his picture. "Char worked for four hours, with such deep concentration, holding our son's jacket and his picture," she recounted. "It was like Kim had something to say to her, he wanted something to come out." I picked up immediately that Kim had been murdered, and gave his mother the names of the men who had done it. They were arrested, convicted of the murder and are now serving twenty-five years to life.

Unfortunately, not all the cases I'm brought in on come to such a neat and tidy conclusion. Even though I can often see exactly how a crime was committed and by whom, the police need physical evidence that sometimes is not forthcoming. I believe my real job is to help the families find a little peace and perhaps bring some closure to the pain they're in. With luck, at the same time I can occasionally give the authorities a little "nudge" in the right direction.

# Finding People When You Need Them

Intuition can help us find people we need to see in situations other than police investigations. So many clients tell me things like, "I had to speak to so-and-so in order to finish an important project, and guess who I ran into in the parking lot?" I believe our sixth sense can help us be in the right place at the right time. And in some circumstances, it can give us a little more assistance than that!

A gentleman named "Neil" once told me quite a story about using his personal "homing" instinct to locate someone. Neil's wife had gone on maternity leave from her job as an ad salesperson. While on leave, she continued to service her accounts, call in ad copy, and take care of her customers, but when she returned to work, she was denied the commissions on these accounts. She filed a grievance with the labor relations board, and the dispute was placed in front of a mediator.

Neil thought the whole case was cut and dried, but unfortunately the owner of the company lied and the mediator ruled against Neil's wife. "The ruling came in the mail and when I read the mediator's reasoning—it was so ridiculous and his summation of the testimony so incorrect—I was fuming," Neil said. "Around suppertime I told my wife, 'I've got to leave for a few minutes.' She asked, 'Where are you going?' 'I can't tell you because I don't know,' I replied.

"I got in the car, drove all the way across town and turned left into a supermarket parking lot. I got out of my car, walked into the store and down a long aisle to where the meat counter was—and there was the mediator standing right there. I walked up to him and said, 'Sir, we received your judgment today,' and I tore him to shreds verbally as I have rarely done before. Then I turned around and walked out. It felt so good!

"When I left the house that night, I didn't know where I was going or who I was meeting; I just knew I had to get in the car and drive. When I saw the supermarket, even though I had never been in that store before, I knew I had to go inside, and I knew I had to walk down that aisle. It's almost impossible to see a mediator once a case has been decided, and normally they're very hard to reach by phone either. You have very little opportunity to redress any grievance you have about any decision that has come down. But because I followed my gut instinct, I was led directly to this man so I could let him know how he had misrepresented the facts about my wife's case."

## The Answer to That Burning Question, "Now, Where Did I Put My Keys?"

This ability of our intuition to "hone in" on missing things and people is useful in more ways than helping solve a crime or locate a missing person. Have you ever lost something important, like some vital papers, and spent a half hour or more looking for them? Intuition can be extremely useful in these kinds of situations. Try stopping for a moment and tuning in intuitively to where they are. Get your logical mind out of the way, ask the question, "Where are those papers?" and then notice the first thing that pops into your mind. You may not find the missing object all the time, but by paying attention to your intuition, you're more likely it.

A young friend of mine was getting ready to go with her boyfriend to the video store, and he was running around like crazy looking for his membership card. He was getting frustrated and tearing up the apartment when she told him, "Stop!" She looked at him for a moment, and without knowing why, walked up and put her hand in one of his jacket pockets. Voilà! There was the card. "This happens with him all the time," she tells me. "One day he had lost a book and was hunting all over for it. I took a second to get quiet, and a picture popped into my head of him reading in bed. I said, 'Look by the bed,' and there it was. Now, you might think that I had seen the book in the bedroom, but actually it had fallen off the nightstand and was wedged behind the bed. I'm pretty good at finding something intuitively if I don't go crazy looking for it and give myself a minute to visualize. Then I'll get this mental picture and I'll go right to where the object is."

Intuition can not only help us find things we already possess, it can guide us to things we are destined to have. Several people I know have been led by their intuition to discover the place where they're supposed to live. My producer friend Stuart says, "Whenever I rent an apartment or house I save the realtor so much time, because the moment I walk in I can tell if I'm supposed to live there or not. It's a complete gut reaction. I either say, 'I could never live here,' or, 'This is where I'm going to live.' I always just go with that gut reaction, and it's never been wrong."

My sister Alicia once went looking for a Viking range—but her intuition led her to a whole new house instead. Several years ago Alicia and her husband wanted to renovate the house they'd lived in for twenty years. Alicia loves to cook, and she had always wanted a Viking range—one of the big, professional models with tons of burners—in her kitchen. So they called in designers and drew up plans for a new kitchen, which would have a Viking range in it. But every time they got ready to tear out the kitchen and start remodeling, something would get in the way. Alicia would joke about it, saying that she wanted to just wake up one morning and have a new kitchen and range appear.

After about the sixth delay in a row, Alicia was getting frustrated and beginning to believe the remodel would never happen. That particular day, a patient walked into her office and put a picture in her lap, saying, "I hear you're looking for a house with a Viking range." And there it was—a picture of a beautiful condo in the patient's housing complex, with the exact Viking range Alicia wanted in its kitchen. "Not too many people buy Viking ranges, or even know what they are," Alicia said later. "And yet there it was—exactly what I had been looking for." Alicia told the patient, "I'm not looking for a house. We're just redoing our kitchen." But the patient replied, "Why go through all that aggravation? Here's the range you want; it's just got a different house around it. And I know you would love this condo complex. It would be so perfect for you and your husband at your stage in life."

So Alicia took the photo home to her husband, thinking she would show it to him just because it was an interesting "coincidence." Imagine her surprise when he said, "Let's go take a look"! They both went out to the condo that weekend, and as soon as they walked into the kitchen her husband said, "Oh my gosh, Lee, it's your range!" The price of the condo had been reduced that very weekend. Needless to say, they bought the condo and are living in it very happily to this day.

But the story doesn't end there. The woman who bought Alicia's old house was led to it intuitively as well. The house was put up for sale in the middle of January—not the best time to sell a house in Michigan. On the second weekend it was on the market, the phone rang and a woman said, "I'm sitting out in front of your house with my sister. We're lost. We turned the wrong way. I'm looking to buy a house and we saw the sign in your yard. We're so sorry, but we're here right now. Is there any chance we could come in and look?" The woman loved the house and bought it within a few weeks.

# Buried Treasure in San Juan Capistrano

Martha Gresham also uses her intuition when it comes to deciding where to live and when to move. But a few years ago I gave Martha a reading in which I saw her buying a house that would have a major effect on her life—and provide a few unexpected dividends as well! I told her, "I see an old house with columns on the side and beams inside. It's run down and looks like bees or something have gotten into the side of it. I think you're going to buy this house. It's going to happen very quickly and you're going to have to close the deal in a very short time. And by the way, I see something like a treasure in the basement—some kind of silver treasure in dirt, maybe under a rock."

It's a good thing Martha is polite, or else she would have told me I was crazy. She had just bought a gorgeous condo in a very exclusive community—the kind of place you almost have to wait until someone dies before you can get in. She thought she was never going to move, and here I was telling her about this rundown house with a treasure in the basement! A week and a half later, however, Martha's daughter called her from San Juan Capistrano, California, not too far from where Martha was living. She said, "Mom, I just saw an old house that I think you should look at. It's a neat old place with about two acres of land, right on Ortega Highway. Why don't you go by and take a look?" So Martha drove over the next day—and saw the house I had predicted she would buy. There were the columns, there were the bees which had gotten into one side of the house, there were the beams inside. "I got goose bumps—and then fell in love with the place," Martha told me later. "I could walk around and see what it would look like finished. Even though the old man who owned it told me it was in escrow, I immediately put in an offer on the house. The other deal fell through, and the house was mine."

But I was also right when I saw that Martha would have to close the deal in a very short time. She had to sell her condo *and* offer the owner of the house a different piece of property in trade, and the entire transaction needed to be completed in forty-five days. There were a myriad of details that had to be handled quickly. In the middle of all this Martha called me again and said, "I can't seem to get this thing put together, but I just know I'm supposed to have this house." I told her, "There's something with papers in another town. I see a Vicky who's leaving on a trip tomorrow, and those papers are being pushed into a back drawer. You should call her right now." Martha knew that the property swap was being handled by a bank in a different part of California. So she called the bank and asked for Vicky.

"How do you know Vicky?" the bank manager asked.

"If I tell you, you won't believe me, but I'm going to anyway," Martha replied. "A psychic told me that she's getting ready to leave to go someplace."

"That's right," he said, surprised. "She's leaving tomorrow for Hawaii."

"Well, please tell her this transaction has to be done before she leaves or I lose my house," Martha said. Happily, Vicky was able to finish everything that day. "I never could have put this deal together if you hadn't seen I could do it," Martha told me afterward.

But Martha's "karma" with this house was far from over. Remember I said there was a treasure buried in the basement? Well, a few months later Martha called me in great excitement. "You'll never guess what happened," she said. "We started renovations on the house as soon as the sale went through, and my husband, Dick, has been supervising the work. Yesterday I flew to San Francisco to pick out carpeting and get a few other things for the renovation. I never call my husband in the morning when I'm on the road, but this morning I had an incredibly strong feeling that I should call him. In fact, I was getting ready to catch a cab and had the cab driver wait so I could call Dick.

"As soon as Dick answered the phone I asked, 'What are they doing this morning on the house?' He told me they were getting ready to dig up the basement so they could put in a concrete floor. I said, 'Well, don't forget what Char said about buried treasure. You'd better get down there right away and see if they dig up anything.'

"As soon as Dick hung up the phone, he walked around to the back door so he could get to the basement. Just then, the worker who had been digging down there appeared at the top of the basement stairs. Dick told me the man's eyes were as big as saucers as he said, 'I just dug up a metal box.' Dick and the worker went down into the basement and opened the box. It was filled with thousands of dollars' worth of silver coins. They continued to dig and found a second box, also filled to the brim with silver coins. Dick was so excited and wanted to call me— only he didn't have a phone number where I could be reached in San Francisco!

"That night when I came home the coins were spread all over the dining room table. Needless to say, I was extremely excited. If you hadn't made the prediction that we would find a treasure in the basement of this house, I'm sure we never would have looked." I'd also like to point out that Martha's own intuition tipped her off as to the day and almost the exact hour when the treasure would be unearthed!

Time after time, people who listen to their own intuition, their own "gut instinct," find their lives enriched and made easier. When you mislay something, when you need to make an important decision, when you're unsure of what do to next, stop and take a moment to check with your own inner voice. Look for the thought that comes from somewhere other than your own conflicted mind, that feeling that says, "That one, not this one!" When you take that extra moment to keep yourself aligned with what the universe wants for you, you may be surprised at the results—you may find your own treasure, buried or not!

# 23

## Easing the Pain of Passing

One of the few certainties we possess is the fact that we will all pass from this plane to the next. Speaking with our loved ones on the other side can help ease some of the pain after the transition. But sometimes we are also given the consolation of knowing beforehand when that transition will occur. Though possibly painful, this foresight can be an enormous gift, allowing us to say our good-byes, handle unfinished business, and in general prepare ourselves for the loss of the physical presence of our loved ones.

Remember I said earlier that I will never predict death in a reading? That's because I don't play God with my gift, and I believe there are too many factors involved that could change destiny—including the force of will of loved ones. A few years ago my dear friend Mary Sarko was going through a difficult time: her husband, mother, and father were all in the hospital at the same time. Mary has no children, nor any brothers or sisters, so it seemed to her she was losing all her closest loved ones at once. Now, Mary's husband was actually the most seriously ill. He even had a near-death experience where he saw his deceased mother and daughter waiting for him. He was really happy and ready to go—but Mary refused to let him. She said to him as he lay in his hospital bed, "Don't you dare leave me!" Her will was so strong, and his love for her was so great, that she literally pulled him back into life.

Was he supposed to die but didn't? I'm convinced that he could have gone but chose not to—because Mary is such a strong person and loved him so deeply. However, I do believe that at times our loved ones will let us know when it's their time to go, and sometimes our intuition will give us clues to that effect. "For years my husband used to tell our kids, 'Take good care of Mommy because Daddy's going to die at fifty,'" one of my students recalls. "Sure enough, he dropped dead at fifty." The universe can also prepare us to cope with sad times. A few years ago I was in Cleveland, Ohio, for an appearance on one of the morning TV shows. I was in a limousine because they were taking me to SeaWorld to do a spot, and suddenly I had the thought, "The next time I ride in a limo it will be at a funeral." I didn't want it to be my dad, but I thought it would be. Two weeks later, he died.

Some people seem to be especially sensitive to the energy that surrounds someone whose death is imminent. I've heard stories of young children who love being around someone—a grandparent, for example—and then all of a sudden they get very upset whenever they get near this very same person. Could they be picking up on the energy of someone who is getting close to their time? One gentleman told me a story of running into a neighbor in a local coffee shop. "I was standing in line waiting for my coffee, and I spotted this woman making her way to the door. As I watched her go, I had this thought—*I'm never going to see her again.* She gave no outward appearance of being ill, but I couldn't shake this feeling. Three days later some of my neighbors came by, collecting for a flower contribution for this woman's funeral. She had been taken ill around nine or ten o'clock in the evening, the same day I had seen her in the coffee shop, and died that night."

A few years ago a young student of mine was living with her parents in Brooklyn, and her grandmother lived in the apartment above them. My student was visiting friends in upstate New York for a long weekend, and returned around 1:30 in the morning. "It was a long drive and I was really tired," she remembers. "I came into the house, sat down on the bed and started taking out my contacts when I got this really weird idea that I should go upstairs and say hello to my grandmother. Now, my grandmother always loved company, but this was 1:30 in the morning, and I knew she would be long asleep. I'd just seen her a few days earlier, right before I left for the weekend, and I knew I could see her the next day. And I was really ready to go to bed. I could have easily just ignored the feeling, but instead I thought, *No, don't be lazy. Once you're upstairs, you'll be happy because she'll be happy to see you, and that'll be that.*"

So she went upstairs and woke her grandmother to say hello. They chatted for a bit (her grandmother could keep her eyes open only for a moment, but she kept talking even with her eyes closed), and then my student said, "Okay, Grandma, I'll see you tomorrow," and went downstairs to bed. The next morning, she went straight to work and didn't get a chance to see her grandmother first. And later that day, her grandmother was out walking and got hit by a truck. She was taken to the hospital and went in and out of a coma for about two months before she died.

My student told me, "The next day my two sisters, my brother, my parents were all saying, 'I should have picked her up today.' 'I was going to come by today.' 'I wish I had seen her.' And I felt so lucky that I had been moved to go upstairs and say good night to her that night. That was the last time I saw my grandmother as she really was."

## "I Felt His Spirit Pass through Me"

Messages of imminent parting may take many forms. A client once told me that she had been sensing her deceased father close by over the last few months, and believed it might be because her mother (his wife) had not been doing well. "Perhaps he's there either to help her through this time, or to encourage her that it's not her time yet. Or perhaps he's there to help her pass. I don't know—but it's a consolation to have his spirit so near." Sometimes people will report seeing their loved ones' faces actually become younger and more tranquil as they approached the time of their transition. "My father had been sick for a long time, and on the day he died, he looked better than he had in months," one woman told me.

Jeannie Starrs–Goldizen has lost both her husband and son, and in each case she was alerted to their passing. "My husband Marty was in the hospital in Phoenix, Arizona, for some surgery," she remembers. "While he was in the hospital a clot in his leg broke loose and caused a pulmonary embolism. The doctors threw me out of his room while they were working on him, so I went outside the building. It was about 98 degrees, and I was almost convulsing from nerves. All of a sudden I looked up and saw a shooting star. At the same time I could actually feel something go through me. It was a feeling I can't put into words; it was completely warm and serene. I said to myself, 'Okay,' and walked back inside the building. Just as I got to Marty's room, the doctors were coming out. I said, 'Yes, I know, he's dead.' They just looked at me as if to say, 'How—?' I told them, 'Never mind how I know; I just know.'"

When Jeannie's son Clint died, she also received several intuitive warnings. The night before he died, she was awakened from a sound sleep. She came out of her room, gray and shaking like a leaf. Her two daughters asked, "What's wrong?" and Jeannie said, "Your brother's going to die."

The next day Jeannie went to her job in a medical office building, and about 1:00 she went into the ladies' room. "Standing at the sink I saw a bright light, light blue in color, surrounding a white aura that was spreading out from my body," she told me. "I knew something was standing there. I asked, 'Okay, why are you here? What's going on?' Then all of a sudden, I knew it was another sign."

That night around 8:00 a state trooper showed up. Jeannie said, "You're here to tell me my son's dead." The state trooper's face was a real study! He asked, "How did you know?" and Jeannie said, "Let's just say I had a visit." Clint had indeed died earlier that day. These kinds of messages not only give us a physical experience of our loved ones' passing, but they also confirm that there is an energy which leaves the body after we die.

## Easing the Way

Sometimes we're given the gift of knowing that someone we love is getting ready to pass away—from a prolonged illness, for example. Being around a loved one during this time is often one of the most difficult experiences we can face. But it can also be a time of enormous love, healing and faith. And when we connect intuitively with the love surrounding us at those times of transition, we can help make the passing easier for ourselves and our loved ones on both sides of the divide. We can let them go with our blessings, knowing that their death is a release from pain and suffering on this side. Death is not so bad; suffering is. When someone you love is suffering and you know that their continued existence on this plane will only mean more pain, then please—love them enough to let them go.

My friend Hope had such an experience last year when she lost her father to pancreatic cancer. "He had been sick a long time with a lot of different ailments, but he was diagnosed with the cancer only eight weeks before his death," she remembers. "My whole family kept vigil at the hospital, but I just sort of took over. It was very important to me to be with him, and most of all, to give him permission to go. I wanted to let him know that we would be okay, that my mother would be taken care of, that no one was disappointed with him and we loved him, and that it was okay not to keep fighting. It's hard when somebody you love is dying. On one level you don't want them to go, and you have to convince yourself and that person that it's okay, they did a great job while they were here, and they'll continue to do a great job on the other side.

"That time with my dad was a very beautiful, intimate experience. I talked to him the whole time. I told him that I truly knew he did the best he could and I was sorry for whatever hardship and heartaches I may have caused him through the years. To be able to do that, to be able to talk about it was really so wonderful, instead of pretending it wasn't really happening. We all felt so much peace at the end. And it was funny—my dad kept raising his hand and waving to people that no one else could see. My brother thought it was a reflex, but I knew he was waving to people he loved who had already passed and were waiting for him."

This feeling of the presence of departed loved ones at the time of passing is one of the most common experiences shared by those of us in touch with our own intuition. My student Marilyn was in the room when her aunt died at the age of one hundred. Marilyn told me that it was as if she could see her grandmother (who had died many years before) holding her aunt in her arms as soon as her aunt stopped breathing.

# Forgiveness and Love

So how can we help those who have left us for the other side? It begins many times with forgiveness and ends, always, with love. The greatest energy, the most healing energy, the most powerful force in the universe, is love. We can continue to give our love to the people who are gone—first and foremost, by thinking of them and keeping them in our thoughts. Thought is our channel to the spirit world; it's the way spirits communicate with us and vice versa. If a departed loved one pops into your head for no apparent reason, it's usually because they're nearby. It's a great opportunity to connect with them again and send a little love their way. When I want to send love to departed spirits, I start with putting a white light of protection around myself first and then around them. Next, I say a prayer for them, asking for blessings from the highest level of goodness, love, and wisdom we call God. After all, prayer is just another kind of thought, one with direction and a higher purpose. Finally, I send my love and good wishes their way, letting them know I love them, telling them I'm okay and all is well.

Our thoughts and good wishes can absolutely benefit our departed dear ones. Most of the world's spiritual traditions know this—it's why we light candles for the dead and mark the anniversaries of their births and deaths every year. It's just like fueling their battery with the energy of your love. Don't you feel better when someone thinks about you or asks after you? How pleasant is it when someone asks you sincerely, "Hey, how're you doing?" You can be depressed or sad or feel the whole world's giving up on you, and then one person can say, "Is there anything I can do?" and everything feels somehow lighter. It's all about loving and caring and giving to others, no matter where we are, no matter the distance of time or space or astral plane that may separate us. Love is the through line that will always connect us—to each other and to the highest level of universal goodness.

# 24

*ᴧ*

# Conclusion: Life
# Is a School,
# And We're All
# Here to Learn

Imagine you're back in high school or college, taking several different courses on required subjects. You read the books, go to lectures, study the material, and learn it at least well enough to pass the tests you are given along the way. While you're taking those classes, they're a major part of your life. You're completely into history or geometry or English literature or biochemistry or music theory or ceramics. You give it all the energy you need to absorb the material—and then you move on.

Our lives here on earth are like that. Life is a school and we've been put here to learn certain lessons—different lessons each time we return. These "life lessons" are designed to help us evolve as souls. If we work hard and study hard and do what we're supposed to while we're here, then we "graduate"; that is, our spirits grow to higher and higher levels. If we fail to pass our lessons, we're sent back again and again for remedial work, perhaps with more supervision and bigger penalties.

Think back to those courses you took in school. Two years after you graduated, how much did you recall about biology or history or English or math? Probably not a lot. You may be able to call up that knowledge if you need it, but you're certainly not as involved with it as you were when you took the class. That's kind of what happens when we pass over to the other side. For a while, we retain all those details of our lives here, but eventually we take the memories and lessons we learned and either evolve to a higher level or reincarnate so we can learn a whole new set of lessons here.

We're always being tested. We're always being tasked to learn more, to be more, to love more, to care more compassionately for ourselves as well as others. Intuition is simply another tool we can use to help us pass the tests we're given and to learn the lessons we're asked to learn. And if we master our intuition, we may be able to use it to help others with their lessons, too.

It does seem that some people's tests are harder than others. I can't tell you why—maybe it's karma from a past life, maybe they need a *big* example to make them learn a crucial lesson, maybe the hardship they're going through is somehow serving others. But I believe that God never gives us anything that we can't handle. And sometimes, quite honestly, the biggest tests we can face come from following our intuition. There have been times when I've had a strong gut feeling that goes against all logic, and I've had to decide if I truly believe in my own sixth sense enough to follow my instinct. I will say, however, that most people usually come out right in the end when they follow that inner voice.

My friend Gary told me once, "For many years I spent a lot of time worrying about my future and regretting the past. I thought about the things I should have done, and by doing that I was ignoring the present. But then I realized there are always going to be good times and bad times, and the bad times are usually the lessons we need to go through in order to enjoy the good times. The past is nothing but the experiences we needed to enjoy the present and the future."

In this final chapter I want to share with you a few lessons that I think we all have to learn as we progress through our lifetimes on this earth. I hope that putting them down in this form will help you "get" these lessons as quickly as possible.

## Lesson #1: We're responsible for our lives.

It's not about predicting the future, it's about the choices we make along the way. We can't always know what's really predestined, and we can't always know which of our choices are changing or fulfilling our destiny. It's up to each of us to take responsibility for our lives and take action so we can learn whatever lessons the universe has in store for us. One of my students, Sarah, told me, "People have to be responsible for their own actions. You can't pass the buck and say, 'My religion says I can't do this,' 'my job says I can't do this.' No, *you* make your choices, you're responsible for your own life. And a lot of people don't want to hear that. I tell anyone who comes to me for a reading, 'Look, I accept responsibility for what I'm saying, either right or wrong. But you've got to take what you hear and do what you want with it. It's your life.'"

Even with all the talk nowadays about personal responsibility, we still seem to have become a culture of excuses. "I'm this way because I was abused," "I'm that way because I'm fat," "I never had the opportunities," "What other choice do I have?" and so on. A lot of people who are part of the "New Age" movement use the excuse of fate and predestination. "It was written in the stars that I would never be financially successful," or "never find my soul mate in this lifetime," or "get cancer." But most of the time that kind of talk is only an excuse for not taking action. Yes, some things are predestined because we need to learn a particular lesson, but destiny can be changed in many ways—both large and small—through our own efforts. You may not be destined to meet your "soul mate," but that doesn't stop you from forming incredibly close and wonderful relationships. You may have a lot of trouble with money, but you can quite possibly accelerate the timeline for learning how to amass it and handle it so you can at least be comfortable. You may even be fated to come down with a devastating disease, but if you learn the lessons that come with it—patience, willingness to fight for your health, accepting the help of others, cheerfulness in the face of pain, to name a few—your life and the lives of those around you may be richer as a result.

My client "Rosalie" once said, "It takes a great deal of courage to take personal responsibility, with all the pain and fear that can go with it, and go through the tough lessons. Just keep asking, 'What can I learn from this?' I ask myself that question all the time. It helps me keep focused on what I'm learning and not all the other stuff that may be happening at the same time." Another student adds, "Once when I was embroiled in some particularly nasty litigation, I told my lawyer about this philosophy. I said, 'You know, even if we lose this case I know I will learn something that will help me in the future.' And he said, 'If you truly believe that, then you're invincible.'"

## Lesson #2: "Judge not, lest ye be judged."

One of the most important lessons I think all of us need to learn—or maybe keep learning—is not to judge others. The beauty of life is that we're all different, with different needs and gifts and abilities and choices. You don't know why someone acts the way they do. You can't understand them until you've lived their life, or perhaps their lives as they've come back to this earth plane again and again. I'm not saying we should tolerate acts that hurt others. But we spend so much time and energy judging other people, criticizing them for who they are, who they aren't, what they have or don't have, and whether they fit our ideas of what someone "should" be.

This is especially true when it comes to sex. I think a big problem in our world is not accepting others' sexual preferences. Some people are heterosexual, others are bisexual, and still others are homosexual—so what? But because of society's judgments, a lot of people are fearful because they can't be in touch with who and what they really are, or they're angry because they feel they aren't accepted because of their sexuality. Or they won't accept themselves because their parents would say, "Oh my God, not my son, not my daughter!" When people negate or repress their true sexual energy, many times it will take them out of balance and cause problems in their lives as a whole. We need to be at peace with ourselves as far as this important energy is concerned. And that means being able to express ourselves freely and openly, with the caution that we cause no harm to others. Sexual energy is important—we need to be in sync with it, to understand it, and to be truthful about it, because in truth we're freed. I believe that we can't help who we are or what our needs are. We can't help if we're not built gorgeously, or we're not bright in the conventional sense, or if our sexual preference goes against what society declares is "normal."

I think we have a primary responsibility to look at *all* people with understanding and compassion. Intuition transcends every race, creed, color, sexual preference, socioeconomic class, political affiliation, and religion. It's up to us to learn to look beyond what separates us and find what makes us alike. After all, every spirit is made up of the same energy, and the last I heard, energy molecules had no interest in judging other molecules.

When we don't judge people, when we try to see the best in them instead, it allows them to see the best in themselves. It's kind of like raising a child. The best thing we can offer our children is an atmosphere of non-judgmental and unconditional love. We're all children—we all need that kind of nurturing and support, if not from other people, then from ourselves.

Again, I'm not talking about allowing people to hurt each other. But as some wise spiritual master once said, "We can hate the sin while loving the sinner." We can do our best to point people to the kind of attitudes and behavior that will lift them to higher levels of goodness, light, and love.

So let go of your expectations about people. Let go of having to be the one "in control" as far as others are concerned. Let go of the attitude, "I know what's right." Let the people you love grow in their own ways. If they ask us, yes, offer your wisdom, the benefit of what you've learned during your time on earth. But the best thing we can give them is our love—not our advice, and certainly not our judgment.

## Lesson #3: The secret of life is balance.

To paraphrase the great poet Khalil Gibran in his book *The Prophet:*

Without the energy of Hate we don't understand the full energy of Love.
Without Sadness we don't understand the full energy of Happiness.
Without Evil we don't understand the full energy of Good.
Without Chaos we don't understand the full energy of Peace.

Everything is a cycle of energy perpetually flowing between yin and yang, positive and negative, feminine and masculine, giving and receiving. Everything has an opposite in this world. Where there's evil, there's good. Where there's love, there's hate. Where there's chaos, there's peace. A battery doesn't run unless it has a positive and negative charge. Some people on this earth are destined to cause chaos and harm. But must *we* become evil? Must *we* create chaos? Do *we* have to become abusive murderers or torturers? Of course not. However, we do need to recognize that evil does exist. There's good and bad in almost everyone, and when the bad gains the upper hand, watch out.

We need to understand that evil exists so that we can fight negative tendencies in ourselves and others. Remember, good has more power than evil. We want to work toward the goal of getting the positive and the good and the loving to band together to try to bring peace to the earth. We need to learn to fight negatives consciously, in our souls and in our thoughts, and then rise above them to the point where we learn true self-love. Then we can keep goodness, happiness, and peace in our hearts consistently.

Balance is the key in keeping ourselves together. It's important for all of us to be balanced emotionally, psychologically, physically, and psychically. When we're out of balance in any area, there's more of an opportunity for negative energy to affect us. If we're out of balance physically, we get sick. If we're out of balance emotionally, we get upset or depressed or manic. If we're out of balance psychologically, we have all sorts of behavioral problems. If we're out of balance psychically, we open ourselves up to negative energies from the astral plane. We also need to keep a balance between our minds and emotions. I believe that true wisdom arises from the perfect balance of knowledge and feeling.

Part of being balanced is taking care of yourself, especially when you're using your intuition. It's so easy in this work to get very drained, to keep putting yourself out in service of others because it's so needed. But you have to be aware of how much your "battery" is being depleted by the effort, and then take the time to recharge yourself in whatever way works for you. I take long walks, call friends up to chat, read, see a movie. But I know what my limits are, and I ask other people to respect my boundaries. You see, there's a difference between being selfish and having self-love. Selfish says "my needs first"; self-love says "my needs matter." To keep in balance, you have to take your needs into account while you're helping others.

When we're in balance, it's much easier to stay in tune with the highest levels of wisdom and goodness. We're not so caught up in our own stuff and it's easier to give to others while taking care of ourselves. And it's easier to take things lightly! If you take anything too seriously, you're not balanced. Often intuition can use our sense of humor to get past the conscious mind and give some profound messages. I remember being on the phone with a friend and making a joke, only to have him ask, "Why did you say that?" It turned out the joke was somehow related to what was going on with him at the time, and it gave him a very profound message.

I like to tell people, "Look, I don't have all the answers, but I know there's a place where you can find balance, where you can find a happy medium. Because that's what I am—a happy medium!"

## Lesson #4: Change and growth are not optional.

Nothing ever stays the same. Our nature, our purpose—both here and on the other side—is to keep growing and changing until we attain the highest level of wisdom. We all need to learn to change with change. It's one of the most important lessons we can master.

Sometimes change will cause us pain. It may mean we will have to leave behind places, things, and relationships that no longer serve us. When I first began to study intuition and become a professional psychic intuitive, I was lucky that most of my friends and family were very supportive. But there were others who told me I was silly or deluded, and I should go back to teaching junior high. I had to stop seeing those people; their attitude was keeping me from making the very changes that I needed.

We've all had friends or family members who have refused to let us change something we felt was important, or who didn't recognize a change that had already occurred. It takes courage to look at the people in your life and realize when those relationships are damaging you or holding you back. But when someone is stopping you from growing, it's time either to confront him or her or let them go out of your life. I believe friends and relationships come into our lives at specific times for specific reasons, and when that reason is no longer valid, the friendship either changes or disappears. Trying to hold on is like going to college and trying to keep every single friend you made while you were in high school. You can't do it; you, and they, will be changing too much and too fast.

Like riding a raft down a river, intuition gives us the ability to stay afloat amid constantly changing circumstances. Every move by another person can have an effect on your own course, and because the future can change at any moment due to one person's choice or decision, it's crucial to be in sync with the energy around us at all times. It's the difference between going with the flow and trying to row upstream against the current. When we're in tune with the universe, when what we're doing feels right, the future seems to make more sense, even though the currents of our destiny are shifting all the time. We can sail through the changes of our lives to reach our ultimate goal.

## Lesson #5: We're all in this together.

We're all components of a whole, and we need to understand that we possess the power to destroy or heal not only our own lives but also the lives of those around us. We're all in this together. My growth will help you to grow, and vice versa. We need to pay attention to each other, do our best to help each other, pull together in large ways and small ways.

I remember a few years ago the Detroit Red Wings ice hockey team won their second national championship in a row. I watched the last game, and when they won the whole team carried one player around on their shoulders. Was it the team's top scorer? Was it the goalie who made a spectacular save? No—it was Vladimir Konstantinov, a player who had been in a terrible car crash the previous year. He had sustained severe brain damage and never played another game since that accident, yet the Red Wings wanted to recognize his contributions to the team the previous year. They wanted him to know he would always be on their team.

I believe the reason people love watching sports is partly due to the team effort displayed on the field or court or ice. We love to cheer for "our" team; it feels so good to be a part of that energy. Well, what if *everybody* was on your team? We're all part of the team that makes up the universe. Your actions affect me, and mine affect you. It's our job to pull together and help our teammates as much as we can, whether it benefits us directly or not.

There is a wonderful lady who has looked after my mother for several months. One evening I was driving her home and I started hearing her spirits and loved ones talking to me. I pulled over and said, "Can I give you a reading?" and proceeded to pass along these messages to her. I wanted to touch her life in this way, not for any fame or material gain, not because it's my job, not even because she'll take good care of my mom (since she does that anyway). I wanted to do it because she's on my team, the team of humanity, the team of spirit. My job—the job of everyone on earth and on the other side—is to help others.

So remember the people who are on your team. And remember that even those who have caused you pain were on your team as well. It's like playing another team in sports: your competitors are also on your team because they're giving you something to compete against! In the same way, the people who oppose us are on our team because they're causing us to grow. So even when someone appears to be put on earth specifically to drive you crazy, relax; and realize that, in the cosmic sense, they're on your side. It makes life a lot easier when you can see everybody as part of your team!

## Lesson #6: Use the gifts God gave you to make things better.

Princess Diana's brother, Charles Spencer, said in his eulogy at her funeral, "Diana, your greatest gift was your intuition, a gift you used wisely." Diana used her intuition with grace and compassion to help those in need. The impact of grief around the world at her death was overwhelming, and was compounded a few days later by the loss of Mother Teresa.

What a profound experience it was to watch life stop as the entire world acknowledged these two great women. For a few brief moments, millions of people were joined in one universal consciousness—one mind, one thought, one prayer. If our world could only come together more often without prejudice, greed, or jealousy, concentrating on healing one problem at a time, we could stop so much suffering. Perhaps that was one of the best lessons of that experience.

I believe Princess Diana and Mother Teresa made their transitions almost at the same time so the entire world could learn from their example. Both these women were given extraordinary gifts of the spirit. They both had courage, and selflessness in caring for others; they both overcame enormous obstacles in their lives to become models of compassion. And each of us possesses a spirit with the capacity to live up to those same standards.

We are all part of the energy of God in this universe. To reach the highest levels of energy, to merge into that God-consciousness, we must take the gifts we are given and use them to help others and make things better. Whether we're reaching out to the less fortunate on this plane, or acting as guardian angels or spirit guides on the other side, we only grow when we use the best of who we are to help raise the level of goodness universally. When we learn the lesson of *being* our best to *do* the best, we will have taken a large step toward our ultimate goal of the absolute goodness, wisdom, and love that is God.

## Lesson #7: Contentment and gratitude make for a very rich life.

Some of my clients are not very happy people. They come in for readings and tell me, "Why don't I have the relationship I want?" "Why am I so broke?" "Why can't I find the perfect job?" I say, "Look, if you want to be happy you need to practice contentment and gratitude. Did you wake up this morning? Can you use your legs and arms? Do you have a roof over your head and food on your table? Then you're luckier than a lot of the people on this planet. Look at Somalia, or Russia, or India, or the homeless on our own streets. Those people feel lucky when they have enough sustenance to keep body and soul together. There are parts of the world where people feel lucky when they can get through a day without being shot."

Ingratitude is a sure way to cut yourself off from ever getting anything else. So what if you don't have the lover or car or job you want? If you're grateful for what you have now, you're a lot more likely to attract greater abundance from the universe. We've got to be grateful for what we've been given and content with what we have. Contentment has to do with our attitude. Look at the cup as half-full, not half-empty. When you see it as half-empty, you inevitably start blaming yourself, other people, destiny, the universe—and blaming will get you nowhere. Yes, we should keep striving. Yes, we should have goals like a relationship or a job or more money or helping more people. But we can still enjoy what we have in the moment even while we're working to grow and become more.

Gratitude opens the heart like nothing else. When you learn the lesson of living in gratitude and contentment, your transition to the spirit world will seem easy and natural—because that's the energy in which the highest spirits live all the time. With gratitude, you are connected to the highest possible level of the universe. You are connected to the very consciousness of God.

I believe we are given the gift of intuition to help us learn these lessons, as well as many others, as we progress through our lifetimes. Remember, when we die we won't judge ourselves based on how wealthy, beautiful, or successful we are. We'll judge ourselves based on our deeds, how much we loved ourselves and others, and whether we're able to look in the mirror each day with a clear conscience.

My prayer is that we all use our powerful intuitive abilities to master the lessons we're here to learn, and to contribute in some way to creating the highest good, both here and on the other side. I hope this book has helped open your eyes to what is possible when you use your God-given intuition responsibly, freely, and with good purpose. May your intuitive journey lead you to discover the greatness of your own soul, while filling your life with enormous contentment, peace, and joy!

# Appendix

‿

# Ten Frequently
# Asked Questions about
# Intuition and Psychics

I hope you've discovered a lot by reading this book. More important, I hope you're using your own intuition in as many ways as possible. To help you as you continue your journey of self-discovery, I thought I would answer some of the most common questions I encounter from both my students and clients. These questions may give you additional guidance in using and shaping your own intuition, as well as dealing with professional psychics.

## Q. How can I tell the difference between intuition and wishful thinking?

There are two ways thinking can interfere with intuition. One is wishful thinking—your desires get in the way of what you may really sense is true. In some cases, you may go into denial if what you want and what you sense don't match. The other kind of thinking that interferes with intuition is what I call "gloom and doom." Your intuition may be telling you everything will be fine, but you're either so scared or so convinced that things will fall apart, you can't see the sunshine for your self-created thunderclouds. (Some people are always waiting for the other shoe to drop!)

The key to distinguishing between intuition and wishful thinking is experience. The more you use your intuition, the stronger your "intuition muscle" becomes, the more confident you are, and the better you become. I tell my students to experiment with using their intuition in as many circumstances as possible. However, I also tell them to use common sense when putting their insights into action!

Usually when your intuition is accurate you'll get a sign of some sort. A phone call may come in that reassures you, or you may go out shopping and run into somebody who's associated with the person or situation you wanted to know about. Or you might have a dream that tips you off. When you put your intuition into action, you'll quickly see the difference between real guidance and wishful thinking simply by what happens. Then you can go back and check how you came to that accurate intuition.

Everyone's mind works differently. Observe your own mind and see how you get your intuitive information, and how you get stuck sometimes in wishful thinking. Then do your best to follow your own intuitive process. Learn from the best teacher of all—yourself.

# Q. Often when I'm emotionally involved in an issue myself, I can't seem to "tune in." How can I get an answer to the question?

Removing ourselves emotionally from an issue we care about can be very difficult. That's one of the reasons most psychics can't read for themselves nearly as well as they do for others! Here's an exercise I've found very helpful when you're really close to something and need an answer:

1. Put your issue in the form of a question. (Remember, it should be a single-part question—not "Am I going to get married and to whom?" but "Am I going to get married?")

2. Write your question on a piece of paper and fold it up so you can't read the question.

3. Write four other questions on four separate pieces of paper. These questions can be about you, about family, friends, the universe, whatever you want. Fold each piece of paper so you can't read the question written inside.

4. You should have five sheets of folded paper. Now, mix these papers up and write a number from one to five on the outside of each one.

5. Put the folded papers in a hat or a bowl. Without looking at them, mix the papers up again and then choose one. Don't open it, don't look at the number written on the outside—just hold it in your hand and let thoughts and impressions float into your head. Keep the intention of getting an answer to the question written on this particular piece of paper, whatever it is.

6. Write down your impressions, or say them into a tape recorder. When you're done, look at the number on the outside of the piece of paper and write it down next to your answer (or say it into the recorder).

7. Follow steps 5 and 6 with each of the remaining four pieces of paper.

8. Now, open up each question and see how you answered it. Pay particular attention to the answer you gave to the question that was so close to you.

This exercise helps get your conscious mind completely out of the way so your intuition can provide you with its wisdom. I've also found that the universe will eventually tip you off about almost every question, but you have to be aware of everything around you. A sign will usually show up—especially when you're thinking about something else! Remember the old saying "A watched pot never boils"? The same is true with the answers to our questions. Not all questions have immediate answers; the cards may still be shuffling. Often the best thing we can do is to ask the question, then forget about it. Let the universe give you the answer in its own good time. Just keep your eyes and ears open for the answer when it comes.

## Q. Why don't I ever dream about my loved one who has passed on and whom I cared about more than life itself?

Probably because you want it too badly, and you may be holding their spirits too close. Spirits need to feel free to be able to come back and communicate with us.

Usually I find that those we love come into our dreams when it's absolutely necessary—when they have an important message to convey, or when we're having a particularly difficult time. After all, if I dreamt about my father every night, I wouldn't pay attention to the dream! But when he comes in, I'm extremely alert because I know he's trying to tell me something important.

My sister Elaine says she has dreamed about our father only twice since he died in 1984. In the second dream he was holding something she couldn't quite see, and he said to her, "Honey, I have something for you." The next day Elaine found out that her daughter-in-law was pregnant for the first time, and that little boy was named after my father.

Even if you don't see your loved ones in dreams, however, know that they are around you much of the time. All you have to do is think of them with love and they will be right there with you.

## Q. What do I do if I feel I'm out of sync with the universe? What if I feel there are all kinds of barriers in my way?

Barriers to our desires can be the universe's way of protecting us. How many stories have you heard about people who were delayed at home or work and missed a plane as a result, only to find out later that the plane crashed? When they were racing to make the airplane, I'll bet they felt the universe had it out for them—but I'll bet they changed their minds pretty quickly when they heard the news about that flight.

If you're feeling out of sync with the universe, the first thing to do is check your intuition. See if you have a feeling why things aren't going your way. Maybe you're supposed to be taking a new direction. Maybe you're supposed to be staying right where you are while all the other possible factors align themselves to support where you're destined to end up. Maybe you're in denial about what's really in your best interests. Check your wisest self and see what it says, then do your best to follow its good advice.

# Q. Why aren't there always immediate answers to questions?

Because whatever the question is, whatever the experience is going to be, it's still in the process of developing. Not all things are predestined. We live in a universe where there is free will and choice, and if you're not getting an answer that usually means there are still people who haven't made their minds up, or factors that haven't come together. Things could still go one way or the other, so how can you get a definite answer? You may even still be able to influence the outcome by your own thoughts or hard work.

Then again, sometimes we're not supposed to know an answer. Sometimes we're supposed to live and do the best we can with a situation so we have the experience to reflect on in the future. We learn our greatest lessons from living through our greatest trials. Trust the universe to have your greatest good at heart, and do your best no matter what life throws your way.

# Q. How can I help the people I love to progress?

There's an old saying, "You can lead a horse to water, but you can't make him drink." If someone you love is in pain—or worse, causing someone else pain—yes, do your best for them. Offer them alternatives, show them other ways to fill their needs, share your own insights and experiences with them. Maybe letting them know that they'll feel the consequences of their actions both here and in the hereafter will help them to change. But realize that *they* have to make the choice to change or stay the same.

The only soul you can be responsible for is your own. If you find yourself in a situation that's dysfunctional or unhealthy, you have to realize that the only one you can really change is you. Either leave, or change yourself, or accept it and stop playing the victim because you chose to be there. But realize that those you love are responsible for their own lives. You can help them all you want, and I absolutely believe you can make a huge difference in someone's life by opening their eyes to the consequences of their actions. But you can't do it for them. Be a role model and a guiding light, and let them choose to follow your lead—or not.

# Q. How can I tell if a spirit is high or low?

I believe this is a valid concern. Not all spirits have our welfare at heart, and as someone once wrote, "The Devil can assume a pleasing shape." That's why before a reading, or if I feel a spirit around me, I take a minute to say my prayer of protection and put a white light all around me. Once that's done, I believe that even if there's a low spirit assuming a pleasant disguise, my intuition will tip me off. Either I'll just have a feeling that something's not right, or something I notice in my environment will warn me—I'll look through the *TV Guide* and my eyes will fall on a movie title, *The Amityville Horror,* for example. But it's up to us to be aware of the signs the universe is giving us.

Even if I feel a spirit is coming from a good place, I'll still say my prayer of protection and look for confirmation in signs from the universe. A spirit can mean well and their guidance still not be the wisest. (Remember the grandmother in Chapter 6 who wanted her granddaughter to marry a nice Jewish boy when she was in love with someone else.) When you're dealing with spirits, always check out whatever you're getting using good old common sense.

# Q. How can I tell if a psychic or intuitive is genuine or not?

Going to a good psychic or intuitive for a reading should be like going to any other professional. If you pick a doctor or dentist or even a plumber out of the Yellow Pages, you're taking your chances on their abilities! Most of us prefer to go to someone who's been recommended by a friend or colleague or someone we trust. I believe the same should be true of a psychic.

Once you contact the psychic or intuitive, you should look for a sense of being in rapport with them. Again, it's just like going to a doctor—you want to feel that this person is someone you can relate to and trust. If your personalities just don't jive, find someone else with whom you feel more attuned.

Finally, I believe during a reading you should get a sense that what the psychic is telling you is correct. They'll explain something about your past that feels right, or they'll talk about something going on in the present that's more than coincidence, and that helps you feel in sync. I find in my readings a lot of times I'm just confirming something that my clients already feel or know. You have to trust your own radar to feel if a psychic is coming from a good place. Then see how the reading plays out in your own life. It's hard to judge a psychic because the future has to happen to confirm what you heard in the reading. But all *good* psychics are happy to be known by their track record—that is, the accuracy of their readings.

By the way, there are a lot of great psychics who can't be specific about names or initials, but who are still very accurate. Rely on your own sense of the accuracy of their reading, and don't worry too much if they can't tell you the name of your great-uncle Eugene.

# Q. Are some people easier to read for than others?

Yes. I've had several people call me for readings and tell me afterward, "You're the first person who could ever read for me." In the same way, there are other times when I feel there's negative energy trying to block the person I'm reading for. I don't know if it's themselves sabotaging their own happiness, or they don't feel they deserve real healing, or if there's a real energy block there, but something's getting in the way. I can still read for them, but it's a lot harder. I have to match my energy with theirs, to go to whatever level they're operating on.

There are also those people who are skeptical and they won't work with you. I'll say, "Is there an R initial?" and they'll answer immediately, "No. I don't know anybody with an R." I'll say, "Well, do you know a Robert?" "Uh, well, that's my father, but I haven't talked to him in ten years." They won't answer truthfully even when I'm right!

I can usually pick up something on every single person, but it's very helpful if people are open-minded, thinking about all areas of their life, not just focusing on one particular question or area. Recently on a radio call-in show I was reading for a woman, and I asked her several questions about someone with a B initial, but she kept saying there was no one like that in her family. Finally, I said, "Are you sure there's not a Bob or Bobby?" She answered, "Well, Bobby Joe is my husband." She didn't want me to talk about him so she wasn't thinking about him. She wasn't concentrating open-mindedly about what was going on.

So if you want to get the most from a reading, come in as open-minded as possible. Yes, check out everything after you've been given the information, but don't block the flow of information with your own judgment, lack of concentration, or lack of focus. Remember, a reading is a team effort—you, your psychic, the universe, and the spirits!

# Q. What's the best way to prepare for a session with a psychic?

Every psychic is going to be different in the way they will read for you. I ask my clients to write down a list of names of people they know, both living and dead. That way, if I give them an initial or spell out a name for them, they don't spend a lot of time wracking their brains trying to come up with something obvious. I also ask clients to write down any questions they might want answered— but not to tell me the questions unless I ask them to. Usually in a reading my clients find 90 percent of their questions have been answered without their ever having to ask anything of me directly.

I also suggest that you avoid being too verbal during a reading. I find people sometimes feed the psychic information where really the psychic should pick it up themselves. I would let the psychic bring up situations without giving them information. And when you ask a question, even in writing, remember to make sure it's specific and has only one part. Don't ask something like, "Am I getting married and to whom?" There are two different answers to that question, and it makes it a lot harder to tune in. I also suggest that people make a list of any friends or relatives who have passed over and they would like to contact. At the end of a reading, I'll say, "Do you have any questions?" and the client will ask, "Did you get anything from my mother [or uncle or fiancé]?" At that point I'll tune in and ask for that spirit to come through. If they're around, I'll get an initial, name, or symbol which will let me know it's really them. Sometimes the spirit will answer immediately, sometimes it won't. Sometimes they're busy elsewhere and just have to be called—like calling someone to come to the phone!

Most people go for a reading because they want answers to questions about their lives or about people who have passed. However, sometimes we get answers that we didn't come for but which are more important. A client recently came for a reading because she thought her husband was cheating on her. But I was picking up a health problem, and I said, "I'm seeing a cyst in someone's breast, either yours or your sister's. Both of you should have it checked." The client went to the doctor, who found a lump which proved to be malignant and she had a mastectomy. That was more important to her than her husband cheating (although we did address that issue as well). So try to remain open to whatever the psychic is telling you. Just check it all with your common sense afterward!

The one thing I always tell people to do, whether they're coming to me or consulting another psychic, is to say a prayer of protection before the reading. You want the psychic to give you information that's coming from the highest level of goodness, wisdom, and love, and asking for protection and surrounding yourself with a white light will help ensure that.

For further information about Char, to subscribe to her newsletter, or order her self-help audiocassette, you may contact her at:

| | |
|---|---|
| Website: | www.Psychicchar.com |
| E-Mail address: | Charcom@flash.net |
| Office Telephone Number: | (248) 356-5360 |
| Office Address: | Char Communications, Inc. |
| | P.O. Box 250518 |
| | Franklin, MI 48025 |